T0289531

Pennsylvania Stories—
Well Told

Tioga
Athens
Meadows
New Milford
BRADFORD
Rome
Montrose
Equinunk
Mansfield
TIOGA
Towanda
SUSQUEHANNA
Elk Hill 2,693
Troy
Wellsboro
Monroeton
Stevensville
Hop Bottom
Forest City
Royal
TIOGA S.F.
TIOGA S.F.
Blossburg
Canton
Wyalusing
Laceyville
Susquehanna
Morris
New Albany
LACKAWANNA
Liberty
Dushore
Tunkhannock
Carbondale
TIADAGHTON STATE FOREST
Forksville
SULLIVAN
Evans Falls
WYOMING
Blakely
WYOMING STATE FOR.
Laporte
Scranton
Steamtown N.H.S.
Lake Ariel
Trout Run
Harveys Lake
Old Forge
LYCOMING
RICKETTS GLEN S.P.
Dallas
Pittston
Moscow
Red Rock
Kingston
Williamsport
Montoursville
Plymouth
Wilkes-Barre
Benton
Nanticoke
S. Williamsport
Muncy
Jersey Shore
Shickshinny
Glen Lyon
Pocono Pines
Turbotville
Millville
Berwick
COLUMBIA
LUZERNE
MONROE
Milton
MONTOUR
Bloomsburg
Conyngham
HICKORY RUN S.P.
Lewisburg
Danville
Catawissa
Hazleton
Brodheadsville
BALD EAGLE ST. FOR.
UNION
Northumberland
CARBON
Mifflinburg
Sunbury
McAdoo
Jim Thorpe
Selinsgrove
Shenandoah
Mahanoy City
Lehighton
Palmerton
Middleburg
Shamokin
Tamaqua
Trevorton
Mount Carmel
NORTHAMPTON
BALD EAGLE ST. FOR.
SNYDER
NORTHUMBERLAND
Nazareth
Pottsville
Northampton
Richfield
Herndon
SCHUYLKILL
MTS.
Valley View
Tremont
Allentown
Tower City
Schuylkill Haven
LEHIGH
Liverpool
Hamburg
Lykens
Pine Grove
Emmaus
Millersburg
WEISER S.F.
Kutztown
Newport
BERKS
Fleetwood
Bloomfield
DAUPHIN
PERRY
Linglestown
LEBANON
Myerstown
Boyertown
Marysville
Womelsdorf
Reading
Hershey
Lebanon
Schuylkill
Souderton
Harrisburg
Hopewell Furnace N.H.S.
Pottstown
Carlisle
Middletown
Lititz
Ephrata
MONTGOMERY
Mechanicsburg
Elizabethtown
New Holland
Norristown
Dillsburg
Valley Forge N.H.P.
CUMBERLAND
Mount Joy
CHESTER
Lancaster
YORK
Downingtown
Columbia
Dover
Philadelphia
Strasburg
Gap
Coatesville
ADAMS
York
West Chester
LANCASTER
Susquehanna
DELAWARE
New Oxford
Quarryville
Chester
Spring Grove
Red Lion
Kennett Square
Gettysburg Natl. Mil. Park
Hanover
DEL.
Stewartstown
Shrewsbury
Delta
Oxford
Wilmington

WILLIAM ECENBARGER

Pennsylvania Stories—

Well Told

TEMPLE UNIVERSITY PRESS
Philadelphia • *Rome* • *Tokyo*

TEMPLE UNIVERSITY PRESS
Philadelphia, Pennsylvania 19122
www.temple.edu/tempress

Copyright © 2017 by Temple University—Of The Commonwealth System
of Higher Education
All rights reserved
Published 2017

Library of Congress Cataloging-in-Publication Data

Names: Ecenbarger, William, author.
Title: Pennsylvania stories—well told / William Ecenbarger.
Description: Philadelphia : Temple University Press, 2017. | Includes
bibliographical references.
Identifiers: LCCN 2016049907 (print) | LCCN 2016053189
(ebook) | ISBN 9781439914656 (hardback : alkaline paper) |
ISBN 9781439914670 (ebook)
Subjects: LCSH: Pennsylvania—History—Anecdotes. | Pennsylvania—
Biography—Anecdotes. | BISAC: HISTORY / United States / State &
Local / Middle Atlantic (DC, DE, MD, NJ, NY, PA). | LITERARY
COLLECTIONS / Essays.
Classification: LCC F149.6 .E25 2017 (print) | LCC F149.6 (ebook) | DDC
974.8—dc23
LC record available at https://lccn.loc.gov/2016049907

♾ The paper used in this publication meets the requirements of the
American National Standard for Information Sciences—Permanence of
Paper for Printed Library Materials, ANSI Z39.48-1992

Printed in the United States of America

9 8 7 6 5 4 3 2 1

To all English teachers,

especially **Bertha R. Marsh**,

who told me in the ninth grade that

I should become a writer

Contents

Pennsylvania Stories—
Well Told

Introduction

ONE OF THE PRINCIPAL SUBJECTS of this book, John Updike, once called his native Pennsylvania "the least eccentric state." I must disagree.

I first became aware of Pennsylvania the Quirky as an adolescent in New York listening to the Yankees when they played the Philadelphia Athletics. Many Sunday baseball double headers ended in suspension, since no inning could start after 7:00 P.M. because of the state's "blue laws" against worldly activity on the Christian Sabbath.

About this same time I was pleased to learn that the town of Mauch Chunk, Pennsylvania, had changed its name to Jim Thorpe. Only later did I discover that the famous Native American athlete had never been there—not even once—and, indeed, had never heard of Mauch Chunk.

And speaking of names, can any state top this number of peculiarities? Slippery Rock, Eighty-Four, Rough and Ready, King of Prussia, Burnt Cabins, and Walnut Bottom (not to mention Intercourse, Blue Ball, Climax, Desire, and Pillow)?

There are many dialects of the English language in Pennsylvania. Philadelphians root for the "Iggles," and their top elected official is the "maire of Filufia." Around Lancaster, in Pennsylvania Dutch country, many sentences end with an interrogatory— "Doncha know?"—and people go to the carwash because "the car needs cleaned." In Pittsburgh, the question asked to find out whether you have eaten yet is "Jeet jet?" and the nation's capital is "Warshington."

As a statehouse correspondent, I watched the Pennsylvania legislature spend millions of dollars in a matter of minutes without debate while arguing for two years over whether the official state dog ought to be the Great Dane or the Beagle.

Where else but in Pennsylvania would a state's two National Football League (NFL) franchises, the Philadelphia Eagles and the Pittsburgh Steelers, merge during World War II and play as the "Steagles" because of manpower shortages? (Chicago also had two NFL teams in those days—the Bears and the Cardinals—but there was never a team called the Bardinals.)

Only Pennsylvania would nominate an unknown schoolteacher to the state's second-highest office because he happened to have the same name as a popular politician.

Where else would the first day of deer-hunting season be an unofficial state holiday, closing schools and offices?

What other state would build an infamous mental institution-warehouse a few hundred yards away from the birthplace of Dr. Benjamin Rush, who was known as "the father of American psychiatry" for his enlightened and humane views?

Nevertheless, Pennsylvania, for all its eccentricities, also has greatness, starting with William Penn. Like many other colonials, Penn made a promise of fair treatment to the Native Americans; unlike other colonials, he kept it. Pennsylvania was the birthplace of our nation and its Constitution and the site of the greatest speech in American history. It has some of the richest agricultural land in the world, and its famous turnpike helped shorten World War II.

Alas, Pennsylvania also has a dark side. Historically, its state government has been populated by rogues of almost unimaginable venality, and the stain of corruption remains at the State Capitol today. Indeed, the cost of the construction of that magnificent Capitol more than a century ago was the occasion for one of the greatest scandals in the history of Pennsylvania. And that, of course, is saying something.

Pennsylvania's care for the needy, indigent, and mentally ill has sometimes fallen to levels unworthy of a civilized society. One example of this, Philadelphia State Hospital, is detailed in this book.

Another topic in these pages is the Ku Klux Klan (KKK), and it is an unfortunate truth that too often hate groups such as the KKK have found friendly venues in parts of rural Pennsylvania. In fact, one of America's first outbreaks of racial violence occurred in Lancaster County on December 27, 1763, when a group of white settlers, undeterred by the local population, broke into a jail and killed and scalped the remaining members of the Conestoga tribe—three old men, three women, five young boys, and three small girls.

My first job was in Harrisburg, where the State Capitol, with its dome modeled after St. Peter's Basilica in Rome and its main staircase modeled after the staircase in the Paris Opera, is almost surely the most beautiful of the 50 State Capitols. And is there a greater example of Frank Lloyd Wright's genius than Fallingwater, his masterpiece in the Appalachian Mountains of western Pennsylvania?

I came to love Pennsylvania's abundance of sonorous Native American names that glide off your tongue: Nesquehoning, Conestoga, Juniata. No less an authority than Charles Dickens thought the most beautiful word in the entire English language was Susquehanna.

Between 1980 and 1995, I wrote more than 100 articles for the *Philadelphia Inquirer Magazine*. I ranged far and wide for my research: spent five days at Heritage U.S.A, the headquarters of the television evangelists Jim and Tammy Bakker in South Carolina; watched air traffic controllers at work in the control tower at Chicago's O'Hare Airport; rode a mule down a 1,000-foot cliff into a leper colony in Hawaii; cruised the Yangtze from Shanghai to Chongqing; hiked through a New Zealand rain forest; and explored language preservation in Iceland.

But most of my articles were set in Pennsylvania, whose greatness and eccentricity made it a fertile source for the long-form journalism that I was doing at the magazine. Over the years both colleagues and relatives have encouraged me to publish a collection of some of these Pennsylvania stories. I have picked 12, using two criteria: reader response at the time the articles appeared and my own retrospective appraisal.

I have prefaced each article with a note that includes any new information about the topic, explaining how I came to write the article, and listing any problems and amusements I encountered along the way. A final observation: Pennsylvania is, in the most literal sense, not quite as great as it used to be. Population loss and its shrinking industrial sector have earned it membership in the Rust Belt, and it has gone from being the nation's fourth largest state to its sixth largest, with an accompanying drop from 27 to 18 congressional seats.

But it remains happily eccentric. After all, what other state would have as its most famous weather forecaster a groundhog who is right only 40 percent of the time?

ALLEGHENY New Kensington Homer City CAMBRIA Ebensburg Alt
Black Lick Nanty Glo BLA
ittsburgh Monroeville Blairsville Seward S Allegheny Holli
Fork Portage Railroad
McKeesport Johnstown NHS
Bethel Park Latrobe Johnstown Johnstown Roar
sburg Clairton Greensburg Westmont Flood Nat. Mem. Claysbu

Intimate Strangers

Mike Lucas Was Struggling to Build a Life.
Bob Casey Was Fighting to Keep His.
This Is Their Story.

Bob Casey and I arrived at the State Capitol in Harrisburg at about the same time: I arrived as a just-out-of-college reporter with United Press International (UPI) in November 1962, and he arrived as a freshman state senator from Scranton two months later, in January 1963.

As a state government reporter, first for UPI and later for the Inquirer, *I covered Casey as a senator, as state auditor general, and as a thrice unsuccessful candidate for governor. No one ever tried harder to become governor than Bob Casey.*

Politics was not kind to Casey. After losing his first bid for the governorship in 1966, he carefully built a reputation for ability and honesty as auditor general that elevated him to near–folk hero status. But in his next try for governor in 1978, there occurred one of the most incredible chapters in the incredible history of American politics: Casey was literally pollaxed.

Originally published as "Intimate Strangers" in the *Philadelphia Inquirer Magazine*, November 6, 1994.

Casey's opponent in the Democratic gubernatorial primary was Pittsburgh's mayor Peter Flaherty. But running for lieutenant governor on the Democratic ticket was an unknown teacher and ice cream parlor owner from the Pittsburgh area. His name was Robert P. Casey.

Despite being unable to get time off from his principal to campaign, and despite spending only $4,000 on his campaign, voters in the lieutenant governor primary picked the name Robert P. Casey from the middle of a crowded field of 14 candidates and gave him the nomination. The Real Bob Casey, who had been heavily favored in the polls, finished second to Flaherty in the gubernatorial primary. The only plausible explanation was that voters thought they could get Flaherty for governor and the Real Casey for lieutenant governor. This was confirmed in random samplings of voters across the state.

Bob Casey was elected governor on his fourth try, in 1986, and reelected in 1990. Then, midway into his second term in 1993, he was diagnosed with familial amyloidosis, a rare genetic disorder that causes proteins to invade the heart and other vital organs. Nearing death in June, Casey received heart and liver transplants. The donor was 34-year-old William Michael Lucas, who had been beaten to death in front of his own home in Monessen, Pennsylvania.

Bob Casey and Mike Lucas never met, but their lives intertwined in a remarkable way.

Though he continued to experience the symptoms of familial amyloidosis despite the transplants, Casey lived for another seven years, dying in 2000 at 68.

This article, titled "Intimate Strangers," won the 1995 June Roth Award for Medical Writing from the American Society of Journalists and Authors.

O N THE SUNNY, PLEASANT EVENING of June 6, 1993, a makeshift motorcade of four cars winds past the old Wheeling-Pittsburgh Steel Company mill in Monessen, Pennsylvania, and begins climbing the narrow, hilly streets of the residential section.

Up, up, up they go—a dark blue Pontiac Trans Am, a gold Oldsmobile Cutlass, a black Plymouth Horizon, and a maroon Chrysler LeBaron convertible with a white top—in tight, purposeful formation, to Clarendon Avenue, where they stop quietly just short of number 440. Two men emerge and walk to the back of the house. The others, perhaps a dozen or more, get out noiselessly and wait behind a hedge, out of view. It is about 6:30 P.M. Danger gathers with the shadows.

Inside the house, 34-year-old William Michael Lucas—known to everyone as Mike—is watching television with his girlfriend, Maria Hughes. He is sprawled on the gray living room carpet nibbling popcorn, his favorite food; she is curled up like a cashew in the big orange chair. There is a knock at the back door.

Mike Lucas gets up and sees his longtime friend, Chris Garry, 22, through the screen. He thumbs his hat back and says, "Hey, man, what's up?" Lucas opens the door, but the man accompanying Garry holds a revolver to his side and orders him to walk out front.

Several days earlier, Chris Garry had been watching television with Mike Lucas in the same living room. Garry had joked with Lucas's mother about the old days when he came here as a child for lunch and dinner. Now Garry is the local drug dealer, and he has stolen about $10,000 worth of cocaine, which he has hidden in a cherry tree behind his house. To explain the shortage to his suppliers, Garry has claimed the cocaine was stolen—by Mike Lucas.

The three men come around to the front of the house where the others are waiting. When Lucas sees the group he turns to Garry and says, "Chris, why are you doing this to me?" Terror is baked on his face. The men form a circle around Lucas. There are quarrelsome voices climbing over each other. Then someone hits Lucas in the head with a pistol, and he falls to the sidewalk.

A few minutes later, Maria Hughes looks out the living room window and thinks she sees a group of young men playing football. In fact, they are taking turns kicking the head of Mike Lucas. After about 10 minutes, a neighbor yells, "What are you doing? Stop! Stop! Stop!" The attackers jump into the cars, and the motorcade roars off, leaving a blue vapor of exhaust fumes.

Maria looks out the window again and sees Lucas on all fours, trying to stand up. The entire upper half of his body is crimsoned in blood. She runs for towels, and when she returns Lucas has begun staggering up the 32 steps to the front porch. A neighbor asks if he's OK, and he nods affirmatively. Together Maria and Mike struggle to the bedroom, where she wipes off his bloody head with a towel.

ABOUT THIS TIME, some 150 miles to the east, Governor Robert P. Casey and his wife, Ellen, are attending Sunday evening mass at St. Patrick's Cathedral in Harrisburg. As they kneel in the flickering light of altar candles, the Caseys are especially prayerful because, for the first time in nearly two years, there is hope. The 61-year-old governor is struggling with familial amyloidosis, a rare genetic disease that causes his liver to spew out poisons that are slowly killing him.

Casey has been feeling bad for several years, but in recent months there has been a drastic change for the worse. He is experiencing dizziness, and his weight has dropped from 185 to 152. His legs have been blue below the knees from failing circulation, and he sometimes has trouble negotiating steps.

Back in April he cut his right shin badly while emerging from a van to make an economic development commercial. A state trooper bandaged the leg on the spot, and Casey finished his day's work. Later the wound took six stitches at the Hershey Medical Center, but it bled all night long. The next day Casey made an appearance on behalf of a new children's health insurance program, and before he even started, his right shoe was filled with blood.

Just weeks before, his son, Matt, had graduated from the University of Notre Dame. There was a Phi Beta Kappa ceremony for him about 100 yards from the hotel where Casey stayed, but the governor was too tired to attend.

Despite the pain and the misery, Casey kept up a busy schedule of official duties. The previous week, he had spent two days and a night in a whirlwind tour of Hazleton and then had gone home and worked until midnight because the legislature had approved the budget.

Increasingly, however, Casey's health is not only topic A, but topics B, C, and D, as well. No matter how many times he shuffles his thoughts, the knowledge that he is dying keeps coming to the top of the deck. Casey has scoured medical journals and called the nation's most prestigious medical centers seeking the scientific breakthrough that would save his life. All the experts have had the same death sentence: Amyloidosis is progressive, untreatable, incurable.

Then, out of nowhere, a glimmer of hope appeared.

On June 4, Casey sat at his desk with a yellow legal tablet and black felt pen. He made two columns—one headed "risks"; the other, "benefits." At the top of the latter, he wrote, "Can't get any worse."

———

FRANCES LUCAS COMES HOME from work about 8:00 P.M. to find her son's left shoe and hat lying in the street. A trail of blood leads up the steps to the front door. Inside, her son is standing with his head swathed in a blood-soaked towel. The police have arrived, but there is confusion over getting an ambulance. She decides to drive him to the hospital herself.

He starts to walk down the steps to her car, but he passes out. She and Maria drag him to the car and prop him in the front seat. He awakens and with an earnest, pinched face says, "Why did they do this to me, Mama? I didn't bother nobody. We gotta find out who did this." It's five miles to the hospital, and on the Donora Bridge, Lucas's body goes limp. His mother stops in the roadway, runs over to the passenger door, shakes him awake, leaps back in the car, and speeds off. Two minutes later, she has to do the same thing again. She fights off the rising lump of panic in her chest, but she can't get a single thought out of her mind. *Oh, it can't happen again. Not to me. Once is all I can bear. Please, God, no.* Twenty-one years ago, Frances Lucas's other son, Eugene, was shot in the back and killed on a Monessen sidewalk.

She ignores a red light and roars into the emergency entrance of Monongahela Valley Hospital, where she works as a receptionist. Luckily, there's an empty wheelchair. Somehow, she gets her staggering, drooping 200-pound son into it and pushes him inside.

"Frances, what happened?" asks Dr. Michael Waters. He looks at the battered head. "I don't think there's brain damage, but we'll have to run some tests." She goes off to telephone her daughter, and when she returns, Waters is downcast.

"His brain is hemorrhaging. We need to airlift him to Allegheny General immediately." Michael Lucas, wrapped in bandages and pain, teetering on the rim of consciousness, is placed aboard a helicopter. The last thing he says is, "Mama, would you run home and make me some popcorn?"

———

IT WAS BACK ON APRIL 14 that the book arrived in the Governor's Office. Along with several other gifts that day, it was placed in a storage room at the Executive Mansion, waiting to be logged in.

There it would have stayed were it not for a follow-up telephone call on May 24 from State Treasurer Catherine Baker Knoll, who had delivered the book to the Governor's Office six weeks before.

"By the way," she asked at the end of an unrelated conversation, "what did you think of the book?"

"What book?"

Casey sends for the book, a 364-page autobiography titled *The Puzzle People*, by Thomas E. Starzl, the world-renowned liver-transplant pioneer. The title page is inscribed in an energetic looping of black ink: "To Governor Robert P. Casey with admiration for your efforts to improve health care in our state of Pennsylvania." At the bottom of the page is a postscript: "I hope to meet you sometime in the future."

————

ON THE VERY DAY Knoll calls Casey, about two weeks before Mike Lucas's savage beating, Thomas Starzl drives his 1978 Honda Prelude—the same vehicle that brought him from Colorado to Pittsburgh in 1980—and parks behind his office, which is on the second floor of a Pizza Hut near the University of Pittsburgh. It is a neighborhood of graffiti, vacant storefronts, bail bondsmen, astrology readers, and regular drug busts.

Starzl began researching liver transplants in 1956 in a garage in Florida. No one else thought such a thing possible, but he stuck with his belief—through failures, ridicule, and vilification from his peers. When Starzl performed the world's first liver transplant 30 years ago, the patient, a three-year-old boy, died on the operating table. The next four patients did not live long enough to leave the hospital.

Today, to many of his patients, he is St. Starzl. His successes attracted enough patients and medical talent to make the University of Pittsburgh the transplant capital of the world. Before he retired from surgery, Starzl trained a whole generation of "liver swappers," who are spread across the nation. He now heads the University of Pittsburgh Medical Center's Transplantation Institute.

Starzl, whose lean and trim physiognomy belies his 67 years, sits down at his institutional steel desk behind a Pisa of file folders. Thin-lipped and intense, Starzl looks like a man who takes the Hippocratic Oath seriously. The heat and the window air conditioner are battling to a draw, and as Starzl is loosening his collar, there's a call from the governor of Pennsylvania.

Casey thanks him for the book and the kind words of the inscription. They discuss the book for a few minutes, and Starzl thinks, *I can't waste any more of this guy's time. He's busy.*

"Well, Governor, I certainly appreciate your call. It was an honor to talk to you." Starzl injects a terminal inflection in his voice, as though the call is over.

"Wait!" says Casey. "I have amyloidosis. What do you know about it? Is there anything you can do for it?"

Starzl asks Casey for details of his illness. He is amazed at the depth of the governor's knowledge. "I'll call you back in five minutes."

Starzl runs up to the third-floor bookcase and pulls out a red volume titled *The Metabolic Basis of Inherited Disease.* It is a hulking ark of a book, barnacled with footnotes, but Starzl quickly turns to page 2448, reads for a few minutes, then calls Casey back.

"God, a liver transplant will cure you."

———

THE FIFTH-FLOOR Trauma Intensive Care Unit at Allegheny General Hospital in Pittsburgh is a cave of noise: clangorous conversations between doctors and nurses, screams of anguish from the afflicted and of grief from the beloved. Every room holds a tragedy: traffic accidents, shootings, suicides, and, in room 548, Mike Lucas.

The page-a-day calendar says June 11, and tomorrow is Frances Lucas's 65th birthday. She sits at the bedside of her son, where she has been for six days, except for brief and fitful periods of sleep on a sofa in the waiting room. All week, doctors have been trying to save Lucas's life, including two operations to relieve blood clots from his brain, but hope is fading. He is being kept alive on a respirator.

Lucas's sister Yvonne has come here from her home near Washington, and she spends hours talking to him in a one-way conversation. Vonda Frezzell, the mother of Lucas's 13-year-old son, sings hymns and reads to him from the Bible. But most of the time, there is silence save for the hum of the air conditioner, the beeping monitors, the low zzzzz of fluorescent lights, and the ticking of the clock.

School photographs of Mike Lucas show a 300-watt smile and graceful, gentle features that seem to demand that a violin be placed in his hands. But bad luck stomped through his life.

He was a terrific basketball player in grade school and seemed a sure bet for a college athletic scholarship someday. But at 12 he broke his hip and leg playing football and was in a body cast for six months. He went on to play sports at Monessen High, but in the grandstand they said Mike Lucas had lost his nerve.

He is remembered by most of his high school classmates as very friendly, very bright, very unmotivated. He had a gang of friends (when gang meant something good), and they would get together regularly to sample adult corruptions—alcohol and cigarettes.

He came from a solid, middle-class family that regularly attended the Wayman African Methodist Episcopal (AME) Church in Monessen. His father and his grandfather worked in the steel mill, and his mother was a receptionist at the hospital. The Lucas home was a refuge for troubled children in the town, white and black.

Mike was the youngest of five Lucas children. He was close to his sister Yvonne, who is six years older and would talk to him regularly about the problems of growing up. They called it "gettin' deep."

But it was Gene—10 years older, athletic, extroverted, kind— who was his idol. When Mike was 13, Gene was gunned down outside a tavern in a dispute with the bar owner over a loud juke-box. Mike never got over his brother's death, and for the rest of his life he carried the tragedy around with him like a wound in his chest.

After graduating from high school in 1977, Lucas held different jobs and studied for different careers, but he never quite got it all together. He moved back and forth between Monessen and the Washington area, where his sister lived. He would enroll in a school of some sort, but then an attractive job would come along and he'd drop out to take it. The cycle repeated.

Everyone remembers him as a kind, decent human being. He loved children and always carried candy is his pocket to hand out. He loved to cook; his specialty was spare ribs in a sauce whose recipe he would never reveal.

In 1987, Lucas got a full-time job at the National Children's Hospital in Washington as a data-entry clerk; later, he did paralegal work in a Washington office and attended a community college. When he lost his job in 1988, he became a crack user. After pleading with him for more than a year, Yvonne and Frances confronted him and ordered him home to Monessen.

By 1992, his mother and sister believed he had overcome his cocaine habit. He had a job with a telemarketing company, and he was spending time with his 12-year-old son, Eugene Frezzell. Living at home with his parents, Lucas cooked meals, read the Bible every day, and set out with religious fervor seeking a job he felt was commensurate with his ability.

Now, in room 548 of Allegheny General, Mike Lucas lies unconscious. His mother stares out the window at a parking garage across the street. The hours drag by like centuries. There is a video screen with green, blue, yellow, red, and purple lines waving through it like little streaks of lightning. They monitor her son's blood pressure, heartbeat, brain waves, and other vital signs. Green, yellow, and black tubes run into his head, feet, and chest. On the television, a game show audience shouts advice.

———

A SCANT TWO MILES from the room where Frances Lucas keeps a vigil at the bedside of her comatose son, Bob Casey is awaiting further tests in room D-462 of University-Presbyterian Hospital. It's Saturday afternoon, June 12.

It's a basic room, no different from any other except for the plainclothes State Police officer stationed just outside the door. Warm slices of sunlight are coming through the venetian blinds, and there is an air of optimism. Finally, something is being done.

But the light vein suddenly turns varicose when Starzl appears, grim-faced, with John J. Fung, transplantation chief at the Pitt Medical Center, and Jeffrey Romoff, president of the medical center.

"I don't have to see any more tests," says Starzl. Casey's cardiac index is 1.6, which Starzl considers incompatible with life. "You're in grave danger of sudden death. You'll need a heart and liver transplant."

It is a lathered moment, and the air seems incapable of sustaining anything inconsequential. But Casey takes a bite of cheesecake, gives his voice a determined upward slant, and says, "Well, if that's what we have to do, let's go."

He has, however, emphasized one important point: "I know somewhere there's a book of rules about who gets an organ and who doesn't. I want absolutely no preferential treatment, and I want those rules followed to the letter."

Starzl tells him, "You're in for the fight of your life. This will make your worst campaign look like a walk on the beach. But you're going to win."

"It could take months to find a donor," warns Romoff.

"Wrong!" says Starzl, leaning up against the door. "One week— maximum."

"Tom," protests Romoff, "that's on the outside of optimism."

As if delivering an order, Starzl points his finger at Romoff and says, "One week." He wheels and disappears down the hallway. Starzl has kept close tabs on organ availability in the Pittsburgh region, and he knows that under the existing rules Casey will go very high on the list.

That night, Casey became one of 31,000 Americans awaiting a donor organ. Each day, seven people on the list die without finding one. But under the prevailing policy at Pitt, Casey is jumped high on the list because first consideration goes to patients needing dual transplants.

The governor falls asleep with the uncomfortable feeling that his survival depends on someone else's untimely death. Human beings have become useful to one another in ways never imagined 50 years ago, but the world of organ transplants relies heavily on tragedy. Seat belts and air bags in cars, handgun controls, and improved emergency medicine all work against the transplanters.

Starzl has overseen four heart-liver transplants, and none of the patients is still alive. But new drugs to fight organ rejection make Casey's prospects more promising. Nevertheless, Starzl encounters determined opposition within the Pitt establishment. There is concern that the institution itself will be harmed if the surgery fails and two organs are wasted. Casey, it is argued, is too old and too sick.

Starzl announces he wants no one on the transplant team who doesn't believe the surgery will be successful. He gets rid of all defeatists and assembles an all-star team of surgeons. "If I'm going to go to the South Pole on a sled," he explains, "I don't want anybody along who doesn't believe we can make it."

———

FRANCES LUCAS FINALLY WENT HOME on Saturday, her birthday, after spending almost a week at the hospital in Pittsburgh. But about an hour after she got to Monessen, she received a telephone call informing her that her son had "taken a turn for the worse."

And thus on Saturday night, June 12, two women sat beside hospital beds two miles apart, inextricably linked by grief and hope, and two men hovered between life and death. There was a common denominator between them: Monessen, Pennsylvania.

America's once mighty steel industry pulsed all up and down the Monongahela River, and Monessen, 30 miles south of Pittsburgh, was an industrial boom town. The mill ran along a two-mile strip on the river bank—a hot, noisy place that shaped the destinies and paychecks of everyone in town.

But the mill closed in 1986, and today Monessen is just another decaying steel town. Its population is about 9,000, half what it once was, and unemployment is twice the national average. Monessen is a mill town without a mill, high on the misfortune 500.

Today idleness hangs over the city like a biblical curse, and there is only one thriving enterprise in plain view: Drugs are sold on street corners, day and night, to sulking young men, stone-eyed with boredom, trapped in the rubble of failure.

For Bob Casey, Monessen was a symbol of Pennsylvania's fallen economy, and he made the revival of towns like it the keystone of his 1986 gubernatorial campaign. On his first full day in office in January 1987, Casey came to Monessen and promised to do everything in his power to help towns all across Pennsylvania hard-hit by the closing of mills and mines.

Within the limitations of his power and the state's resources, Casey made good on his promise, building highways, assisting new businesses, and creating job services centers such as the one on Schoonmaker Avenue in downtown Monessen. Mike Lucas spent a lot of time there in 1992 and 1993, enrolling in a training program and firing out applications for more than 100 jobs.

Then, weeks before Casey entered the hospital for a liver transplant, weeks before Mike Lucas was savagely beaten and left bleeding on his sidewalk, the governor came to the jobs center to give awards to five former welfare recipients who had gotten jobs through the center. But by this time, Lucas had become discouraged. A job with Bell of Pennsylvania had fallen through at the last minute, and he dropped out of a local business school. Hope was a doused fire. Mike Lucas became just another victim of the scourges of American society: unemployment, drugs, and violence.

As Bob Casey and Mike Lucas lay in their hospital beds, there was a very important difference between them: Part of Casey's evaluation for a transplant was sardonically called the "wallet biopsy." In the world of transplant surgery, money not only talks; it keeps up a running conversation, and anyone who either lacks the necessary insurance coverage or cannot come up with a down payment of about $150,000 will not be transplanted—no matter how near death.

Casey has the gilt-edged health insurance plan that covers all 85,000 state employees, and he passed the wallet biopsy with flying colors. Mike Lucas was unemployed and among the 35 million Americans without health insurance. Had things been reversed, Lucas would not have qualified for a transplant from Casey.

At 9:30 on Sunday morning, the Center for Organ Recovery and Education (CORE) in Pittsburgh is notified that a potential donor is nearing death at Allegheny General Hospital. Two hours later, CORE approaches Frances Lucas about using her son's organs for transplant. "I just don't know," she says. "I just don't know." Statistically, only about half of all family members approached to authorize organ donation agree. Among African Americans, the number is substantially lower: Poor blacks suspect their family members' lives are cut short for the sole benefit of rich, usually white, recipients.

For the rest of the day, tests are run on Lucas to see whether he has any brain function. All tests are negative, and at 6:31 P.M. William Michael Lucas is declared brain dead and becomes another drop in America's Niagara of homicides. If the law of averages prevailed that night, 75 other American citizens were shot, stabbed, beaten, and otherwise killed by fellow human beings.

There is no greater pain than having a child die before his or her time, and now Frances Lucas felt that pain for a second time. It grabbed her by the throat; it had mass, density, and it slammed into her over and over again. The sadness beyond all telling. The sorrow for which there is neither a name nor relief.

Gently, she is approached about the organs. She wants to get the question off her mind. She wants one less thing to think about. "OK," she says. There is a full-length novel in her sigh.

It is about 11:00 P.M. She doesn't know who will get the organs, and she doesn't plan to tell anybody about her decision. At least not now.

About this time, Ellen Casey is getting ready to retire for the evening in the hospital room just across the hall from her husband. Two Casey sons, Matthew and Patrick, are preparing to leave the hospital.

Suddenly, John Fung, the Pitt transplantation chief, appears in the doorway wearing powder-blue surgical scrubs and in a state of high agitation. He clears his throat and says, "We have a donor." Little zephyrs of excitement sweep the room.

"Where?"

"Right here in Pittsburgh."

Casey is afloat on a sea of good luck: He is the only patient in the Pittsburgh area awaiting a multiple transplant. It is a fortuitous co-incidence that the organs have been found so quickly and so nearby.

Ellen Casey looks down at Fung's surgical clogs; they are battered and blood-spattered.

"Nice clogs," she says.

"They're my good-luck clogs."

About 1:30 A.M., Casey signs over his gubernatorial powers to Lieutenant Governor Mark S. Singel, surrendering the office he has spent most of his adult life trying to reach. The six other Casey children are notified and summoned to their father's bedside. Margi and Mary Ellen drive from Connecticut to Scranton, where they join Bobby, Erin, and Kate on a flight to Pittsburgh. Chris has just driven from Massachusetts to Washington, and he promptly drives up in a rental car, arriving about 3:30 A.M.

The Casey clan—mother, father, and eight children ranging in age from 23 to 40—crowd into the tiny hospital room and stay up all night talking. Margi, the oldest child, barks out an order to the others: "Don't you dare cry." Then she begins to cry.

The blue-and-white privacy curtains are drawn around Casey, and he is prepped for surgery. About 6:00 A.M., the children come in one by one to say good-bye to their father. Ellen Casey says, "I love you. I'll see you when you get back." She hopes she's right.

Casey is placed on a gurney and wheeled out of the room. Ellen and the eight children follow him down the hallway with a security aide, State Police Sergeant John Kulick, who gives Casey a St. Joseph's prayer card that Kulick carried into battle in Vietnam. It is a prayer for deliverance from danger.

Casey reads it. Casey is pushed into operating room number 6 through the big double door, which closes behind him.

———

A FEW HOURS BEFORE, the pathologist Adrian Casavilla made a neck-to-abdomen incision, and then a foot-long incision across the abdomen of Mike Lucas's body. A beating heart, a healthy pink liver, and two kidneys are exposed. Casavilla snips and hands each organ to a nurse, who immerses them in a cold solution. The organs then are placed in an Igloo cooler—the kind you'd use to take beer and soda to the beach—and rushed to Pitt Medical Center in a CORE van. The ventilator that has kept Lucas alive is turned off; his body is then stitched up and washed while the nurse calls the funeral home.

And thus Mike Lucas, an unrepeatable existence, is now dead and will be buried in Monessen. He is giving the gift of life to the governor of Pennsylvania, who once tried to help him.

———

STARZL HAS ASSEMBLED A TEAM that includes an American born in Russia (John Armitage), a Vietnamese refugee (Si M. Pham), the son of a Chinese immigrant (Fung), a Japanese (Satoru Todo), and a Greek (Andreas Tzakis). They will attempt to transplant the heart and liver of an African American into an Irish Catholic. The organs were removed from the donor by an Argentine (Casavilla).

The seventh heart-liver transplant ever attempted in the United States begins about 7:00 A.M.; Armitage picks up the Bovie, an

electric knife known to surgeons as the fire stick because it si-
multaneously cuts and cauterizes, and makes a foot-long vertical
incision down Casey's chest. Now there is no turning back; it's a
nervy, life-or-death adventure in which all five surgeons are taking
a considerable professional risk because of the doubters among
their colleagues.

They find a heart so diseased that it is able to pump only one-
fourth the normal amount of blood and could have failed at any
moment. Scrubbed, gowned, masked, and gloved, Armitage and
Pham work confidently. The only sounds are chirping monitors
and chatter among doctors and nurses—"This way. . . . Sorry. . . .
Hold it. . . . That's it. . . . Thank you. . . . OK, OK."

Casey's old heart is removed about 10:30 A.M., and by 12:45
P.M., the heart that first beat inside the womb of Frances Lucas 35
years before is inside the governor of Pennsylvania, competently
sending his blood on its appointed rounds through his body.

The Casey family is waiting in the hospital room, watching the
television for bulletins on the surgery. It reminds Matt Casey of
an election night, waiting for returns to see whether his father has
been elected. About 1:30 Armitage comes to the door, mouth in a
crescent of pleasure, and says to Ellen Casey, "How 'bout a hug?"

Later, Jeffrey Romoff, the administrator, stops in, eyes brim-
ming with tears. "I've never seen anything like it," he tells the
family. "Usually we have to pump the heart to get it started. We
just touched it with a drop of warm blood and it started up."

But back in the operating room, Casey now has a foot-long
incision in his abdomen, and the liver team headed by Todo has
taken over. On a small table Mike Lucas's liver, looking rather
like a large roast in a butcher shop, floats in a stainless steel pan.
The liver, whose very name is derived from the verb "to live," is a
virtuoso jack-of-all-trades, a prodigious holder and processor of
blood that performs 500 vital metabolic functions in a single day.

Transplanting a liver is considerably more involved than transplanting a heart. Tucked beneath the body's rib cage, the liver is

much more difficult to reach, and there are more arteries to tie and sever.

Around 7:00 P.M.—12 hours into the operation—Fung goes over to the table, picks up Lucas's liver, and carries it the way a waiter carries a soufflé. "Here's the liver. Everybody back." When the liver is in place, the heart is still beating regularly and evenly—and the liver is "pinking up," a sign that it is getting an adequate blood supply.

Casey is brought into the recovery room about 8:45 P.M. Later, Starzl comes in as Casey is awakening from the anesthetic. His arms and hands encumbered by intravenous tubing, Casey reaches up and touches Starzl on the cheek. No words are spoken.

Within a day of his death, the mortal remains of William Michael Lucas—heart, liver, and two kidneys—were pumping, filtering, and metabolizing in the bodies of the governor of Pennsylvania plus an unidentified 61-year-old man and an unidentified 36-year-old man—commingling in a common pulse of being.

And in a world of oil spills, serial killers, starving children, and ethnic cleansing, there has been an affirmation of the moral immensity of a single soul.

————

WHEN THE LUCAS FAMILY ARRIVES at the Wayman AME Church at 11:00 A.M. on June 18, it is overflowing with more than 300 people; indeed, there are more mourners standing outside than there are in the packed church. People are politely asked to step back so the family can go up front near the casket, where the body of Mike Lucas lies. He is dressed in his favorite black dress hat to hide his wounds.

The church, which Mike Lucas's great-grandfather helped to build, is small and does not have air conditioning. The congregants fan themselves, but heat pours through the open windows like melted butter. Because of the large gathering, the service starts late, but at 11:25 the piano and the choir lead the multitude in song:

Where I'm goin'
I'm goin' up yonder
I'm goin' up yonder
I'm goin' up yonder
To be with my Lord.

The impress of faith is everywhere. The old *Cooley High* gang is there: Delvan Miller, Jeffrey Hill, and JoJo Heath, all still living in Monessen; Willis Love, who works for the Olympics organization in Atlanta; Mark Hall, a USAir employee in Newark; and Craig Giles, a minister in suburban Pittsburgh who is conducting the service.

In his eulogy, Giles seesaws between sadness and anger. In low, fathoming tones, he says, "Mike was not perfect; Mike was no angel. But Mike was a good man who loved life and loved people. The last time I saw him was at my grandmother's funeral. He said he was looking forward to a new beginning."

Then his voice flares like a match. "We've got to change things from within as well as from without. . . . Our children can rap but they cannot read; our children have gold chains but no jobs. . . . Every four hours an African American male is murdered—and 90 percent of the time the murderer is another African American male. . . . We keep poisoning one another with addiction. . . . The Ku Klux Klan is no longer the number-one enemy; today, it's the boys in the 'hood."

In closing, Giles attempts to sing the theme song from *Cooley High,* but he breaks down in tears. Instead, he reads the lyrics, and the words come out in agonizing slowness:

How do I say good-bye to what we had?
The good times that made us laugh outweighed the bad
I thought we'd get to see forever
But forever's gone away.
It's so hard to say good-bye to yesterday.

Frances Lucas and Yvonne Lucas tuck the blanket around the body, and the casket is closed. A long stream of cars heads toward Belle Vernon Cemetery, where Mike Lucas is buried next to his brother Gene.

When everyone else has left, the gang stands around the grave holding hands and praying. Then, just as they had done as adolescents, they repeat the lines from *Cooley High*: "This is for the brothers who aren't here."

Epilogue

Robert P. Casey was released from the hospital on July 27, 43 days after his surgery. He battled infections and viruses for five months, but on December 21, 1993, he reclaimed the governorship, and he expects to serve out his term, which expires in January. His doctors say there is no reason he cannot live at least 10 more years.

Christopher Garry, the man who led Mike Lucas's attackers to his door, was convicted of third-degree murder and sentenced to 10–20 years in prison. Other charges have been filed, but as of October 10 no one else had been tried in Lucas's death.

Frances Lucas has postponed plans to retire because she is still receiving medical bills for her son's hospitalization and treatment. She cannot afford a headstone for his grave.

Passing the Torch

Former Klansman Roy Frankhouser Still Dreams of
the Day When Men Will Be Judged by the Color of Their
Skin rather than the Content of Their Character.

*I first came across Roy Frankhouser in the 1960s in the process
of covering civil rights rallies and protests, which were growing
in size and number all over America. I interviewed him often
enough to realize that, compared with the motley bunch of losers
who made up the bulk of the KKK, he was intelligent. But his was
an intelligence that seemed unfocused. As I wrote in this profile,
"This large, untidy store of information seems unsynthesized. His
ideas are perfectly square blocks in solid colors; there is no asymmetry, no nuance, no mystery."*

*The other unusual and frankly intriguing part of Frankhouser
was that when he spoke privately of his hatred for blacks or Jews,
he was unconvincing. His voice had neither affect nor inflection.
His words were a slow-moving stream, without vigor or intent.
Only when he stood before a crowd at a cross burning did his eyes
dance with enthusiasm and passion.*

Originally published as "Passing the Torch" in the *Philadelphia Inquirer
Magazine*, March 13, 1994.

For three decades Frankhouser managed to get headlines, albeit rather small ones. He was a Klansman, Minuteman, and Nazi who was arrested more than 100 times. He lost an eye in a bar fight; watched a neo-Nazi friend blow his brains out when he learned he was half Jewish; participated in ill-attended rallies of pimply, surly adolescents; and spent several years in a federal prison.

When I approached him in 1994 and said I wanted to profile him for the magazine, I think he figured it might be an avenue toward some twisted form of respectability. I spent about a month interviewing Frankhouser and following him to various hatred-spewing venues. During this time, I came to loathe his lack of personal hygiene and his proclivity for stealing items from my car, including money and sunglasses. I never challenged him on it because I wanted to keep him talking.

To keep my own perspective, I continually reminded myself that Frankhouser represented a group that had bombed a church and killed four little girls on a Sunday morning in Birmingham, orchestrated thousands of lynchings of black men and boys throughout the United States, and organized beatings and lawlessness that terrorized innocent people.

After the article appeared, he never contacted me to say whether he liked it or whether he felt it had brought some newfound virtue or propriety.

Frankhouser died in a nursing home in West Reading in 2009 at age 69.

THE SOLITARY, robed figure writes at a desk, intent as a monk copying sacred texts. A pewter-colored cross holding a writhing Christ rests near his left hand, and on the wall behind him is a framed likeness of Jesus. There is somber music, and twitching candles bathe the room in a fragile semi-darkness, silhouetting the graying, avuncular man with a face like a benediction. . . .

But this is no monastery. The room is festooned with Confederate flags, swastikas, knives, swords, daggers, revolvers, and helmets with the stylized thunderbolts of the Third Reich. The music is by Richard Wagner, the Jew-hating genius beloved by Hitler; it bespeaks bloodshed, demons, and death.

And this is no monk. He is Roy Frankhouser, who has spent most of his 54 years in this tiny house he inherited from his father in a frayed-sleeve, out-at-the-elbow section of Reading. Link by link, he runs down the chain of memories: *The first-floor front room smelled of Vitalis and Bay Rum where my father cut hair and warned me about niggers and kikes, and the back room was where I lived after they let me out of that . . . orphanage, and here on the second floor just above the window are the bullet holes from when the Black Panthers tried to kill me but only hit the plastic turtle bowl, and right above me here on the ceiling are the bloodstains from the time poor Dan Burros blew his brains out.*

With his only eye, Frankhouser glances at his watch. Abruptly, he snuffs the candles and descends the steep stairs for the weekly meeting of the Reading-Berks Pale Riders, Ku Klux Klan.

In his hometown of Reading, Roy Everett Frankhouser Jr. is known by nearly everyone. "That's Roy Frankhouser," they'll whisper when he walks by, as if no other explanation is needed.

But Frankhouser's renown extends well beyond Reading. In the world of extreme right-wing politics, he is Big Time. He has been on an intimate, first-name basis with virtually every national leader over the past 40 years: George Lincoln Rockwell, founder of the American Nazi Party; Robert Shelton, Imperial Wizard of the United Klans of America ("I don't hate niggers, but I hate Jews. A nigger's a child, but the Jews are dangerous people"); J. B. Stoner, chairman of the National States Rights Party, who believes AIDS is a gift from God to rid the earth of gays and blacks; Robert Bolivar DePugh, head of the Minutemen, the anticommunist guerrilla force that built up hidden arsenals all over the United States in the 1970s; Robert Miles, founder of the Mountain Church of Jesus Christ.

Frankhouser's standing in America's pantheon of hate was achieved despite a 10th-grade education; his assets include a booming stentorian voice that seems to swell and fill all available space, a memory like a microchip, and a well-honed skill at manipulating human beings.

Frankhouser—who is as squat as a Russian war memorial and walks and breathes with difficulty—has bits of knowledge from everywhere. He recognizes a Beethoven sonata, knows the year the Spartans and the Persians fought at Thermopylae, and can recite an Allen Ginsberg poem. But this large, untidy store of information seems unsynthesized. His ideas are perfectly square blocks in solid colors; there is no asymmetry, no nuance, no mystery.

For the past 10 years, Frankhouser has had more crosses to bear than to burn. He lost his cherished Klan title of grand dragon of Pennsylvania and then began an ill-fated relationship with Lyndon LaRouche, the right-wing extremist. He has spent most of the past five years in various prisons for various reasons. Though he was designated "Klansman for Life" in 1991, many younger leaders of the current white supremacy movement don't even know him. He might be content with a role of éminence grise, though perhaps a more appropriate term is *der Alte* (German for the old one). But instead he's attempting a comeback. And Roy Frankhouser, who joined the Ku Klux Klan at 14, is now working with young people.

As prescribed by the Kloran, the official book, the local unit of the Klan meets in a klavern, which in the case of the Reading-Berks Pale Riders is the front room of Roy Frankhouser's house. All of the windows have been painted over. About 30 folding chairs are lined up in rows of five facing the red-draped altar. On the altar is a red wooden cross illuminated with small light bulbs; the Klan symbol, an unsheathed sword with a drop of blood in the middle; and a Bible opened to Chapter 12 of Romans, in which St. Paul enjoins the faithful: "Bless those who persecute you; bless and do not curse them. . . . Live in harmony with one another. . . . Repay no one evil for evil, but take thought for what is noble. . . . [L]ive peaceably with all. . . . Never avenge yourselves, but leave it to the wrath of God; for it is written, 'Vengeance is mine, I will repay,' says the Lord."

Behind the altar is a closed door marked "White Only."

About 25 people are present; most are male, and most appear younger than 21. There are two young women and three adolescent girls who look as wide-eyed and innocent as deer frozen in headlights. Three young men exchange collusive whispers. They have swastika tattoos on their arms and wear camouflage fatigues and combat boots. Two older men have a backwoodsy look, with jeans and red flannel shirts, and they squint like cowboys in a cigarette ad.

Satiny robes rustle as they are slipped from hangers covered by plastic dry-cleaning bags. Some reek of kerosene from past nocturnal cross-lightings. The Klansmen and Klanswomen help one another with their robes and then peer through the slits of their cone-shaped hoods.

Patrick, 11, is aglow and resplendent, as though he had just donned a new Easter outfit. Frankhouser helps him on with his hood and says, "Always remember as you grow up, young man, stick your hand up in the hood to get rid of the stiffness before you put it on." Patrick is rapt with attention, feeding gluttonously on each word.

Tara, 17, pulls her ponytail outside her hood as Frankhouser asks whether she remembers the night three years ago when she was initiated into the Klan under a tall, flaming cross. "Yeh," she says. "That was great."

"These young men and young women are looking for someone who genuinely cares about them, and I do," says Frankhouser. "They're tired of being pushed around at school by blacks. Many of them have problems at home. That's why they seek strength from some outside organization. Sure, I have problems with a few of the parents. What I tell my kids is to tell their parents that it was they who messed up the world to the degree it is today, and now it's up to their children to try to straighten it out. That usually works."

As the meeting time approaches, Frankhouser is issuing crisp orders, and finally he shouts, "Ten-Shun!" The meeting is called to order; there are a prayer ("Keep ablaze in each Klansman's heart the sacred fire of a devoted patriotism to our country and its government"), reports ("We marched in three cities, suffered two casualties, and lost one vehicle"), and announcements ("The convoy leaves for the cross-lighting immediately after this meeting"). Twenty minutes later, the lights are dimmed for the closing ceremony. Left arms are extended fully and tilted upward, Nazi-style, and Frankhouser shouts, "White power!" The Klansmen, in a single melting voice, repeat, "White power!" The feeling of belonging is tangible, and reality and fantasy seem to have merged.

Outside the front door, Frankhouser encounters two leather-jacketed adolescent boys who have come by out of curiosity. An opportunity for recruitment. He gives them KKK matchbooks; decals that say, "The Ku Klux Klan Is Watching You Right Now and We Don't Like What We See"; and a booklet titled *Great Achievements of the Negro Race* that is filled with blank pages and carries on the back cover the acronym SPONGE, for "Society for Prevention of Niggers Getting Everything." The boys snicker. Frankhouser invites them to the next meeting. "We'll have some pizza and show you a movie." They stand there sullenly, sucking on Marlboros, and say they might make it.

Just before World War II, Reading was a hotbed of pro-German activities. The entry of the United States into World War II was sternly opposed, and a corollary was the fear of an international Jewish conspiracy against Aryans, an idea that began 200 years ago during the French Revolution and had been brought to America in the 1930s by Henry Ford, the auto tycoon, who was rewarded with a favorable mention in Hitler's *Mein Kampf*. Charles Lindbergh, the aviation pioneer, made several trips to Germany just before the war and was presented a medal by Hermann Goering, Hitler's air minister and founder of the Gestapo. When the United States declared war in 1941, Lindbergh blamed the "Jewish-owned media."

Many Americans agreed, and one of them was Roy Frankhouser Sr. *My father idolized Lindbergh. I always tried to emulate my father. I'd see him in the barber shop, listening to Hitler on the short-wave radio, and he'd say, "We're in the wrong war. We shouldn't be fighting Germany." When I was very young, I went to visit my grandmother in West Chester. She told me not to play with the black boys, but I did anyway, and they beat me up in an alley and took my money. It was just a few pennies. I was five or six.*

The elder Frankhouser was an anti-Semite and racist. *The first time I remember hearing him rant and rave against niggers, I was probably about five years old. I sang for him a song I had learned in Sunday school. It went something like, "Be they yellow, black or white, they are precious in His sight." He got really angry and started slapping me around.*

Frankhouser's parents got divorced in 1949, when he was 10 years old, and during an ensuing custody battle the boy was sent to the Berks County Children's Home for three years.

That's where I learned to rebel against authority. I developed a terrible hatred for tyranny and injustice. I was beaten many times. I hated the place. They wouldn't let me read comic books, and I loved war comics. I got caught reading a comic book in the shower, and the matrons sicced two Boston terriers on me. They bit me repeatedly. I yearned to live with my parents. I came to admire strength. I lived in a society that seemed to be absolutely weak. They could break up my family and throw me into a home, so where was the all-American life? What kind of country was this?

He left the home when he was 13 and lived alternately with each parent. The next year he went to a classic film series at the Reading YMCA and saw *The Birth of a Nation*, a 1915 production considered a technical masterpiece for its inventive uses of the camera. But it also romanticized the Ku Klux Klan and painted its members as noble-minded knights who turn to violence only as a last resort. *I became a racist when I saw that movie, and I fell in love with the Ku Klux Klan. I still show it to young people*

all the time, and they never fail to applaud all the way through it.
Frankhouser joined the Reading Klan in 1954, the year the U.S.
Supreme Court ordered public school integration. *For the first
time in my life, I felt like I belonged.*

Meanwhile, Frankhouser had inherited his father's love for
Germany and for Nazism. *My one criticism of Hitler is that he
burned books. Whenever you burn knowledge, no matter how
you look at it, you're destroying your ability to make choices in
order to survive. . . . I don't believe the Germans had any system-
atic plan to destroy the Jews. The people who brought the world
Beethoven and Brahms couldn't do anything like that. I'm not for
the annihilation of the Jews. Some of my best friends are Jews.
I admire the Israeli army. They're the real Nazis of the Middle
East.*

*But not everybody feels as I do, and I fear for the Jews. If the
Jews knew what was coming—and, believe me, it's coming surely
as the dawn—they'd realize that what's going to happen in America will make Nazi Germany look like a Sunday school picnic.
We'll build better gas chambers, and more of them, and this time
there won't be any refugees.*

When Frankhouser was 17, his mother signed papers allowing
him to join the U.S. Army. He became a paratrooper with the 82d
Airborne Division. But after Frankhouser had been a soldier for
about a year, President Dwight Eisenhower ordered federal troops
into Little Rock, Arkansas, to enforce school desegregation. *I told
my commanding officer I cannot serve in an Army that fixes bayonets against its own citizens.* He was honorably discharged.

About 45 crow-miles from the Liberty Bell, in a flat, fallow farm
field near Rising Sun, Maryland, about 200 people have assembled
on a Saturday evening; they represent klaverns from Pennsylvania,
Maryland, and Delaware. The place is crawling with Klan official-
dom: klexters, klokans, klarogos, kleagles, kludds, klokards. It's a
veritable who's who of klandom. You can hear the traffic whizzing
by on Interstate 95. Cars and pickups, most of them older models

and some of them rusting out, are in the makeshift parking lot, which is marked by a Confederate flag. Towering over the gathering, like a village cathedral, is a 50-foot log cross wrapped in kerosene-soaked rags.

A few Klansmen have donned their robes and hoods, but most still wear black combat boots, camouflage fatigues, and black T-shirts. Nearly everyone, including the women, is tattooed. They stand talking in small groups, their voices arched like the backs of cats.

Frankhouser, who in 1966 addressed a KKK rally in this very field—*Black power is a plot to kill every white child!*—has set up a folding table and is selling Klan paraphernalia: T-shirts, caps, rings, and earrings (clip and pierced). He asks a pretty, freckled woman, "Would you like a nice ring?" and, without waiting for her answer, he suddenly pops out his left eyeball and shows it to her. "Wouldn't that make a great ring?" She steps back, in mock-horror, and laughs. Then he sticks the plastic eye on the tip of his nose, and she is convulsed with laughter.

A swastika-sleeved man, wearing a black Nazi SS uniform and jackboots, greets Frankhouser. He walks with his feet splayed, duck-like, and he is fat—a mountainous Jell-O of jowls, chins, and paunch. Beneath a musketeerish moustache, he twitchy-smiles, but his eyes are blank and give nothing away:

> Lemme tell ya a great story, Roy. You'll appreciate this. We was comin' home one afternoon and passed a bus with a Star of David on it. We couldn't believe it. A kike-mobile! Well, we slowed down and started givin' 'em "Heil Hitlers" and shouting, "Six million more! Six million more!" and you know what those hook-nosed bastards did? They started crying. Imagine. We cracked up. We couldn't stop laughing. A whole busload of hysterical kikes, screaming, pounding on the windows, tears running down their cheeks. And then the frosting on the cake—the bus driver was a nigger! When

the nigger saw our armbands, his eyes bulged out, and that bus took off like a rocket. We couldn't stop laughin'.

Within earshot, three little girls and two little boys, somewhere between the ages of 3 and 5, are catching frogs and lightning bugs in jars. One of the girls has pink ribbons in her hair and wears a black KKK T-shirt; one of the boys has a red T-shirt that says, "Hey, Nigger," and depicts a white hand giving a middle-finger salute.

The Supreme Court's 1954 school desegregation decision gave the Klan—which had prospered and declined twice since its founding in 1866—a new call to action. And among the new recruits was Roy Frankhouser.

One of Frankhouser's heroes quickly became Robert Shelton, the Alabama salesman who became the tough, violent leader of the Klan during the Civil Rights Movement and whose followers, among them Frankhouser, beat black and white Freedom Riders on public buses in Birmingham and Montgomery. *I used a crowbar. I beat the s—— out of those Freedom Riders.* Shelton was looking for leadership in the North, and he saw Frankhouser as a bright young man. So he made him grand dragon of Pennsylvania, head of the state Klan.

Frankhouser was arrested repeatedly for his anti–civil rights demonstrations—in Baltimore, Pittsburgh, Atlanta, Philadelphia. *Frank Rizzo arrested me five times. He would always grab me by the collar, drag me into the squad car to put on a show for the reporters and photographers, but then we'd joke around, and he'd tell me not to worry. I liked Rizzo a lot.*

Another hero was George Lincoln Rockwell, who had recently organized the American Nazi Party. *I called him up, and he said, "Come down to Washington." Four of us went down from Reading. We brought our German helmets, rifles, and bayonets. When Rockwell walked in the room, I said, "Achtung! Present arms." We all did, but it was a low ceiling, and our bayonets stuck in the plasterboard. He slapped me on the helmet and said, "Enough of this Hollywood crap. I'll teach you how to be Nazis," and he sent us to the White House to pass out leaflets. Eventually I spent about six months at his headquarters and got fairly close to him. He was a great man. Dedicated to the cause. I cried when he was assassinated.*

Frankhouser, who was in his mid-20s, became close friends with another fast-rising star, Daniel Burros. The two Rockwell Nazis met frequently in New York and Reading. They would talk about the need to preserve the white race in America and discuss ways to achieve it while listening to music, especially Wagnerian operas. Burros had some minor artistic talents; he enjoyed drawing pictures of Jews dying, and he usually carried with him a small bar of soap labeled "From the Finest Jewish Fat."

In 1965, Burros was leading the New York Klan's anti-Jewish crusade when the *New York Times* dropped a bombshell: Burros was half Jewish. The story broke while Burros was in Reading, and on a Sunday morning in October at Roy Frankhouser's house, Burros shot himself, in full view of Frankhouser and Frankhouser's girlfriend and future wife, Regina. His last words were "Long live the white race. I've got nothing more to live for."

I was angry because he broke my bed and my gun cabinet. Then he saw the revolver on the bureau, and he grabbed it. Good God! At first I thought he was going to kill Regina. Then bang! He's shot himself. In the chest. But then he was standing there as if nothing happened. I thought he missed. Then I saw the hole in his shirt. He was swaying, sort of. What the hell is going on here? It was surreal. It all seemed to be happening in slow motion. Then he raised the gun again, this time to his head. Shot himself right in the temple and fell on the floor. Regina was screaming. All the while, Wagner was playing. . . . God, it was awful. He was my best friend.

While the sun is a ball of blood low in the Maryland sky, the aliens—prospective members—are summoned to the sacred altar, which is a waist-high table covered with a Confederate flag, for the ceremony of naturalization. There are nine of them—a young man, a young woman, and five teenage boys and two teenage girls. In their robes and unhooded they look like a choir. For this naturalization ceremony, Frankhouser, also robed, takes the part of klokard, or teacher. The 100 or so observing Klansmen, none of them hooded, stamp out their cigarettes and shuffle to attention.

Frankhouser, his face crimsoned by the retreating sun, reads from the Kloran and begins asking a series of questions; each requires an affirmative response from the aliens. "Are you a native-born or naturalized white, Christian, American citizen? . . . Do you believe in and will you faithfully strive for the eternal maintenance of white supremacy? . . . Louder! I can't hear you! . . . Do you believe that this is a white man's country, and should so remain, and will you do all in your power to uphold the principles of white supremacy and the purity of white womanhood?"

In a 15-minute ceremony, the aliens swear obedience, secrecy, fidelity, and klannishness. They promise secrecy for all fellow Klansmen (except in cases of treason, rape, malicious murder, or violation of the Klan oath), and they commit themselves to uphold America's flag, its Constitution and laws. At the end Frankhouser declares them fit for the Klan. "By virtue of the authority vested in me, I dub thee Klansmen, the most honored title among men." Each is tapped on the shoulder with the flat blade of the sword. The aliens have passed through the mystic cave to become citizens of "the Invisible Empire," gaining access to the Klan's ceremonial language, greetings and responses, avowals and warnings. Each robed figure stands in mysterious oneness with his or her fellow Klansmen.

The sun drops below the horizon and jerks the world into night. An owl fills the field with questions.

In his 54 years, Roy Frankhouser has been arrested about 75 times; he has endured almost as many beatings, including one that cost him his left eye in 1965. His FBI file runs upward of 50,000 pages.

In the 1970s, Frankhouser became intelligence chief and Pennsylvania coordinator for the Minutemen, the paramilitary group headed by Robert DePugh. He maintained a secret underground weapons cache in Schuylkill County that included semiautomatic weapons, explosives, and rockets. He was charged with stealing dynamite in 1973, but he managed to beat the rap by claiming at his trial that he was actually a government informer and that he had participated so he could continue in that role.

When word of his undercover activities reached his right-wing brethren, Frankhouser was ousted as grand dragon, and his glass eye was auctioned off for a paltry $5 at a KKK rally in Greenville, South Carolina. *It was an extra one, and I donated it to them so they could raise money for the poor.*

Government records show that Frankhouser was an agent of the U.S. Treasury Department's Bureau of Alcohol, Tobacco, and Firearms for about two years—indeed, his superior wrote several memos describing him as an excellent infiltrator and confidential informant capable of "great personal risk." And there are some lingering suspicions today among right-wing extremists over Frankhouser's government activities in the 1970s. *I had to act as a double agent to find out what was going on. I kept a lot of people out of jail by warning them what the Feds were up to. . . . If I really were an informer, I wouldn't be here today. I'd be long dead.*

Despite his fall from grace among some of his right-wing brethren, Frankhouser managed to land on his feet when he began an 11-year association with Lyndon LaRouche, the right-wing presidential aspirant, serving as a political and security consultant. As his influence with the organization grew, he was sent to Germany to overhaul LaRouche security operations in Wiesbaden.

In 1985 the federal government began investigating complaints from LaRouche contributors that amounts were charged to their credit cards far in excess of those they authorized. In February 1988, Frankhouser was convicted of obstructing justice for his part in the scam. He spent nearly three years in federal prison.

Less than a year after his release, Frankhouser was involved in the stabbing of a young Klan member at a meeting in suburban Harrisburg. *The guy was a child molester. . . . I should have killed the creep.* Awaiting trial in Cumberland County Prison on aggravated assault charges, he quickly got in a fight with a black prisoner and was placed in solitary confinement. *It's the most dreadful thing in the world. I went crazy in there.* He was sent to a state mental hospital for evaluation but was declared fit to stand trial. Last April, nearly a year after he had been detained, a jury found him not guilty of the stabbing because he had acted in self-defense.

Along with Frankhouser's legal problems, the poverty and loneliness that have dogged him throughout his life increased exponentially. He lives a marginal existence in Reading, holding down a variety of part-time jobs, including livestock auctioneer and janitor. *I finally got some oil in the tank so I could have some heat. I got tired of watching my own breath.* He is divorced and the father of three adult children, whom he seldom sees. *I've always tried to shield them from my political activities, but I would like to see them more often. This hurts me very much. Why don't they just stop by? But maybe they did stop by and I wasn't there.*

On the moon-drenched field in Maryland, the Klansmen stand in disordered ranks, listening to guest speakers. The first is Barry Black, pastor of the New Covenant Church of God, wearing camouflage trousers, combat boots, and a black shirt with a clerical collar. "Niggers are raping our women with impunity. . . . We're sick and tired of it all. Let's go get that filthy kike out of the White House." Then Bob, leader of a Delaware Klan, huge tattooed arms, goatee, black T-shirt, and jeans; he might be central casting's idea of a rebel biker: "Clinton, our faggot-loving, Jew-loving president. . . . We made America, and now we ride around in old cars while the Jews and kinky-haired faggot niggers ride in Mercedes."

Scholars of racial prejudice say that children get their first indoctrination from language—specifically from certain powerful words freighted with emotional impact—such as "nigger." Dave is 19, lives near Reading, and is Frankhouser's favorite protégé. He has short brown hair and wears jeans, a flannel shirt, and a black leather jacket. He looks like the young man who lives up the block.

"My father hated niggers. My whole family . . . my parents, my grandparents, my great-grandparents, they all hated black people. They remember when Reading was all white and prosperous. . . . Everybody had jobs. Then the niggers moved in, and Reading went down the tubes. You can't walk the streets at night. . . . It ain't safe."

"Dave is one of my most promising young people. There are many others. Most of them have problems at home, and they seek strength from some outside organization. We're their second fathers and mothers."

Dave's eyes are double barrels of liquid rage. He speaks in a low monotone. "I'm a high school graduate, but I can't find a job. I have applications everywhere. . . . The niggers are getting all the jobs. It disgusts me. . . . I'm livin' at home. I go to the supermarket and I see them buy steaks. They drive up in Mercedes and BMWs. You wonder, where do they get their money? Well, a lot of them are dealing drugs. These people have no morals or anything." His eyebrows descend and nearly unite in disgust.

"I feel like part of a lost generation. No one cares what I think or what I believe in. Here in the Klan, they care. I feel a kinship with those Confederate soldiers who started the KKK. They were left out just like I've been. The South was saved by the Klan, and now it's time for the Klan to save the whole country." *The Human Relations Commission goes on the air making appeals for racial harmony. Race-mixing is being taught in the schools. . . . We have a right to the youth, too.*

"Mr. Frankhouser is a really good person. He taught me the truth, the real truth, about my ancestors . . . that there was actually no Holocaust . . . that the Jews made the whole thing up so they could get back at the Aryan people."

Dave is interrupted by an insistent voice from the altar: "Hey, Roy! Roy Frankhouser! Come on up here and say a few words. . . . Folks, this here's Roy Frankhouser."

Frankhouser steps up to the altar. At first he is reserved, reluctant, almost shy, but before long he has turned as mean looking as a Gestapo thug, and he is ranting like an evangelist with a full tent. "You're damn right I'm a racist, and I'm proud to be a racist." His voice seems to slip into just the right vitriolic pitch, like a needle in a groove. His cheeks quiver with rage. "We need to say, 'Niggers, we can't stand this smell anymore.'" The cheering comes in salvos; there is a fusillade of hoorays, damn rights, and amens. A wave of applause washes over him. Frankhouser basks in the warmth.

Frankhouser's Pale Riders are part of one of many Klan factions across the nation (United Klans of America, Confederate Knights, White Knights, Territorial Knights), and the Klan itself is part of a white supremacist coalition that includes the Posse Comitatus, the National Association for the Advancement of White People, and—the shock troops of the entire movement—the skinheads, splintered into such groups as White Aryan Resistance, the Fourth Reich Skinheads, and the Confederate Hammer Skins.

There are about 300 such groups nationwide, and their members are mostly low-income, poorly educated whites who see racial purity as the only salvation in an increasingly desperate situation and as a source of a sense of belonging, identity, and importance. These groups are usually led by individuals who are intelligent, likable, and articulate—sequoias among saplings.

Frankhouser runs his klavern with a military hand, referring to his fellow Klansmen as "the troops" or "my men" and to their activities as "missions." He regularly hands out medals for "heroism" among klavern members, and if someone is injured, the medal comes with a "wound cluster."

The klavern's missions usually involve a public protest aimed at various grievances, with a goal of maximum publicity. *We demonstrate, educate, and agitate.* Frankhouser is careful to inform police well in advance of any public activity—as a means both of protecting himself and his followers and of attracting the press and onlookers. As he learned from George Lincoln Rockwell, the more hecklers, the better the publicity. Last fall, klavern members journeyed to Auburn, New York, to take part in a white power march, but they were met and driven out of town by a mob of some 2,000 counter-demonstrators. Several of Frankhouser's members, including a woman, were injured. *We got our a—— kicked. I need time to restructure them mentally. I don't dare take them into the field now. Either they'll be too aggressive or totally cowered.*

Although even Klansmen refer to the ceremony as a cross burning, Klan purists call it a cross lighting to avoid any appearance of sacrilege.

Cross lighting became a Klan ritual about 1915. The idea apparently was adopted from Sir Walter Scott's poem "The Lady of the Lake," in which burning crosses were used by family clans in Scotland to signal one another.

Frankhouser, holding a blazing torch, begins the ceremony by barking a series of dismounted drill orders to the robed Klansmen and Klanswomen, who are assembled in ranks. "Halt! Right face! Left face!" Frankhouser's orders are snappy and precise, but the response is disorganized, almost comic.

At Frankhouser's command, the Klansmen converge on the cross, each taking up an unlit torch from a pile near the base. They form a wide circle and rotate around the cross slowly; as they pass Frankhouser, he lights their torches and says, "I give you the sacred light. Proceed." When all the torches are burning, they stop, and Frankhouser says: "Behold, the fiery cross is still brilliant. All the troubled history has failed to quench its hallowed flame." He ignites the cross. Flames leap up the post and spread over the horizontal bar; the Klan members step forward and place their torches at the base of the cross.

Frankhouser, his one eye borrowing glitter from the fire, intones: "We light the cross with fire to signify to the world that

Jesus Christ is the light of the world. Where the holy light shall shine, there will be dispelled evil, darkness, gloom, and despair. The light of truth dispels ignorance and superstition as fire purifies gold and silver, but destroys wood and stubble, so by the fire of the cross of Calvary we cleanse and purify our virtues by burning out our vices with the fire of His word. . . . Who can look upon this sublime symbol or sit in its sacred light without being inspired with a holy desire and determination to be a better man?"

"Amazing Grace" plays over the loudspeaker—"*how sweet the sound.*" The cross continues to burn. The heat can be felt 30 feet away, and the Klan members sweat under their heavy robes and hoods. They spread their arms wide and look into the sky filled with acrid smoke. "*I once was lost but now am found.*"

The sound of the flames licking at the cross is ghastly. "*Was blind but now I see.*" The air is varnished with the smell of kerosene and burning wood. Large black tatters of burned burlap flap from the cross. "*How precious did that grace appear.*"

Frankhouser asks, "What's the solution?"

"White revolution!" comes the chorused response.

"White power," shouts Frankhouser.

"White power," comes the response.

"White power!" "*'Tis grace that brought me safe thus far.*"

"White power!" "*And grace will lead me home.*"

"White power!"

"White power!"

Frankhouser stands silhouetted against the burning cross, dreaming of the day when men will be judged by the color of their skin rather than the content of their character. Less than a mile away, Americans are speeding along Interstate 95 on their way to ballgames and family reunions, unaware that, nearby, significant events are taking place, important rites are being celebrated, and young minds are being molded. On the official Klan Kalendar, it is the day of Desperate in the month of Sorrowful in the year 78 A.K.

The Shame that Was Byberry

To Behold the Horrors of This Philadelphia Mental Hospital Is to Wonder: Just Who Are the Lunatics?

As an undergraduate, I wrote a term paper for an abnormal psychology class on the book and movie The Snake Pit, *which took its name from the medieval practice of lowering the insane into a pit filled with snakes in the hope that it would return them to sanity. A few years later, I read Ken Kesey's great novel* One Flew over the Cuckoo's Nest, *which would become a great film starring Jack Nicholson in 1975.*

My exposure to these books and films came at a time when deep changes were taking place in America's approach to psychology in general; in particular, challenges to the efficacy of mental facilities centered on the controversial concept of deinstitutionalization.

So when Governor Robert Casey announced in 1987 that the Philadelphia State Hospital, known as Byberry, would be closed after 80 years of housing mental patients, it occurred to me it

Originally published as "The Shame that Was Byberry" in the *Philadelphia Inquirer Magazine*, July 10, 1988.

might be a good time to do an article on the dark history of this institution. When the state Public Welfare Department said it would allow me complete access to reports and studies, I went for it.

Byberry was permanently closed in 1990. A nearby farm, which was used to provide food for the facility, was made into a state park and named after Benjamin Rush, a signer of the Declaration of Independence, who was born there in a stone farmhouse. Rush is considered "the father of American psychiatry" and was an early advocate of enlightened and humane treatment of the mentally ill. It is an almost unbelievable irony that a little more than a century after Rush's death, Byberry would be built a few hundred yards from his birthplace.

The farmhouse was accidentally demolished in 1969 during the construction of a nearby apartment complex. When I interviewed Tom Keels, the Philadelphia historian, he noted that the stones have been moved several times, and "what remains of them are scattered around Fort Washington State Park."

On the brighter side, Benjamin Rush State Park provides visitors with an area to enjoy the natural beauty of open spaces, along with some Pennsylvania woodlands, places for study, recreation, and the solace of gardening. The park features one of the world's biggest community gardens, as well as a large area devoted to flying radio-controlled model airplanes and 3.5 miles of multiuse trails that meander through open meadows and shady wooded areas.

BYBERRY. It's a word that belongs in a nursery rhyme, arching melodiously from the throats of playground children aflame with the joy of living. Byberry was a rustic town in Pennsylvania, so called because it was not unlike a town named Byberry in England. But Byberry also became an institution in Pennsylvania— and it was not unlike an institution in England known as Bedlam.

Bedlam. It was short for London's Royal Bethlehem Hospital, which was Henry VIII's final solution for the insane of sixteenth-century England. It was a place of such repulsive horror that the word lost its specificity and came simply to mean any place of great uproar and confusion.

Byberry. It is short for the Philadelphia State Hospital, that drab, cold, gloomy mausoleum 15 miles north of City Hall, just across Poquessing Creek from Bucks County. It was opened in 1907 and operated much of the time on the theory that circumstances that would drive a sane person mad might drive a mad person into sanity.

Byberry. Like the Holocaust, it is impossible to amend, impossible to accept. Now the state is moving to close it forever, and a political debate is emerging over what to do with the valuable land it occupies. Perhaps we should allow it to stand out there on Route 1 as a reminder that in a bureaucracy there is no problem too big to be avoided, that the humans given responsibility for other humans cannot sit back and admire their intentions, that injustice always walks softly—and we must listen for it carefully.

Byberry. It pulls you in and wrings you out like a rag. It's a lake where all the world's tears have flowed. The history of Byberry reads as though it were written by Dante and then rewritten by Kafka, with Poe looking over his shoulder. Byberry's story is freighted with tragedy. All institutions fall short of the aspirations of those who create them, but seldom in the twentieth century has this occurred with such devastating effect on its guiltless residents. There are a few heroes, and they're not hard to spot. And like all true stories, this one has no end.

Byberry, Pennsylvania, was settled and named by the four Walton brothers, who came to America from England in 1675 and began farming the land. It is an irony and a coincidence that in 1745, Benjamin Rush was born in Byberry, a few hundred yards from what would become, nearly two centuries later, the grounds of Philadelphia State Hospital. Rush would go on to become "the father of American psychiatry," and just before his death in 1813, he heralded the advent of a "humane revolution" in the treatment of the mentally ill. His optimism was premature.

Although Byberry didn't become part of Philadelphia until 1854, there were important developments in the city 100 years earlier in the treatment of the insane. Quaker morality led to the establishment of America's first general hospital in Philadelphia in 1751. Benjamin Franklin petitioned the Provincial Legislature, which took the radical step of voting public funds for Pennsylvania Hospital. One of the new institution's goals was the "Cure of Lunaticks."

Pennsylvania Hospital was the first institution in America where the insane were viewed as sick people in need of medical care rather than as criminals. In 1841, it would open a separate institution for the mentally ill—the Pennsylvania Hospital for the Insane. Patients in colonial days received the latest treatments, which included bleeding, induced vomiting, purging, and scalp blistering. Difficult cases were put into ankle irons or a "maddshirt," which was an early version of the straitjacket.

These treatments were expensive, and the hospital had a very selective admissions policy. The idea of a dual system, one private and one public, began to emerge. If you were insane and poor, you were likely to end up in the Philadelphia Almshouse, which cared for the impoverished, the orphaned, and the aged, as well as the insane. The almshouse opened in 1732 and was moved and expanded several times. In 1838, it was established in the Blockley section of West Philadelphia, and it is this institution, which would come to be known as Blockley, that is the direct antecedent of Byberry.

On the night of February 12, 1885, the Insane Department at Blockley was destroyed by fire. Nearly all of the 22 patients who died were fastened by their arms and legs to the walls of their rooms, and in the panic no one could find the keys to set them free. The city fashioned makeshift facilities in their ashes, but it began to look around for a site for a new hospital.

More than 20 years later, on November 16, 1906, the Philadelphia City Council approved the purchase of 874 acres of farmland and farm buildings in the extreme northeastern section of the city; it was as far away as you could get from City Hall and still be in Philadelphia. Most of the homes and farm structures had been built in the 1870s. Two Blockley attendants were sent out to begin preparing them for patients.

On July 3, 1907, six patients were taken from Blockley to the new facility—Byberry City Farms—and placed in the care of two attendants. They came in one of the city's first motorized ambulances, and the first patient to step out was William McClain, who was an alcoholic.

From this time on, there was a steady movement of patients from the overcrowded Blockley facility to Byberry City Farms, where the patients would perform agricultural tasks thought to be therapeutic. One of the first treatment devices was called the sweatbox, a body-size contraption filled with electric lights with just a hole for the patient's head. Sweating was thought to be therapeutic, too. Construction of new buildings began in 1912. In August and September 1925, all remaining patients at Blockley, about 1,300 in all, were moved out to the new site, and it was given a new name: the Philadelphia Hospital for Mental Diseases. But it already was called Byberry.

———

Extract from the 1925 annual report of the Philadelphia Hospital for Mental Diseases: "Relatives and patients alike praise the bright sunny cottages with refreshing views of open country that do indeed surpass the gloomy wards of old Blockley."

———

Memoir of Dr. Walter G. Bowers, written in 1946, about early years at Byberry Farms: "When an attendant was discharged or reprimanded for being cruel and mistreating the patients, he was discharged by the Chief Physician. It was the practice of the attendant to call on the Assistant City Director of Public Health and Charities who usually sent him back to the resident physician with a note requesting that he be reinstated and frequently with an increase in pay.

"To bear this out, a case is recalled where an attendant chocked [sic] a Negro patient by twisting a towel around his neck with such force that both eyeballs ran down over his cheeks. It was necessary, a few days later, to summon an eye surgeon, who enucleated both eyeballs, with as a result, permanent blindness to the patient. The attendant was discharged and later reinstated.

"This and many other similar occurrences are recalled which are very distasteful to anyone who has humanitarian principles at all. In other words, it was a treatment of the dark ages and not the treatment in a civilized community."

Bernard Landy's story: Born in 1906, second of three children. Father a clerk, mother had history of mental illness and died at 49 in a mental hospital.

Seclusive and quiet as a child, which led to being teased by friends; this brought on nervousness and then aggressive behavior. Sent to live with aunt in South Philadelphia, began breaking furniture, and ran from the house babbling to strangers. Police called in, sent him to Byberry on December 12, 1923. 17 years old.

Report on Landy dated January 30, 1924: "Suspicious, anxious, irritable. Says he wants to get busy at once and make some sort of a man of himself."

No further file entries until 1967, when because of reduced patient load he came to the attention of hospital staff; after one year of regular therapy, he was released on June 30, 1969. The final entry in his file reads: "Appears to have lived fairly comfortably without any serious incidents for his past 46 years of institutionalization."

———

In 1925, the new state Bureau of Mental Health issued its first order to local hospitals; it limited the use of restraints on patients, requiring a written order from a physician and a specified period for restraint. Detailed records were supposed to be kept by all hospitals. These rules were ignored flagrantly and repeatedly at Byberry.

The attendants were either the political appointees of the corrupt City Hall political machine, who didn't show up for work at all, or they were undesirables recruited directly from the police courts and given their choice of going to jail or working at Byberry. Certain of these attendants came to be known to the patients as "sluggers."

Physicians' committees, welfare organizations, and auditors condemned the treatment at Byberry throughout the 1930s. Grand juries regularly inspected local institutions, and year after year they came away from Byberry sickened and issued reports with words such as "horrifying," "wanton neglect," "deplorable," and "unspeakable." But most of the money appropriated to improve conditions at Byberry was siphoned off into political graft, and by 1935, Philadelphia had an international reputation for political corruption almost beyond imagination.

The mayor throughout much of this period was J. Hampton Moore, who dismissed all allegations as the wild rantings of "sick-i-atrists." In 1932, Mayor Moore suggested at a luncheon of the Retail Merchants Credit Association that many Byberry patients were freeloading on the taxpayers: "On visiting days, the roads outside are black with automobiles. Sometimes there are as high as 150 automobiles belonging to relatives of the patients. These relatives can afford automobiles and bring candy and cake and delicacies to the patients for whom you taxpayers are paying."

A few weeks later at Byberry, the attendants staged a hunger strike to protest their food, claiming the vegetables had worms, the meat was rotten, and there were often mice in the drinking water. And the attendants received better food than the patients.

The reformers agitated for a state takeover of the hospital, but the politicians in City Hall resisted for nearly a decade because the shift would have cost them about 700 patronage jobs. But by 1938, the Republicans had run the city into the ground. Subway lines were sealed up because there was no money to buy cars, fire trucks failed to arrive at fires, about one in every three streetlights was out, and the water supply was so nauseating that people lined up with jugs at Fairmount Park springs every day. Finally, on September 29, 1938, a new law shifted Byberry to the jurisdiction of the state Public Welfare Department, and Byberry's long-suffering thousands were delivered from the hands of City Hall politicians—into the beckoning hands of Harrisburg politicians.

———

Letter of resignation, November 16, 1929, Dr. Stephen L. M. Smith, assistant superintendent: "When it comes to a point where the men in charge can't engage even an assistant without the consent of some politician, it is pretty bad. Why, when we would discharge a man for drunkenness or incompetence, back he would come with a letter from City Hall ordering his reinstatement.

"Buildings do not make hospitals. Any doctor would prefer old buildings and high-grade personnel to new buildings and the meddling of ward leaders and other politicians. Patients are not entirely safe under such a system."

———

Presentment of May 1933 grand jury: "Sewage backed up on washroom floors, 200 patients sleeping on cots in hallways, population is 5,500, or 2,400 above capacity. The city treats its prisoners far better than it does these helpless mentally deranged wards."

———

Presentment of October 1934 grand jury: "Words cannot describe conditions at Byberry."

————

Presentment of November 1934 grand jury: "It must be borne in mind that this is not a penal institution. Persons go there because they are suffering from mental illness."

————

Mayor Moore, December 16, 1934: "[Byberry] is one of the best in the country. These alleged eminent physicians would have us put in many physicians and attendants to sit with these 60-year-old inmates until they die at about age 80, give them a pill now and then and maybe hold their hand and kiss them."

————

Presentment of January 1935 grand jury: "Water from leaking roofs dripping directly onto patients' beds. Byberry is a menace to the health of its patients."

————

Mayor Moore, February 17, 1935: "Byberry is not in horrible condition. It is slanderous and libelous to say so. You won't find any of these inmates suffering. They are comfortable and well-housed."

————

Grand jury testimony of dining room attendant, April 8, 1935: "It's easier giving them liquid food because they have no utensils. When they get solid food, they have to grab it with their hands."

————

Grand jury testimony of Dr. William C. Hunsicker, city Public Health director, who under the city charter was the superior of Byberry Superintendent William Rickert, May 1938: "I was taken down to the Mayor, and the Mayor told me that Rickert was a friend of his and he could trust him and rely on him and so forth. But [he said] that Rickert did not know a thing about mental hospitals and that he, the Mayor, wanted some person with experience to help him along."

———

May 26, 1938: William J. Daly, son of City Councilman John J. Daly, is appointed "chief engineer" at Byberry, responsible for keeping the power plant operating. He is paid an annual salary of $3,000; Byberry physicians are paid $2,000 a year.

———

Report of joint legislative committee, July 21, 1938: "Some patients have been wrapped up in straitjackets for as long as three years. We saw about eight or ten patients in a ward set aside for experimentation of the new insulin shock treatment. We saw patients in that ward in various stages of the shock, but we saw no physician in charge at the time. In fact, in our eight hours of continuous inspection of the hospital, we neither met nor saw a single member of the staff in or about the hospital."

———

Governor George Earle, September 29, 1938 (as he signed legislation placing Byberry under the jurisdiction of the state Public Welfare Department): "Today Byberry and all its horrors end— tomorrow brings a new institution, a new hope for these unfortunate patients."

———

State Welfare Secretary Charles Engard, September 29, 1938 (upon assuming control of the newly named Philadelphia State Hospital): "I don't even want to hear the name of Byberry again. The horrors it conjures up will be more easily forgotten if the name is forgotten."

Necrology

March 23, 1929: John P. Dougherty, 73, dies in his Philadelphia home five days after his release from Byberry; relatives tell the coroner he had been beaten badly, but attendants testify he had suffered the injuries in a fall. *November 15, 1930*: Anna Alter, 23, commits suicide by jumping from a bridge linking two hospital buildings. *December 14, 1930*: Mary Matysik, 13, strangles herself with her nightgown after an attendant used it to tie her to a chair—and then went to lunch. *February 8, 1932*: Mary Pugh, 41, dies after being beaten on the head with an iron bar by another patient. *May 12, 1936*: John Price, 17, a paralytic, is bitten by a 14-year-old inmate and dies of blood poisoning. Coroner's inquest blames death on lack of supervision. *July 24, 1936*: Stephen Szarzynski, 38, dies of internal injuries suffered at Byberry. His sister says he told her just before he died that he was beaten by attendants, but hospital authorities say a bed fell on him. *November 25, 1936*: George Baker, 58, dies after being beaten by another patient. *July 23, 1937*: James Godfrey, 37, dies of a ruptured intestine; circumstances are investigated but results are inconclusive. *April 28, 1938*: Reynold Rosenblatt drowns in a bathtub during hydrotherapy.

Dr. H. C. Woolley was named the state's first superintendent at Byberry, and in his first annual report to the new state Board of Trustees, he described what he found there when he arrived: "A medieval pesthouse. Fire-trap buildings. Leaky plumbing. Holes in the floor. Cracks in the walls. A horrible smell. A staff with no morale. Backbiting. Office politics. Favoritism. Inefficiency. Insubordination. Patients without clothes. Cringing patients. Crowded wards. No mattresses. Sleeping on wet floors. Nothing to do all day. Rotten food."

Woolley had been named superintendent by Governor Earle, a Democrat, but in November 1938, the Republican Arthur James was elected governor, and within weeks James met with Jay

Cooke, the Philadelphia Republican leader, to discuss the issue of filling the jobs at Byberry, which was in the 35th Ward. There were about 800 patronage jobs at the hospital.

The new Board of Trustees of Philadelphia State Hospital scheduled its first meeting for December 22, 1938, at the hospital, but one of the members was so sickened by the stench that he requested that the meeting be moved to Center City. The others complied. At that meeting, several trustees told Woolley they would take over all of the hiring and firing at Byberry "so you won't be burdened with the responsibility."

Woolley reddened and then replied, "If you think you're going to turn Byberry back into a political roost while I'm superintendent, you're crazy. You can get in your cars and start out for Byberry right now, because you're the new superintendents."

It was two years before the trustees held another meeting. During that time, Woolley, who remained on the job, fired more than 200 attendants for brutality to patients.

World War II had an enormous impact on Byberry. Shortages of construction materials blocked an ambitious capital-improvement plan, but the war also brought an infusion of idealism into the hospital—the "Conchies." On August 12, 1942, a vanguard of 11 conscientious objectors arrived at Byberry to work as attendants. Others would follow, and many of them would keep diaries of what they saw. These diaries would form the basis for a spate of journalistic exposés after the war. Moreover, hundreds of men suffering from war-related mental illness would be institutionalized, and the treatment they received pricked the national conscience.

By the end of the war, public revulsion against state mental institutions had reached an unprecedented level.

———

Superintendent Woolley (just before he resigned on January 6, 1941, standing at the top of a stairway that is the only exit out of

Building No. 4, housing 89 physically disabled patients): "I wake up at night in horror over this place. I can see myself and members of my staff before a coroner's jury and a grand jury charged with the responsibility for roasting to death aged and blind people. Yet in every report I ever made to the state in my 27 months here, I outlined this condition very thoroughly because it is so horrible. And it still exists."

———

George Elder's story: In 1942, George Elder stood before a federal judge and said he could not serve in the armed forces because he conscientiously objected to war. He also told the judge that he was part Cherokee and felt the U.S. government owed him money because of its past treatment of the tribe. The judge ordered a psychiatric examination, and Elder was committed to Byberry.

The report of his initial examination says he repeatedly referred to the war as "Roosevelt's War," and this led to his classification as a paranoid schizophrenic. Decades of institutionalization failed to cure his pacifism. In 1971, still a patient, he said: "I still don't believe in war, violence, or riots. And I agree with the young people who are protesting."

———

Physicians' dinner menu, August 7, 1945: "Prime rib roast beef with gravy, boiled potatoes, roast corn on the cob, bread (white, rye, whole wheat or raisin) with butter, salad of cucumbers, lettuce and celery, apple-apricot pie and coffee, tea, iced coffee, iced tea or milk."

———

Patients' dinner menu, August 7, 1945: "Hard-boiled eggs, lima beans, beets, white bread, milk or black coffee."

Necrology

February 2, 1940: Alexander Allbritton, 42, is fatally beaten after attacking an attendant. *February 19, 1940*: Amos Holt, 53, hangs himself from bedsheets tied to a pipe. *September 5, 1940*: Peter Pondolph, 71, is beaten to death by another patient. *October 18, 1940*: William J. Williamson, 59, is beaten to death. Two attendants—one a dishonorably discharged sailor, the other a former middleweight boxer known to patients as "the Slugger of Byberry"—are charged with involuntary manslaughter and convicted. *December 20, 1940*: Paul Hallowell, a former city police officer paralyzed from the waist down, dies after being struck by an attendant who was enraged by difficulties in taking the patient's temperature. *December 30, 1940*: David Chodnowsky, 64, dies from injuries suffered in what official reports call a fall. *February 8, 1941*: John Corrigan, 50, dies after a fight with another patient. *March 7, 1941*: John Smith, 32, is fatally beaten by an attendant. *August 6, 1941*: Harry Burnett, 14, commits suicide by taking an overdose of sedatives. *October 15, 1941*: Frank Perri, 81, a senile psychotic, dies of injuries after being beaten by two other patients. *October 29, 1941*: Catherine Lindenmuth, 31, commits suicide in a bathroom in Building No. 12. *March 30, 1942*: Louis Petrone, 34, dies of injuries suffered while being restrained by attendants. *April 18, 1942*: Elias Bogden, 42, hangs himself from a rafter. *November 27, 1942*: The body of Evelyn Griffith is discovered in a tunnel beneath Byberry. She had been missing for a month. *July 17, 1943*: Henry Reynolds, 69, dies after a fight with another patient. *February 20, 1944*: Coleman Patterson, 27, is beaten to death with a broom handle by another patient. *July 12, 1944*: Michael Kirkpatrick, 19, leaps to his death from a 25-foot wall. *October 9, 1945*: Andrew Mullin, 93, dies in a fight with another patient.

Byberry's 1945 annual report states that of its 5,923 patients, two were released as recovered during the year. The Veterans Administration (VA) entered into an agreement with Byberry to treat returning servicemen, but on July 31, 1946, the VA abruptly canceled the agreement because of "abominable conditions" at the hospital. Leonard Edelstein, a conscientious objector who served at Byberry during the war, told state officials in May 1946 that he had witnessed an attendant strangling a patient in 1944, eliciting this response from Welfare Secretary S.M.R. O'Hara: "It seems too bad that now that the war is over, an unfortunate matter of this kind should be brought to the attention of the public in this manner and not through official channels."

But even as O'Hara spoke, the nation was being numbed by a series of articles in *PM*, a New York City newspaper, by Albert Deutsch, who would later publish his findings in the book *The Shame of the States*. The most shocking chapter was on Byberry, and it proved that the state had not improved conditions there since taking it over in 1938. Deutsch wrote: "As I passed through some of Byberry's wards, I was reminded of the pictures of Nazi concentration camps at Belsen and Buchenwald. I entered buildings swarming with naked humans herded like cattle and treated with less concern, pervaded by a fetid odor so heavy, so nauseating, that the stench seemed almost to have a physical existence of its own. I saw hundreds of patients living under leaking roofs, surrounded by moldy, decaying walls, and sprawling on rotted floors for want of seats or benches."

Deutsch asked F. E. Cramer, staff psychiatrist, whether there were many suicides at Byberry. Cramer replied: "No, thank heaven. The plain truth is there just isn't enough privacy here to permit a successful suicide attempt."

The governor of Pennsylvania at this time was the Republican Edward Martin, who was finishing out his four-year term and running for the U.S. Senate. His major campaign issue was that during the war he had built up a $200 million budget surplus, an astounding figure for that day. One of Martin's frugalities was to continue paying Byberry attendants $69 a month, plus room and board. The voters apparently approved of this fiscal conservatism; Martin won the election.

To blunt the Byberry revelations, Martin accused Deutsch of "cheap sensationalism," and two weeks before the election, the Welfare Department released the 68-page booklet "A Pictorial Report on Mental Institutions in Pennsylvania," which purported to show what conditions were really like at Byberry and elsewhere. Some of the 231 photographs showed Byberry patients being treated by psychiatrists, a Byberry patient getting a manicure, and a Byberry patient having her hair done.

That same year, *Life* magazine published a lengthy expose by Albert Q. Maisel titled "Bedlam 1946." It began thus: "In Philadelphia, the sovereign Commonwealth of Pennsylvania maintains a dilapidated, overcrowded, undermanned mental 'hospital' known as Byberry. There, on the stone wall of a basement ward appropriately known as 'The Dungeon,' one can still read, after nine years, the five-word legend, 'George Was Kill Here 1937.'"

In 1946, Mary Jane Ward published a novel, *The Snake Pit*, which took its name from the medieval practice of lowering the insane into a pit filled with snakes in hopes it would return them to sanity. The book and a subsequent film aroused the public as never before about the inhumanity of state mental institutions.

Furey Ellis, a Philadelphia insurance man, was named president of the Board of Trustees in 1947, and one of his first steps was to take groups of state legislators on uncensored tours of Byberry. Ellis's efforts led to a $29 million capital-improvement campaign and the opening of five new buildings within two years.

But the old problems of overcrowding, understaffing, and underpaying continued. In 1951, City Coroner Joseph Ominsky announced an investigation into the deaths of 10 Byberry patients from fractured skulls within a three-month period. A coroner's jury concluded that some of the deaths could have been avoided by better handling of the patients, but no attendants were charged. The state dedicated a $2.8 million treatment building on May 7,

1952, but it would take 14 months to move patients into the building because it had no furniture or equipment; "red tape" in Harrisburg was blamed.

By 1953, Byberry was so crowded that it was forced to limit new admissions to 10 per week. As a result, hundreds of mentally ill Philadelphians were placed in county prisons, where they received no psychiatric treatment and endured the abuse and mockery of criminals. Things improved in 1955 when George M. Leader became governor; he had a strong commitment to mental health, appointed the state's first mental health commissioner at a salary second only to his own, and increased spending by more than 50 percent. But the roller coaster continued. The legislature slashed the Byberry appropriation in Leader's 1957–1958 budget, and 331 employees were laid off.

By 1959, more than two decades after the state took control of Byberry, the patient census reached an all-time high of 6,889. Patients slept in double-decker beds and in basements.

———

Presentment of August 1946 grand jury: "Something should be done about this place. It is inhuman to have people living like that. The sights we saw were terrible."

———

Testimony of Superintendent Eugene L. Sielke before state Senate investigating committee, June 10, 1959: "It's true that there are roaches at Byberry, but not in the treatment rooms. The roaches are a problem in the dietary and warehouse building, and the reason for this is that the state spends only $1,500 a year for extermination services in 130-odd buildings spread over 1,600 acres."

———

Report of special legislative investigating committee, dated October 27, 1966, after a surprise visit to Byberry: "The sensation of this decayed and rotten scent remained in one's nostrils and mouth for hours after leaving the hospital."

———————

U.S. Public Health Service report, 1966: "Byberry is primarily a custodial facility where evidences of hope are extremely rare."

Necrology

April 9, 1946: Laura Bienasz, 54, is beaten to death with a broomstick by another patient. *October 11, 1946:* August Denaple bleeds to death after his throat is slashed by another patient. *October 22, 1946:* James O'Toole, 40, is killed in a fight with another patient over a pack of cigarettes. The fight occurred in the recreation room of C Building; there were 300 inmates and two attendants there at the time. *November 1, 1946:* The body of Sophie Bardynski, 50, is found by hunters near hospital grounds. Missing for three weeks. *June 24, 1947:* The badly decomposed body of Raymond McDonald is found in high bushes at the rear of a Byberry building. Missing for two weeks. *June 28, 1947:* Emma Simms, 59, is beaten to death with a wrench by another patient. *January 2, 1949:* Laura Rudy, 59, is found dead on the front porch of a house in Philadelphia. Byberry authorities said she had wandered away three days before. *March 13, 1949:* Stanley Klusek, 20, is burned fatally after setting his clothing on fire. *May 8, 1949:* Ralph Wilder, 64, is killed in a fight with another patient. *April 12, 1950:* The body of Daniel Heins, 71, is found on hospital grounds. Suffered a fall. Missing for two days. *July 26, 1950:* Joseph Daniels, 57, dies of injuries suffered when thrown to the floor by another patient. *February 10, 1951:* Mary Lee, 37; Agnes Knight, 32; and Florence Hayes, 48, are killed in a fire in Building C-6. The city fire marshal says "precious minutes were lost" because the hospital has only one alarm box, located in the telephone switchboard room, which is about 150 yards from C-6. The fire marshal had recommended improvements for more than a year before the fatal blaze. *June 25, 1953*: Charles McGinnis, 48, is beaten to death by another patient in a washroom. *January 8, 1954*: Matilda Erro, 64, is killed when she is kicked in the head by another patient. In a 10-by-30-foot room with 83 other patients. *November 7, 1954*: Robert Palmer, 83, is found dead in a wooded area near the men's dormitory. *April 12, 1955*: The body of Margaret Mangelli, 27, is found stuffed into a locker in a laundry room. Death by suffocation, apparent suicide. *December 15, 1955*: Leo Zerbe, 44, is fatally beaten by two patients. No attendants on duty. *October 27, 1956*: The skeleton of Helen Permaneska, 67, is found by hunters in a wooded area of Bucks County near the hospital. Missing from Byberry for four months. *April 25, 1957*: The body of William Friedrich, 40, is found floating in Poquessing Creek. *August 27, 1960*: The body of George Barney, 37, is found on the hospital grounds near a creek. Missing for three days. *March 10, 1963*: James Guiles, 63, is killed when hit on the head with a chair by another patient. No attendants were in the day room at the time. *October 16, 1965*: The body of James Downie, 77, is found about a mile from the hospital. Missing for several days. *November 9, 1965*: The body of Thomas Hanstein, 37, is found along the railroad tracks near Byberry. Wandered off grounds and struck by freight train.

The National Institute of Mental Health made an in-depth study of Byberry in 1966 and recommended the appointment of a top-flight psychiatrist as superintendent. Governor William W. Scranton chose Daniel Blain, a former president of the American Psychiatric Association, the organization's medical director for 10 years, and a leading international authority on the treatment of mentally ill people.

Blain took over in October 1966 and soon afterward led two influential legislators on a tour of Building S-1, which was known to the Byberry staff as "the snake pit." They saw hundreds of men sitting on the floor and in corridors. A blind man lying on a bench was yelling. Others were whimpering. Another sat silently in a wheelchair with a sheet pulled over his head.

"You get what you pay for," Blain told the lawmakers.

Blain took other legislators on similar tours, and he continually badgered the legislature for more money—and got it. Two antiquated buildings were closed, bedsheets were changed regularly, food was improved and varied, visiting hours were expanded, the dairy farm was abandoned, and institutional peonage—the practice of having patients work for the hospital without pay—was drastically curtailed.

But most important, treatment was increased and community health centers were established that concentrated on diagnosing and treating mental illness in its early stages. The result was a steady reduction in Byberry's population. On April 28, 1971, the Board of Trustees announced that there were 2,976 beds and 2,477 patients. After nearly 64 years, overcrowding at Byberry had ended.

———

BUT BYBERRY'S PROBLEMS persisted. There were work stoppages as Byberry employees protested low pay and difficult working conditions. In 1980, federal officials threatened to disqualify Byberry from federal aid programs unless conditions were improved. They cited a critical shortage of nurses because of inadequate state funds and said they had found one nurse supervising 150 patients scattered over six wards.

Catherine Sinchuk's story: Catherine Sinchuk was 23 when she was found babbling incoherently in the streets in 1921 by Philadelphia police, who took her to Byberry—routine practice in those days. She continued her babbling, intensely at times, but no attempt was made to treat her condition. She remained at Byberry for 48 years. "Catie" Sinchuk was a "good patient" who crocheted a lot, didn't cause any trouble, and therefore didn't get any attention. In 1969, someone thought her babbling might actually be a foreign language. A Ukrainian-speaking employee was brought in, and Sinchuk's eyes lit up at the sound of the language she hadn't heard for nearly five decades. She said she had come to America from Ukraine in 1913, fell in love with a young man, and became pregnant out of wedlock. She was ostracized by the Ukrainian community; her child died, and then her lover died of pneumonia. She cracked under the strain, and that is when police found her on the streets. For 48 years, no one understood her—or bothered to try. In 1969, after being in Byberry from age 23 to age 71, she was released and lived in a home with Ukrainian-speaking nuns. She died in 1983.

Necrology

December 26, 1967: The body of John Burke, 66, is found by hunters. Missing for three days. Died of exposure. *February 17, 1968*: The partially burned body of Theresa M. Macutkiewicz, 38, is found in the restroom of a Bensalem Township gas station. Missing for two days. Matches found on floor. *April 27, 1968*: Joseph Bergin, 57, is killed when struck on the head by another patient. *July 6, 1968*: The body of Joseph Wilderman, 27, is found in a lavatory closet with puncture wounds in the chest. Two patients stabbed him with a ballpoint pen. *August 22, 1968*: James Hardy, 40, is beaten to death on hospital grounds by another patient. *February 14, 1969*: Richard Chambers, 32, a patient since he was 16, is beaten to death with a shoe by another patient. *July 18, 1970*: The skeleton of a man is found in tall weeds on the hospital grounds. Positive identification is never made. The field had not been mowed for three years. *July 25, 1970*: The decomposed body of Thomas Mulligan, 67, is found in a field of blackberries behind the hospital.

   In April 1987, state Public Welfare Secretary John F. White Jr. formed a special task force to investigate Byberry. In September, the group issued a report in which it said patients were being neglected, beaten, and sexually abused. The report called for "immediate and drastic action to reverse the history of neglect, poor management, absence of treatment, and rampant abuse." In response, White allowed the superintendent to retire and suspended three assistant superintendents and the medical director.

And in December, Governor Robert P. Casey announced plans to close Byberry forever within two years. There were then fewer than 500 patients at the hospital; those who remained would be transferred to other state facilities.

———

Report of the Blue Ribbon Committee established to review the clinical and patient care programs at Philadelphia State Hospital (PSH), September 1, 1987: "PSH, while having sufficient staff and financial resources, has not used those resources well to provide an effective treatment program, stable and continuous contact with the community mental health system, and sound staff organization. . . .

"[The Blue Ribbon Committee] members and staff have minutely reviewed incident reports for the past several years and sadly note a conspicuous failure to follow up on these abuse reports, especially with those few employees who appear to be repeatedly the subject of such reports. . . .

"[There are] clear indications that the selection of superintendents has not been based on criteria related to patient care issues but rather on practical and political expediency."

———

Unidentified Byberry employee (to Blue Ribbon Committee members as they left the hospital): "See you again in four years."

———

Billy Kirsch's story: On March 9, 1988, a federal judge ordered that Billy Kirsch, 27, a Byberry patient for three years who had been bound in restraints for the previous 14 months, be moved out of Byberry, given intensive therapy, and then placed in a group home. Kirsch, who is mildly retarded, had been shackled at his wrists, or ankles, or both, 24 hours a day. Lawyers filed a suit on his behalf alleging that the restraints violated Kirsch's constitutional rights and only caused his problems to get worse. U.S. District Judge James M. Kelly ruled that Kirsch's treatment at Byberry was "professionally unacceptable." Kirsch was placed at the Polk Mental Retardation Center, where he is receiving treatment, unshackled, and reportedly doing well.

————

WHILE HE WAS SUPERINTENDENT at Byberry, Daniel Blain had a dream. It involved a three-century-old farmhouse that sat a few hundred yards from the hospital. It was the birthplace of Dr. Benjamin Rush, the first American to suggest that the insane were suffering an illness and ought to be treated instead of mistreated. Blain's dream was to move the farmhouse onto Byberry grounds and make it a Museum of Psychiatry.

But in March 1969, the City of Philadelphia sent a demolition crew out to the northeastern section of Philadelphia; the men made a mistake in addresses, and Benjamin Rush's house was reduced to rubble by a bulldozer. Blain had the stones brought to Byberry and made plans to reconstruct the house, but he died before his dream was realized. On December 23, 1975, Governor Milton J. Shapp signed legislation setting aside 275 acres of Byberry for Benjamin Rush State Park. But for 14 years, the state has not provided any money for the construction of the park.

Somewhere on the grounds of the Philadelphia State Hospital, there is a large pile of stones. Few people know what they are or why they are there.

The Pencil

What's Portable, Chewable, Doesn't Leak, and Is Recommended by Ann Landers?

On a cold January morning in 1985, David Boldt, the editor of the Philadelphia Inquirer Magazine, *called me into his office and asked me whether I thought I could make any topic, no matter how trivial, into an interesting article. I said I wasn't sure. He looked around the office, and then on his desk, and finally opened a drawer. His eyes went wider, and he pulled out a simple yellow pencil. "Give me an article about this," he said.*

Thus challenged, I spent the rest of the day in the Inquirer *library poring through clips about pencils. Computerization of the* Inquirer *had just begun, and most of the old articles were neatly folded clippings that were filed in brown #10 envelopes. It was tedious work, but finally I came across a story explaining that the humble pencil was developed and marketed in 1765 by a German named Casper Faber. Several envelopes later I found*

Originally published as "The Pencil" in the *Philadelphia Inquirer Magazine*, June 16, 1985.

that Faber's great-great-great-great-grandson was making pencils near Wilkes-Barre, Pennsylvania.

Back at home I read through my volumes of the long-running Paris Review *interviews with famous authors. I assembled tidbits such as that Ernest Hemingway used to sharpen pencils ritualistically as a means of getting his creative juices flowing and that he wrote his first drafts in pencil, standing up.*

Further research showed that Abraham Lincoln wrote most of the draft of the Gettysburg Address in pencil. After several weeks I concluded that the pencil was "the most useful, least appreciated, most stolen article in the world." (That may no longer be true.)

Over several days, I toured the factory and interviewed Eberhard Faber IV, the chief executive of Eberhard Faber Inc., who was a trove of pencil lore.

When I turned in my article, David was pleased.

In the years since, pencil sales declined right along with writing by hand because of computerized word processing. Eberhard Faber Inc. was merged into the Faber-Castell Corporation in 1987, Faber retired, and the Pennsylvania operation was closed down. The plant was reborn as a swimming pool factory until it was demolished in 2010.

> We are perishing for want of wonder,
> not for want of wonders.
> —G. K. CHESTERTON

CONSIDER THE PENCIL. The ubiquitous, yellow (mostly), seven-inch, two-for-a-quarter lead pencil—the simplest, most convenient, least expensive of all writing instruments. The most useful, least appreciated, most stolen article in the world. Servant of poet and banker alike. Mightier than the pen or the sword. Nevertheless, the pencil is taken for granted, as though it had no mystery, no background, no wonder.

The pencil is, perhaps, man's closest approach to perfection. The modern pencil can draw a line 35 miles long, write an average of 45,000 words, and absorb 17 sharpenings. It is nearly weightless and totally portable. It deletes its own errors but does not give off radiation. It doesn't leak and never needs a ribbon change, isn't subject to power surges, and is chewable. Any legal document that does not expressly forbid it can be executed with a pencil.

The pencil has many ancillary uses—lubricating stuck zippers, stirring cocktails, twisting tourniquets, cleaning pipes, propping windows, and scratching backs. Perhaps the most unusual use was developed by Ann Landers, who once advised young women that the way to determine whether they need to wear a bra is to place a pencil horizontally beneath one of their breasts; if the pencil falls to the floor, you don't need a bra.

The ballpoint and felt-tipped pens have chased the fountain pen into hiding, but the old wood-shafted, eraser-tipped pencil is still found in nearly every home and office and tucked behind many ears. The dictating machine, telephone, and typewriter have failed to make the pencil obsolete. The word-processor age is well under way, but no one's writing the pencil off. Indeed, sales are increasing.

About 1.9 billion pencils were turned out by the 17 American manufacturers last year, an increase of about 100 million over 1983. About 50 million pencils were purchased by the federal government last year, but the largest concentration of pencils is found on the floor of the New York Stock Exchange, where one million pencils were reduced to stubs last year.

The pencil's simplicity emerges from great complexity. Thousands of people participate in the making of a single pencil, using about 40 raw materials from all over the world. But very few of these people know they are making a pencil, and not one of them could make a pencil alone.

Pencils are made in most countries (the estimate is that 14.4 billion were produced worldwide last year), but fewer than 3 percent are imported to the United States. The Japanese, the Germans, and even the Soviets (theirs are red) are in the pencil business, but they haven't made a dent in the U.S. market. American negotiators at the SALT II talks in Geneva in 1980 noticed that each day, the freshly sharpened "U.S. Government" pencils they placed at the bargaining table were missing by the end of the session. They finally discovered that the Soviet delegates were taking the pencils, and one of them confessed: "Ours don't work very well, and they don't have erasers."

No one person invented the pencil, but the pencil as we know it today was developed and marketed in the village of Stein, near the ancient German city of Nuremberg, in 1765 by Casper Faber. Today, his great-great-great-great-grandson is making pencils near Wilkes-Barre, Pennsylvania.

The pencil plant of Eberhard Faber Inc. sits on a 27-acre site in the Crestwood Industrial Park near Wilkes-Barre. The evergreens around the low-slung building are mittened in snow, and a huge American flag is snapping salutes in the brisk wind. Beneath it is a smaller flag with a large "E" on it, symbolizing an award from President Reagan last year for outstanding performance by an American manufacturer in exporting. The lead area of the plant is athrob with machinery, and the concrete floor is rink-slippery with powdered graphite.

As every schoolboy and schoolgirl ought to know, there is no lead in the lead pencil, though until about 1970 there were traces of lead in the paint on the pencil. The "lead" of the pencil is composed chiefly of graphite and clay—the more clay in the mixture, the lighter the imprint of the pencil, and the higher its number. A No. 1 pencil is darkest and has the least clay. The modern pencil is erroneously called a lead pencil because the finders of graphite about 400 years ago noted that it marked like lead.

Bags of graphite from Mexico, looking like coal, and bags of clay from Georgia, looking like powdered sugar, are piled on the floor. They are mixed with water in a machine called a Knead-a-Master, and the resulting doughy material is pushed through a machine that makes spaghetti-like strands that are dried and baked in an oven.

The process is industrially efficient but considerably less romantic than the way Eberhard Faber once made its pencils. The clay used to come from Bavaria, not far from Casper Faber's original plant, and its quality was so high that during World War II, American pencil manufacturers stockpiled it for drafting pencils needed to design ships, planes, and other military hardware. After the war, Bavarian clay was one of the first items to be shipped out of occupied Germany. But today the Bavarian mine is nearly depleted, and there are some who think the Georgia clay is better.

Until about 15 years ago, the graphite and the clay were mixed in tumbling machines with flint pebbles, the finest of which were found only on the beaches of Denmark. The egg-size pebbles were selected individually by beachcombers, who were paid five cents each for them. But the development of the Knead-a-Master machines put the beachcombers out of work.

————

THE ANCIENT ROMANS used uncased lead as a marker, but the modern pencil was born in 1564 when a high wind blew down a huge oak tree in Borrowdale, England, exposing the world's first graphite mine. Local shepherds began using chunks of the graphite to brand their flocks. Then merchants cut it into sticks and hawked them on the streets of London for writing. King George II maintained a monopoly on the Borrowdale graphite and prescribed hanging for graphite poachers.

When France went to war with England in the late eighteenth century, Napoleon found his nation cut off from Borrowdale graphite. "Mon Dieu!" screamed the French bureaucracy, whereupon Napoleon commissioned research that resulted in taking inferior graphite, pulverizing it and mixing it with clay, and then firing it in a kiln to produce a hard "lead." Meanwhile, the Borrowdale mine, which contained the richest deposit of graphite the world has ever known, was played out by 1833, but leadership in pencil making had shifted to Germany, where Casper Faber perfected the process of binding powdered graphite and encasing it in wood. In 1765, Faber and his wife set up a factory where they assembled and marketed the world's first commercially distributed pencils.

There was a neophyte American pencil industry in the early 1800s, but none could compete with the German Fabers. After graduating from Harvard in 1837, Henry David Thoreau joined his father's pencil-making business. He pored over books at the Harvard library until he learned that Faber used the fine Bavarian clay to bind the graphite. Thoreau discovered a nearby glass manufacturer that imported the clay, and he surreptitiously arranged to get part of each shipment for the pencil company. Pencils bearing the "John Thoreau & Son" label sold for 25 cents each. Other domestic brands cost a nickel. But Thoreau soon wandered off to Walden Pond, and the pencil company dissolved.

––––––

THE AIR IN THE WOOD ROOM of the Eberhard Faber plant is varnished with the sweet smell of cedar, which is the preferred wood for pencils because it is strong enough not to break, yet soft enough to sharpen easily. No other wood does quite as well. Nearly all of the wood for Eberhard Faber pencils is incense cedar from California's High Sierras. The trees must be at least 25 years old, and 100-year-old cedars are better. Many people believe a hole is drilled in the wood so the lead can be inserted. Actually, the pencil is made like a sandwich. Slats of cedar are cut to pencil length but half pencil width. The wood is grooved, the lead dropped in to one half, and then topped by the other half and glued. Most pencils are then shaped hexagonally. Round ones are easier to hold, but six-sided ones don't roll off the desk. There are constant quality checks in the manufacturing process, for big commercial buyers choose their pencils carefully. The industry estimates that a top-quality pencil will reduce working time by 10 minutes over the life of the pencil.

Casper Faber's heirs continued the family pencil business, and in 1848 Eberhard Faber I, Casper's great-grandson, came to America to establish an import business that included Faber pencils. He became an American citizen, and in 1861 he founded his own pencil business by opening the United States' first pencil factory in New York City on the present site of the United Nations building. Fire destroyed the plant in 1872, and it was relocated to Brooklyn's Greenpoint section, where it stayed for 85 years.

Until the Civil War the pencil was not popular in America, and the favored method of writing was the goose-quill pen. But soldiers on both sides needed something convenient to write letters home with, and the demand for pencils increased dramatically. In addition to Eberhard Faber, there were two other major domestic pencil manufacturers: the Eagle Pencil Company and the Dixon Pencil Company.

When Eberhard Faber I died in 1879, the business passed into the hands of his 20-year-old son, John, who demonstrated his business savvy by promptly going to court and changing his name to Eberhard. Eberhard II headed the firm for 66 years, sharing his authority for most of them with his brother, Lothar.

When Lothar Faber died in 1943, his son, Eberhard Faber III, became executive vice-president, working directly under his uncle, Eberhard II. But two years later, Eberhard III died trying to save the life of his eight-year-old son, Eberhard Faber IV, who had been pulled out to sea by the undertow at the family's summer home near Point Pleasant, New Jersey. The boy was rescued by an uncle, Duncan Taylor.

Eberhard Faber II died in 1946 at 87. The three top Fabers in the pencil business had died within three years of one another, leaving as the logical family successor a nine-year-old boy. The company began a long decline.

———

> All goods coming from my factories I warrant to
> be of the very best material, of uniform quality,
> most carefully finished, and always full count. It is
> my aim to manufacture perfect goods only.
>
> —EBERHARD FABER II
> IN THE COMPANY'S 1892 CATALOG

MOST EBERHARD FABER PENCILS are given eight coats of paint, more than a Cadillac. The plant has machines that can paint pencils in a rainbow of colors, but mostly it paints them yellow. The early American pencils, like Henry Ford's Model T, came in one color—natural wood. But at the 1893 World's Columbian Exposition at Chicago, an Austro-Hungarian firm showed yellow pencils. About this time, Eberhard Faber was introducing what is still the flagship of its pencil line—the "Mongol"—so named because it used Siberian graphite, considered at that time the world's finest. The Mongol was painted yellow to enhance the image.

The yellow pencil became the rage, outselling everything else, and its popularity has never let up. Today about 75 percent of the pencils sold for general writing purposes are yellow, though carpenters have always demanded red pencils because yellow ones are tough to spot in the wood shavings. About 40 years ago, one manufacturer conducted an experiment. It supplied an office with 500 yellow pencils and 500 green ones—identical in all respects except color. A few weeks later, the manufacturer was flooded with complaints about the green pencils—smudgy, weak points, difficult to sharpen. There were no complaints about the yellow pencils. This year, Eberhard Faber is trying to promote a natural finish pencil, but it has gotten resistance from dealers who are reluctant to challenge yellow's long reign.

The pencil business boomed after World War II, but Eberhard Faber became more and more of a stub in the domestic market.

The company missed an opportunity to get in on the ground floor of the soon-to-boom ballpoint pen market, patented by the Hungarian Lazlo Biro, who was negotiating with Eberhard III at the time of his untimely death. By 1949, there was heavy pressure on Julia, the widow of Eberhard III and the major owner of the firm, to sell the company, but she refused and looked warily toward her son, Eberhard IV, now a 13-year-old precocious student at the prestigious Collegiate School in New York City. While she was hospitalized after a major cancer operation, Julia Faber was beset by a potential buyer who managed to get into her room. The intruder was driven out at gunpoint by Duncan Taylor, who earlier had rescued her son from the Atlantic surf.

Eberhard IV took a job as a stock boy with the company in 1952, and he would eat his lunches on the factory roof under the huge sign "EBERHARD FABER"—and dream of a career as a man of letters. By 1956 the company's Brooklyn plant was obsolete, and, lured by a $740,000 low-interest loan from the Pennsylvania Industrial Development Authority, Eberhard Faber moved its operations to the Wilkes-Barre area.

While this was happening, Eberhard Faber IV graduated magna cum laude from Princeton and went off to France as a Fulbright scholar at the University of Poitiers. Later he moved to Paris, took up residence in a fourth-floor walkup, and began writing the Great American Novel. He came back to Princeton in 1961 for graduate work, did a brief stint in the U.S. Army (where his nickname was "Leadhead"), and then went back to Paris to resume his writing career, which so far was all aspiration and no publication.

In 1965, Faber came back to America and the family business, working his way up the ladder as cost accountant, executive trainee, assistant to the treasurer, assistant secretary, secretary, and vice-chairman. But he became unraveled while learning the ropes, and in 1969 he quit the company and moved his wife and two young children to a New Jersey farmhouse, where he played tennis, chess, and poker and occasionally wrote fiction.

There were losses at Eberhard Faber in 1969, and in 1970 there were even larger losses. Management blamed most of the problems on a bad labor situation. But Eberhard Faber IV continued polishing his idleness at the farmhouse, feeling neither restless nor unfulfilled, and some family members began wondering whether he was the sap in the family tree. In 1971 the company hired a consultant, who concluded that the problem wasn't labor but management, and what Eberhard Faber really needed was a management shakeup.

At the time, Eberhard IV was 34, enjoying himself enormously, but he felt the spur of the moment dig into his flanks. He decided to give up on the Great American Novel and work on the Great American Pencil. On June 1, 1971, he became president and chief executive officer of Eberhard Faber Inc.

On his first day in office, he prepared a speech for the company's 500 employees, reassuring them that though the firm was in deep trouble, there were no plans to go out of business. But the largest room in the plant was the cafeteria, which could accommodate no more than 75 people. So Faber gave the speech eight times, and after the last speech to the night shift, he was completely exhausted.

Faber brought in more consultants, revised management organization, improved communications, set new goals, and dropped out of the mass pencil market to concentrate on the commercial, school, and art markets. Within two years, Eberhard Faber was back with the world leaders of the pencil business.

———

ERASERS FOR PENCILS are made by mixing synthetic rubber, a soybean-based filler called factice, and pumice, a volcanic ash from Italy. It is the pumice, not the rubber, in the eraser that erases.

Eberhard Faber was the first company to put erasers on pencils. The idea caught on in the United States immediately, but it has never caught on in Europe. The Europeans claim they shun erasers because they encourage schoolchildren to be careless. But the students, and just about everyone else, carry separate erasers.

Bands of aluminum are shaped into the ferrule, which is the cylinder that holds the eraser to the pencil. A single machine performs the five operations needed to complete the pencil by adding the ferrule and the eraser. A shoulder is cut on the pencil, the ferrule is slipped onto the shoulder and clinched to the wood. The eraser is inserted in the ferrule and riveted.

You can tell a lot about a pencil by its ferrule. An unpainted ferrule indicates an economy pencil, while a painted ferrule with a colored band means top-drawer pencil. The American Pencil Company's "Venus" pencil has a royal blue band, Dixon's "Ticonderoga" has a green band, and Faber's "Mongol" has a gold band on a black ferrule.

The Mongol is Faber's best commercial pencil, and a recent book, *Quintessence*, about familiar and excellent products such as Ace combs and Zippo lighters says the Mongol No. 2 pencils "draw the finest line between certainty and possibility" and "are the instruments of the mind's music." One of the few subtleties in the 1978 movie *Animal House* was that the Omega fraternity house was on the campus of a fictional Faber College, whose athletic teams were nicknamed the "Mongols."

The Cadillac of Faber pencils is the Blackwing, which is heavily favored by composers, including Stephen Sondheim, and Faber's famous Ebony pencils are demanded in the art world.

The story was writing itself and I was having a hard time keeping up with it. I ordered another rum St. James and I watched the girl whenever I

looked up, or when I sharpened the pencil with a
pencil sharpener with the shavings curling into the
saucer under my drink.

I've seen you, Beauty, and you belong to me
now, whoever you are and if I never see you again, I
thought. You belong to me and all Paris belongs to
me and I belong to this notebook and this pencil.

—Ernest Hemingway, *A Moveable Feast*

————

The pencil has made its mark in literature. Hemingway, Theodore Dreiser, Thomas Wolfe, Walt Whitman, O. Henry, Eugene
O'Neill, John Steinbeck, Philip Larkin, James Thurber, and Truman Capote all were partial to the pencil.

Hemingway used to sharpen pencils ritualistically as a means
of getting his creative juices flowing, and he wrote his first drafts
in pencil, standing up. Dreiser wrote *Sister Carrie* in a pencil so
soft that the manuscript had to be specially treated to prevent
smudging. Capote wrote his first drafts in pencil—usually while
lying in bed smoking cigarettes and drinking brandied coffee.

John Steinbeck liked a Mongol $2^3/8$ ("It's quite black and holds
its point well") and Blackwings. Thomas Wolfe used Blackwings
but didn't sharpen them often enough, to the frequent consterna-
tion of his editor, Maxwell Perkins. Wolfe would press down so
hard on the unsharpened pencil that he wore a groove in his middle finger. Archibald MacLeish once described himself as "a pencil
man and a slave to the eraser." He liked Blackwings, and near the
end of his life he lamented in a letter that "people die too absolutely
these days, disappear like pencil marks to an eraser—black wing."

The pencil has been a companion to American presidents since
George Washington, who carried his around in a Morocco red
case. Abraham Lincoln wrote most of the draft of the Gettysburg
Address in pencil. Theodore Roosevelt used a pencil for all of
his diaries and speeches and most of his letters. Herbert Hoover

wrote his autobiography in pencil because it helped him "elimi-nate excess wordage." Franklin Roosevelt liked to doodle with a pencil by drawing little fish. Dwight Eisenhower wrote his mem-oirs in pencil.

———————

A MURAL IN THE RECEPTION AREA of the corporate headquarters of Eberhard Faber Inc. depicts the history of writing, with consid-erable emphasis on the role of the Faber family. If the office of the chief executive officer had a ferrule, it would be bare aluminum. It is small, almost crowded, and unpretentious. A photographic montage of Eberhard Faber I, Eberhard Faber II, and Eberhard Faber III peers across the room to the desk occupied by Eberhard Faber IV. Also hanging on the wall is a painting of a Paris street scene and a painting of the original Faber pencil factory near Nuremberg. A bouquet of sharpened Mongols and Blackwings sits on the desk, and an electric sharpener is nearby.

"You know, my great-grandfather came to America as an agent for the German Faber company," says Eberhard Faber IV, igniting an unfiltered Lucky Strike. "He set up his own company, but the old company continued to prosper. They ran out of males at some point, and today the company is called Faber-Castell. We compete with them in Germany, and they compete with us here."

Around the turn of the century, the two Faber companies were red-hot competitors, and the rivalry led directly to the establish-ment of trademark guidelines in the United States. There was a dispute over which firm made the Faber pencil, and the upshot was that both companies were allowed to use Faber in their name. It was an unusual decision and apparently unprecedented until two restaurants in Philadelphia were allowed to operate with Bookbinder in their names. The Mongol pencil was one of the first products in the United States to have a trademark.

"By the way, there's a story around that the pencil was named the Mongol because my Uncle John, that's Eberhard II, was quite a gourmet and he named it after his favorite soup, Puree Mongole. To set the record straight, the story is apocryphal, and it was named the Mongol to convey the image of Siberian graphite. Eagle did that same thing by calling their best pencil the 'Mikado,' but they changed it to the 'Mirado' after Pearl Harbor.

"But the story about Duncan Taylor driving the would-be buyer out of my mother's hospital room is true. Uncle Duncan seemed to keep popping into my life. When I was at Princeton, there was a big controversy because Alger Hiss was supposed to speak on campus. I wrote an editorial saying it was OK for him to be here, and later someone read my editorial into the *Congressional Record* as an example of communist infiltration of American colleges. When I applied for the Fulbright, I was investigated for subversive tendencies by the federal government. One of the investigators turned out to be Uncle Duncan."

Making pencils is a little bit like spelling Mississippi—it's a question of knowing when to stop. Faber plucks a Mongol No. 2 from the bouquet on his desk, twirls it thoughtfully in his fingers, and says the plant is capable of producing one million pencils a day.

"But one of the big problems I found when I got here was that there were too many companies making too many pencils and engaging in ruinous price wars, and perhaps the most important change I made was to get out of the mass market and concentrate on sales for schools, artists, and offices. We made about 100 million pencils last year. We're the largest maker of erasers in the world, and we also make rubber bands, pens, and markers.

"We emphasize the quality, not the economy of our pencils. Admittedly, we don't have the best prices on pencils. But even so, remember that this Mongol was introduced in the 1890s for five cents, and now it retails for two for 25 cents. There aren't many other products that have been around for 100 years or so, maintained the same quality, and increased in prices only threefold."

Faber administers a silent "touché" with the Mongol, replaces it in the bouquet, and lights another Lucky.

Pencils are a worldwide product, but total imports into the United States are only about 2 or 3 percent. In pencils, the Americans have kept up with the foreign competition. The market is still growing in the United States, but only slightly. The pencil business is booming in the Third World countries because every time they open a school, they need lots of pencils.

"When I came back as president nearly 14 years ago, I thought I'd stay on for no more than one year. But here I am still, and I'm still enjoying it."

There are millions and millions of pencils strewn all over the world with the name "Eberhard Faber" on them, but Eberhard Faber says he doesn't mind. "I'm very proud of my name and feel that it stands for quality, as it always has. This far more than offsets the minor disadvantages of having a name like mine, like being unable to achieve anonymity when it would be desirable."

Faber is so proud of his name that he has passed it on to his son, Eberhard Faber V, who is 18. "We've stopped using the numbers, though, because when people meet us, they don't believe there is such a person—sort of like meeting the Smith Brothers—or they think we'll die if we cut ourselves shaving. People call me Tim, and my son is called Lo, short for Lothar, his middle name. He worked here last summer, and he's going to college in the fall. It's too early to tell if he wants a career in Eberhard Faber."

Faber reaches in the bouquet and extracts a Blackwing, with its distinctive flat ferrule and eraser.

"Try one of these, will you? But I should warn you not to get addicted to them. It's dangerous because they retail for 50 cents each."

If Faber had a tail, he would have wagged it.

The Great Zambelli's Theory of the Big Bang

A Profile of Mr. Fireworks, George "Boom Boom" Zambelli

When I interviewed George Zambelli (a.k.a. "Boom-Boom" Zambelli), he was 61 years old. He continued working for another 18 years, usually showing up at his office at 5:00 A.M. and staying until 11:00 P.M., every day except Christmas. Interestingly, he died on December 25, 2003, presumably not wanting to miss a day of work.

He also continued, right up to the end, his long-standing habit of turning his back on his fireworks shows to view the crowds' reactions.

At his funeral in his hometown of New Castle, Pennsylvania, the family honored him in the only way possible: with a rare daytime pyrotechnic show and a more traditional nighttime display.

He was laid to rest in a mausoleum halfway between the headquarters of Zambelli Internationale Fireworks and the fireworks plant. Nearby today is George Zambelli Memorial Park, where

Originally published as "The Great Zambelli's Theory of the Big Bang" in the *Philadelphia Inquirer Magazine*, June 29, 1986.

there is a memorial plaque and, on a tall pole, four lights arrayed like a fireworks burst.

Dr. George Zambelli Jr. said of his father, "If you asked Dad why he liked fireworks, he would say, 'They are magic.' He thought of himself as an artist who painted the skies. To the very end, that didn't change."

The company is now run by his grandson. Design work is still done in New Castle, but much of the manufacturing has been moved to Asia and Europe.

In the years since Zambelli's death, the company has offered pyrotechnic displays at the Super Bowl, the Kentucky Derby, national party conventions, New Year's Eve at Times Square, the World's Fair, presidential inaugurations, and, of course, some 800 local Fourth of July celebrations annually.

Just before Hunter Thompson, the journalist and author, took his own life in 2005, he wrote a suicide note that asked that the company propel his remains into the sky. Thompson's widow brought the ashes to New Castle, and his wish was granted.

T HEY ARE COSTLY, risky, and unpredictable, with lifetimes no longer than the length of their fuses. They were a diversion of European monarchs, yet the Founding Fathers adopted them to celebrate independence from King George III. They have caused more casualties than the entire Revolutionary War: More Americans have died celebrating their independence than achieving it.

But once again this week, America will reverberate with explosions and, if you listen closely, the softer sounds of jaws dropping and throats oohing. We are ready to trumpet the Land of the Free and the Home of the Brave with fireworks—many of them made by communists.

Halley's Comet comes and goes, but fireworks are always with us. They are as old as civilization. The gun and the cannon are mere offshoots of the fireworks industry. Fireworks have always had a strong association with happiness. They are used to venerate, commemorate, celebrate, inaugurate, and titillate.

Though two-thirds of all fireworks in America will be ignited between this weekend and next, they are becoming more and more a year-round event. The old southern tradition of fireworks on New Year's Eve has spread north and west. Fireworks accompanied Ronald Reagan's second inaugural and Pete Rose's breaking of Ty Cobb's record. And in September, Todd Silver of Puyallup, Washington, used fireworks to propose to his girlfriend. (She accepted.)

The Bicentennial whetted the nation's appetite for fireworks, and in the 10 years since, sales have more than doubled. If there is such a thing as the Golden Age of Fireworks in the United States, it is now. A four-day pyrotechnic extravaganza in connection with the unveiling of the refurbished Statue of Liberty begins Thursday, and it is billed as the largest fireworks display in history. The industry predicts fireworks use during the coming July Fourth weekend will reach an all-time high.

Though the furtive reports of illegal fireworks will still be heard, the celebrations will largely be controlled spectacles. Most states now restrict the use of fireworks by individuals. And Pennsylvania is one of the toughest—only sparklers are allowed.

But there remains a small band of skilled pyrotechnicians to put color and sound in the sky on the Fourth of July. They are nearly all descendants of Italian immigrants who brought their skill with them. They consider themselves artists—painters whose canvas is the night sky.

———

IT's HE. The Great Zambelli. Or, as a recent press release put it, "Mr. Fireworks, George 'Boom Boom' Zambelli, the internationally renowned pyrotechnic king, president of Zambelli Internationale Fireworks Manufacturing Company Inc." He's over there in his white Continental. Behind the wheel. When you've worked around fireworks for 54 years, you like to be in control. He shoots off a skyrocket of a smile and leans over to open the door on the passenger side.

Driving the 50 miles from Pittsburgh to New Castle, Pennsylvania, with The Great Zambelli is as thrilling as any show he's ever done. Tearing along the dotted line at 70 m.p.h., whizzing through amber lights, passing on blind curves, Zambelli reassures his passenger that he's in good hands, both of which he frequently removes from the steering wheel to make a point. The scenery keeps repeating itself, as though on a conveyor belt: darkened steel mills sitting idle like industrial Stonehenges, abandoned gas stations with grass growing in their service islands, narrow wooden houses with men sitting on the porches like shipwrecks on a reef.

"There's Jones and Laughlin. You know how many people used to work there? Six-teen thou-zand. You know how many people work there now? Twenty-three hundred."

There's no economic stagnation at Zambelli Internationale. This is the rush period. May and June are to American fireworks companies what November and December are to other merchants. Most of the year there are about 65 people on the payroll, including perhaps a dozen Zambellis. But during the first two weeks of July, it swells to 1,400 as company "shooters"—the people who set off commercial fireworks displays—fan out across the nation to entertain huge audiences at about 1,200 locations.

Zambelli brings the nose of the Continental to within six inches of a green Honda creeping along at 55 m.p.h. "This guy must work for the government," he says. Deftly he swings out into the passing lane and shoots a glare at the driver that sticks two inches out his back.

"The Statue," he says, "that's going to be something like you never saw before."

This week's Statue of Liberty Fireworks Spectacular in New York Harbor is so big that the sponsors have taken the unusual step of apportioning the work among the nation's three top firms—Zambelli Internationale, Fireworks by Grucci, and Pyro Spectacular. The three are fierce competitors in the big league of fireworks, and this is the first time they have ever worked together.

At 61, Zambelli has retained most of his curly hair, which is flecked with gray. Zambelli Internationale was founded by his father, Antonio, near Naples in 1900, and he brought the business to New Castle in 1920. George began rolling firecracker tubes at age seven, and by 16 he was a shooter.

Zambelli has done them all: The annual July Fourth Washington, DC, show; the Philadelphia Bicentennial Show; Kuwait Independence Day; Ronald Reagan's second inaugural on the White House lawn. He's done the canonization of Mother Seton and the introduction of a new Yves Saint Laurent perfume called Opium. He put together a show for a wake to fulfill the last request of a Maryland priest, and a local steelworker left $750 in his will for a Zambelli show at his funeral. His last wishes were carried out in 1977 with a show that featured 300 rocket-launched American flags fluttering to earth on tiny parachutes.

"We even did a show from the top of the U.S. Steel Building in Pittsburgh," Zambelli says. "Highest building ever used for a fireworks show. It's in the Guinness Book of World Records."

New Castle, Pennsylvania, lies near the Ohio border about equidistant from New York and Chicago, as much midwestern as eastern. Its population is about 34,000, 10,000 below what it was when Antonio Zambelli arrived more than a half century ago. Other Italian pyrotechnicians came here at the same time, and during the 1930s, 25 percent of all American fireworks were produced in New Castle. "All the families came over on the same boat," says George Zambelli, with perhaps a bit of hyperbole. "They were all from around Naples, and they came here because the climate was similar." Later, some of the families moved their operations to other states. Some fireworks companies died because later generations chose not to carry on the pyrotechnic tradition. And one of the plants blew up. But Zambelli remains.

The offices of Zambelli Internationale are in an old downtown hotel that is owned by the family. It is now called Z Penn Centre, and the first-floor directory near the elevator tells you that the tenants include Dr. Donnalou Zambelli, dentist (George's daughter); Dr. Michael E. Drespling, foot specialist (Donnalou's husband); Dr. George Zambelli Jr., ophthalmic surgeon (George's son); the Lauder School of Charm and Modeling, which is operated by Connie Zambelli (George's wife) and Marcia Zambelli (George's daughter and Miss Pennsylvania 1976); and, of course, Zambelli Internationale, which employs Joseph Zambelli (George's brother), Louis Zambelli (George's brother), and Annlyn Zambelli (George's daughter).

Within Zambelli Internationale, George exercises the office of president and the powers of an emperor. The paterfamilias has made his company the world's largest manufacturer and exhibitor of fireworks with the persistence of gravity, the optimism of a seed catalogue, the patience of a child who has just mailed in a cereal box top, an energy level sufficient to build pyramids, and a smile that could sell used chewing gum. George Zambelli is the kind of man who can follow you into a revolving door and come out first.

"Fireworks has always been a family business," Zambelli says. "Hey, it's a dangerous business and you have to trust the person working next to you. That's why we keep it in the family, OK?"

Each family business has its own formulas for various types of fireworks, called recipes, that are guarded as closely as those for Coca-Cola and Colonel Sanders's chicken. The Zambelli recipes were written down in Italian in a little black book, carried across the Atlantic, and now repose in a safe in Z Penn Centre. "Hey, my brother Joe didn't even show me the recipes until about 10 years ago," Zambelli says with a jab at his listener's kneecap.

The basic recipes change as often as the rules of chess. The principal ingredients are base matters—saltpeter, sulfur, and charcoal—which, when combined with other chemicals, are transformed into colored light moving in controlled patterns. The idea is thousands of years old.

No one knows for sure who invented fireworks or their essential ingredient, gunpowder. A case can be made for the Chinese, the Hindus, and the Greeks. We do know that the Chinese were making primitive fireworks by packing saltpeter, sulfur, and charcoal into bamboo tubes 2,000 years ago. These early ears-only fireworks produced such a loud noise that the Chinese became convinced they would drive away evil spirits, and so any important event—death, wedding, birthday—became an appropriate occasion for fireworks.

Though the details are lost in the mists of history, the invention of gunpowder was an event comparable to the explosion of the first atomic bomb. It changed the face of the Earth and the course of its history. When the medieval scholar Roger Bacon stumbled upon the combination four centuries ago, he was so disturbed by its potential for evil that he tried concealing the formula in an anagram. Though there are other claimants to the distinction, the perfection of gunpowder for use in a gun is sometimes credited to a thirteenth-century German monk. The Chinese never saw a gun until 1590, when the crew of a visiting Portuguese warship fired off a few rounds to demonstrate their moral superiority.

Marco Polo found fireworks one of the wonders of the Orient and wrote that the Chinese fireworks made "such a dreadful noise that it can be heard for 10 miles at night, and anyone who is not used to it could easily go into a swoon and even die." He brought fireworks back to the West in the 1300s, and the Italians have been making them ever since.

Soon the Italian fire masters were in demand by the monarchs of Europe. Pyrotechnics came to be patronized by church and kings, and like other royal diversions, fireworks soon filtered down to the masses. But mostly they were a vivid part of royal celebrations. King Louis XIV of France entertained his court with fireworks displays at Versailles that sometimes went on for five consecutive nights. Queen Elizabeth I of England was so smitten by fireworks that she appointed a "royal fire master," and

King James II was so pleased with his coronation display that he knighted his fire master. Russia's Peter the Great was an avid pyrotechnic lover, and in 1881 the coronation of Czar Nicholas III was celebrated by a huge show—despite the fact that he was taking over because his father, Alexander II, had been killed by a nihilist's bomb. Napoleon used fireworks to celebrate his military victories.

New ingredients were added to produce color, and eighteenth- and nineteenth-century Europe was the scene of the most spectacular displays this side of Mount Vesuvius. In 1749, George Frederick Handel wrote his "Musick for the Royal Fireworks" to accompany the firing of 10,000 rockets over the River Thames to celebrate a peace treaty. The piece was played in Washington in 1980 to accompany Zambelli fireworks welcoming the king and queen of Belgium. Handel must have been grinning in his grave. Another great blast from the past was a nineteenth-century show put on by England's Brock family, titled "The Defeat of the Spanish Armada." It involved the construction of wooden frames 80 feet tall and 600 feet wide on which 35,000 individual fireworks were placed. A crowd of 80,000 watched a fiery depiction of naval battles and sinking ships. At Queen Victoria's diamond jubilee in 1897, there was a pyrotechnical portrait of Her Majesty that, through some flaw, unfortunately had her winking at the spectators.

The monarchical love of fireworks did not dissuade our Founding Fathers from adopting them to celebrate the birth of the republic. Indeed, the upstart Americans declared their independence from King George III, who celebrated his birthday every year with fireworks. John Adams, the Boston patriot, was the first to envision fireworks—called "illuminations" in that day—as a way to celebrate independence. Writing to his wife, Abigail, on July 3, 1776, the day after Congress decided to break its ties with King George, Adams said: "I am apt to believe that it will be celebrated by succeeding generations as the great Anniversary Festival.

It ought to be solemnized with pomp and parade, with shows, games, sports, bells, guns, bonfires and illuminations from one end of the continent to the other, from this time forward and forevermore." The American fireworks industry knows of this letter and will use it at the drop of a ladyfinger, especially when confronted by legal attempts to restrict its product.

The offices of Zambelli Internationale seem to be going in one era and out the other. The dignified remains of the old hotel—chandeliers, carved woodwork, and brass doorknobs—coexist with drop ceilings, fluorescent lighting, and the winking cursors of computers. Zambelli's office is in Room 40 of the old hotel, and he sits at a desk surrounded by file folders on the floor. The Zambelli file cabinets bulge with records of past projects—papal visits, world's fairs, inaugurations, telethons, Rose Bowls, Super Bowls, and the return of the hostages from Iran. The walls are filled with testimonials from satisfied customers: Hubert Humphrey, Jimmy Carter, the Reagans, Macy's Department Store, Disneyland, the Dallas Cowboys, Resorts International, the Philadelphia Bicentennial Commission, and the governments of Kuwait, Nicaragua, Belgium, and Bolivia.

The world's largest Rolodex, a foot-square, sits on the desk. Zambelli is talking on the telephone, but he regularly pauses to issue a resurgent stream of orders, each one weighing in at a ton. Female staffers come in and out of the office, dodging around each other in the hallway like cars in a Buster Keaton movie. Occasionally, they return fire by buzzing on the intercom. *BRRRRP!* "The Cleveland Indians want to know." *BRRRRP!* "Bacardi Rum is on the line from Puerto Rico." But it's no contest. The Great Zambelli has them all on the run.

Between orders and phone calls, Zambelli is answering questions from a visitor. One of them is about the danger of fireworks, and he stops abruptly, as though the needle has been lifted from a record. "You can't ban fireworks. They're synonymous with America. Lawnmowers and chainsaws are dangerous, too. What you can do is keep the manufacture and display of fireworks in the hands of experts."

The world's worst recorded fireworks disaster occurred on May 16, 1770, in Paris at a display honoring the marriage of the future King Louis XVI to Marie Antoinette. The show went off fine, but in the excitement a scaffold collapsed, and the crowd panicked. About 800 people were trampled to death. The royal newlyweds distributed money to the families of the victims, but the masses were unassuaged—and eventually got revenge with the guillotine.

Pyrotechnical apologists point out that it was not the fireworks that killed the people, but this was not the case in Paris 21 years before during a celebration of the Peace of Aix-la-Chapelle. French and Italian fire masters fought with one another for the honor of lighting the first fuse, setting off the entire display in the confusion. Forty people died; about 300 were injured seriously.

The issue of fireworks safety has always burned brightest in democratic America, where July Fourth celebrations soon came to be colored red, white, and black and blue. July 5 newspapers were filled with such headlines as "Girl Killed by Firecracker" and "Boy Blinded by Fireworks." July Fourth became known as "Death's Busy Day" and the "Carnival of Lockjaw" because of the large number of infections from burns. The phrase "Have a safe and sane Fourth" was originally an admonition to beware of fireworks. On July 4, 1903, 445 Americans were killed by fireworks, and about 4,000 were injured. The American Medical Association surveyed the period from 1900 to 1939 and came up with 4,290 fireworks deaths, 96,000 injuries. The tolls for fighting the Revolution were 4,044 deaths, about 6,000 injuries. The American Medical Association (AMA) said that in 1927, 21 children died from eating fireworks called crackerballs, which looked like candy.

The record in Philadelphia was worse than the national average. In 1864 a diarist noted that in the city "as a general rule

30 or 40 houses are set afire every Fourth of July." On October 24, 1882, eight people were killed when fireworks exploded near Boathouse Row during a celebration of the bicentennial of William Penn's landing. Jean Baptiste Revelli, the longtime maître d'hôtel at the Bellevue Stratford, was killed on July 4, 1926, at a city-sponsored fireworks show.

The forces for good rallied. For years, the *Ladies Home Journal* made annual appeals to mothers to organize games and parades for children on the Fourth to keep them away from fireworks. There was widespread legislation against the sale and use of fireworks. New Jersey enacted a ban in 1937, and deaths and injuries were reduced by 90 percent the first year. In Pennsylvania, the flames of reform were fanned by the *Inquirer*. A bill banning all fireworks except professional displays was introduced in Harrisburg, and the legislature listened to testimony from adults who had been blinded as children by fireworks and from parents whose children had been killed by fireworks.

The law was signed in May 1939, and the following July Fourth, police stopped cars on the Philadelphia side of the Tacony-Palmyra Bridge and searched for contraband fireworks. It was one of the most effective laws ever passed in Harrisburg. There had been six deaths and 1,702 injuries from fireworks in Pennsylvania in 1938. This was reduced to no deaths and 40 injuries in 1939. There was not a single fireworks death in Pennsylvania for the next 25 years. In 1943, police and fire marshals searched Philadelphia in late June and could not find a single firework in the entire city. Nationally, the AMA recorded only six fireworks deaths in 1946 and then stopped counting.

In 1973, the Consumer Product Safety Commission considered a national fireworks ban, but after three years of debate and legal action, the commission decided instead to place restrictions on the size and charge power of firecrackers and set more rigid safety standards for casings and fuses. The effect of the action was to ban such explosive devices as cherry bombs and M-80s but allow

Roman candles, smoke devices, and sparklers. State laws vary widely, but in general there are 14 states that ban all fireworks, six that allow only sparklers (Pennsylvania is one of these), 28 states that allow Roman candles or other larger fireworks, and two, Hawaii and Nevada, that have no fireworks laws.

South Carolina is the only state on the Eastern Seaboard to permit the sale of a wide variety of fireworks, and about 20 percent of all U.S. fireworks sales occur within its borders. About $1 million of that total is at a single outlet: the Fort Pedro Fireworks Store, which is part of the South of the Border motel complex near Dillon. It's the largest retail fireworks outlet in the nation, and about 95 percent of its sales are to out-of-state residents, who stop on their way elsewhere to pick up items such as Red Rats that skip and fizz close to the ground and Flamboyant Chirping Orioles that shoot up flying wings and bouquets of color. There are more than 1,000 smaller outlets lining the interstates with such names as Cheap Charlie's, Loonie Luke's, and Joker Joe's.

There is a thriving black market in bootleg fireworks, and individuals are able to buy such banned items as M-80s and cherry bombs out of the backs of station wagons. It is also possible to obtain fireworks through the mail, and many are advertised in comic books. Especially dangerous are kits containing chemicals that the amateur pyrotechnician mixes before igniting. Last year, there were about 10,300 fireworks injuries in the United States. The total has remained more or less constant over the past 10 years, despite a dramatic increase in sales. Indeed, in recent years fireworks have posed a far greater threat to the makers than to the users.

Zambelli Internationale makes its fireworks at an isolated 360-acre site about 10 miles from the Ohio River. From the air it looks like a miniature golf course—tiny concentrations widely spaced out and connected by worn paths. These concentrations are concrete block buildings, about the size of a one-car garage. They are called magazines, and each produces a different type of firework.

There are 22 magazines in all. Some are 200 feet apart. A few, where the bigger fireworks are made, are 500 feet apart.

When a magazine door is opened, the smell of black powder leaps out like a lion from a jungle thicket. Two or three aproned workers are in each magazine. Winter has gone into extra innings this day, and many of them have been picked off leaning toward spring in short-sleeved shirts. Though death is but a spark away, the workers seem unconcerned, floating along the current of the day as though this were a garment factory. A young woman sits at a wooden treadle, pulling string around a cardboard canister loaded with explosives. "Paper, paste, and twine are the most important ingredients," says Zambelli. "With the exception of pressing some inner parts, everything is done by hand."

Fireworks are controlled combustion—a blend of chemistry, physics, and aesthetics. Display fireworks are either packed in a tube, about the size of a tennis ball can, or a round shell about the size of a bowling ball. The pyrotechnician decides what the firework should do and then packs the shell accordingly. The way the shell is fused, the arrangements of the "stars" (chemical pellets that produce the colors) and the arrangement of the "salutes" (they make the bangs) are responsible for the effect of the firework.

The shell is placed in a long tube called a mortar. The black powder at the bottom of the shell is ignited; trapped gas propels the shell out of the mortar. The size of the lift charge determines the height at which the firework explodes, which ranges from 300 to 1,000 feet. The stars, about the size of sugar cubes, determine the colors. White is difficult to produce, but a display with the color blue has the master's touch. The blue flame is one of the most difficult because it requires copper chloride, which will emit blue light only when the star heats up to 1,000 degrees. If the star burns any hotter than that, the flame will turn red or green.

Fireworks are not handmade out of some urge for quaintness. There is virtually no machinery in the manufacturing process because of the danger that it will cause an explosion. Static electricity is a constant threat, and Zambelli employees are cautioned not to comb their hair at work. They are also not allowed to wear synthetic clothing that could cause a lethal spark. Workers are in the habit of picking objects up and carrying them to another place. Nothing is pushed.

There have been two serious explosions at Zambelli Internationale. Zambelli's brother-in-law was killed in a 1950 blast, and in 1976, two workmen were injured in an explosion. By industry standards, this is a remarkable safety record. (Zambelli does not have property insurance on his plant because it is too expensive to justify.)

Fireworks plants have long been among the world's most dangerous workplaces. In 1930, an explosion at the Pennsylvania Fireworks Display Company plant in Devon killed 10 employees and wiped out more than 100 surrounding homes. The force of the blast was sufficient to derail and wreck a passing freight train.

Last year was one of the worst in history. Nine people died in May 1985 when a bootleg fireworks operation exploded near Youngstown, Ohio. In June, a legal factory near Hallett, Oklahoma, erupted in more than 300 separate explosions, killing 21 people. Also last year, there were plant explosions in Cantanhede, Portugal (six dead); Monte Carlo (three dead); and Calcutta (18 dead). Since 1976, federal authorities say, 80 people have died in accidents at American fireworks plants. In August, U.S. Labor Secretary William Brock announced that all fireworks plants employing more than 10 people would be inspected because of increased concern for workers' safety. Nevertheless, the American plant record looks good on an international scale. There were 578 fireworks deaths in China just last year.

The old hotel restaurant at Z Penn Centre is still open. Zambelli ignores the elevator and uses the stairs, two at a time, to go to lunch. There's a Manhattan waiting for him at the bar. He takes a quick sip and carries it to a table, where he is joined by his lawyer, his accountant, and his banker, who regard him with a kind of amused awe.

Lawyer notes that the cost of liability insurance for fireworks shows has gone up about fivefold and this year will cost Zambelli Internationale about $750,000. "I hope you haven't already signed too many contracts that you can't factor that in," says Accountant. Zambelli sips his Manhattan, raises a worried tent of eyebrows, but says nothing—and instead steers the conversation into a quiet channel of reminiscence.

"You ought to see Jimmy Carter," he says through a melon slice of a grin, as he recalls the former president's reaction to the Zambelli fireworks show at Carter's inaugural celebration. "He's just like a kid. All excited and happy.

"I'll tell you what people like about fireworks," Zambelli adds, though no one has asked. "What's the first thing you remember getting excited about as a child? Lightning bugs, right?" Banker looks up as though he's just swallowed his fork, but Zambelli doesn't wait for an answer to his question. "Sure, of course, it is. It's the mystique of the night. And then the second thing you got excited about was fireworks, right? That's the mystique of the night, too, right?"

Whatever the merits of the Zambelli Lightning Bug Theory, the principal hypothesis advanced for the appeal of fireworks is that they are an intrinsic part of the festival experience, events that allow people to let their hair down in a culturally acceptable way. In 1966, Dr. William E. Schumacher, state mental health director in Maine, suggested there was a therapeutic value to fireworks. "Fireworks are a wonderful way of getting rid of tensions," he testified in endorsing a bill to liberalize the state's fireworks law. "People ought to have a chance to blow off steam once in a while." Festivals are common to all cultures. The American festivals are the Fourth of July and New Year's Eve, which also happen to be the principal occasions for fireworks.

Mexicans hold about 3,000 fireworks festivals every year, and on September 15, Independence Day, nearly 250,000 people crowd into Mexico City's central square for an hour-long display. The big occasion in Canada is Victoria Day, celebrated in late May. The major British celebration is Guy Fawkes Day, November 5, marking the day in 1605 when Fawkes unsuccessfully tried to blow up the House of Commons. It's July 14, Bastille Day, in Paris, and in the first week of August, the Germans blast off fireworks along a 17-mile stretch of the Rhine. Spain's big bang lasts for a whole week in mid-March in Valencia, and at the Festival of San Fermin in Pamplona, the fireworks are at least as dangerous to participants as the bulls running through the street. An average of 100 people end up in hospitals in Naples with fireworks injuries on New Year's Eve.

Moscow's skies light up 10 times a year with national celebrations, and there are simultaneous pyrotechnics in the 15 capitals of the Soviet republics. In India it's the Festival of Lights on October 27 as part of the Hindu celebration of Divali, and during the first week of August, a Japanese religious organization called Perfect Liberty puts on a million-dollar show at a golf course in the town of Tondabayashi. The small island nation of Malta is one of the world's biggest fireworks users, and they are used in nearly every town on March 31, Malta's National Day. So serious are the Maltese about fireworks that when a national company won a worldwide competition in 1980, the returning winners were met at the airport and carried off by a large crowd.

Americans, too, are serious about fireworks, which they have been setting off at the rate of 2.5 billion pieces a year recently. Banning fireworks is labeled taking the independence out of Independence Day. In 1953, New York police trying to arrest fireworks vendors were surrounded by about 20 angry boys, who prevented the arrest and stoned the police car as it drove away. Substitutes have been tried without success. In 1963 Congress passed a resolution calling for bells to be rung throughout the land. It was called "Let Freedom Ring," but the sound of explosions drowned out the bells.

Two of America's space pioneers were fireworks fans as children and learned from their experience about the laws of motion, chemical oxidation, and other principles that led to the exploration of space by vehicles propelled with liquid rocket fuel. Robert Goddard, the father of modern rocketry, got interested in the field at 15, and his childhood diary for July 4, 1898, reads: "Fired cannon, pop and firecrackers all day. In the evening had five skyrockets, three Roman candles, one large pinwheel, red fire and a Japanese match which I made." And Wernher von Braun tinkered with fireworks throughout his youth.

Jimmy Carter was not the only resident of 1600 Pennsylvania Avenue to marvel at fireworks. In his speech for the Bicentennial, Gerald Ford remembered, "I knew what happiness was when I was a boy. It was the Fourth of July. For weeks we would save up our pennies, nickels and dimes, and then at the last moment, Dad would come through with a couple of bucks for skyrockets." Ronald Reagan recalls, "We'd count and recount the number of firecrackers . . . determined to be up with the sun so as to offer the first thunderous notice of the Fourth of July."

But perhaps America's greatest pyrotechnic maniac is George Plimpton, editor of the *Paris Review* and participatory journalist who published a loving book in 1984 titled *Fireworks*. He believes that pyrotechnics is an art, providing for the eye what music provides for the ear. Plimpton is no paper pyrotechnician. He helped put together the show for Ronald Reagan's inaugural in 1980, and in 1983 he helped choreograph the spectacular show for the centennial of the Brooklyn Bridge—a 9,500-shell, $150,000 extravaganza that was viewed by two million people. In 1981, Sakowitz, the Houston department store, advertised in its Christmas catalogue a $1 million fireworks display narrated by Plimpton, but there were no orders.

For the past 20 years, Plimpton has put on fireworks shows for his friends at his Long Island beach home, and often these events have appeared in newspapers in places other than the society pages. He failed to get a required local fireworks permit in 1972, and he was handcuffed and arrested by police while he was having dinner with 40 or so close friends, including Senator and Mrs. Edward Kennedy. In 1979, something went amiss, and fiery debris began falling on the likes of William S. Paley, Kurt Vonnegut, and others.

Two events of the 1970s figured prominently in the boom in American fireworks. One was Richard Nixon's visit to China and the resulting trade agreements. American fireworks distributors were among the first businessmen to go to China after the establishment of trade relations. The rest of the world can't hold a Roman candle to the Chinese in pyrotechnics, and their fireworks are considered superior to all others. The new imports stimulated American appetites. The great pyrotechnicians, including George Zambelli, now offered displays with Chinese-made items such as "Yellow Birds Fly over a Battlefield"—91 explosions in less than five minutes. Before China was opened up to American business, only 10 percent of all fireworks sold in the United States were imported. Last year, 60 percent of all fireworks used in America came from China alone, an additional 15 percent from other countries.

Then came the great 1976 Bicentennial shows in New York, Washington, Philadelphia, and cities and small towns across the nation. "People discovered the beauty of fireworks during the Bicentennial," says John Conkling, executive director of the American Pyrotechnics Association in Chestertown, Maryland, an organization of 170 manufacturers, importers, and distributors. Before the Bicentennial, American fireworks sales were running about $30 million a year; last year, they totaled about $150 million. Fireworks have been used increasingly in promotions, political rallies, and fancy weddings. Baseball teams have been staging "Fireworks Nights," and they are drawing bigger crowds than Ladies' Days and Bat Nights.

BRRRRP! Bacardi Rum is on the line again from San Juan. "Hey, don't worry, you're in good hands," Zambelli purrs into the receiver. "Have I ever let you down?" Zambelli hangs up, rubs his martyred left ear, picks up the microphone to a dictating machine. "Mr. Robert Santanna. Called you today. Left our 800 number. Blah, blah, blah. Could you get back to us as soon as possible. We need to know the date of your show. Sincerely, George Zambelli, blah, blah, blah."

"Bring me the Kuwait file," he shouts into the intercom. He begins pacing and points to a picture on the wall. "Gorgeous, isn't it? We call that the Crystal Palace. Lasts forty seconds and costs about three thousand [dollars]." He stops at a photograph of the Zambelli family with Jimmy and Rosalyn Carter. "This is at the back door to the White House. You very seldom get there, you know," he says, winking conspiratorially.

"Yup. No doubt about it. It was the Bicentennial. Something happened over that Fourth of July weekend that made people want good shows again. My business has gone up 10, 12 percent every year since."

The Kuwait file arrives. "No, no, no," he says tragically, as though Italy has lost the recipe for pasta. "Not this one. I mean the one with the work papers in it." He drums his fingers on the desk.

This week the Great Zambelli will be at the Statue of Liberty, which his father passed 46 years earlier on his way to New Castle. Other Zambelli experts will be in cities and towns throughout the land. They will be maestros who light up the sky with pyrotechnic paeans to the American dream. A lot can go wrong during a fireworks show. Shells can blow up in mortars; shells can break unexpectedly and send cinders into the crowd; sparks can get into supplies and set the display off all at once.

But the Great Zambelli is a professional, and he doesn't worry about these things. He worries about rain, which can harm the fireworks and keep the crowd away. Zambelli did the 1972 Republican National Convention in Miami Beach and had a finale that spelled out "NIXON NOW!" Rain threatened, and he worried that it would cause a misfire and that the display would come out "NIXON NO!" to his eternal embarrassment. It didn't rain that night, but it did rain in 1980 for the Kuwait independence celebration, causing several delays.

"Imagine that," he says, thumping his forehead with his palm. "Rain in the desert. They wanted to hire me as a rainmaker."

John O'Hara Could Go Home Again

But No Cheering Crowd Would Await
the Once-Despised Novelist in Pottsville.

In the three decades since this article appeared, John O'Hara went from being a virtual outcast in his hometown of Pottsville, Pennsylvania, to enjoying much wider acceptance.

A watershed event in 1998 helped fuel the renaissance: Modern Library, a division of Random House that reprints classic books, placed O'Hara's Appointment in Samarra *at number 22 on its list of 100 Greatest Twentieth-Century Novels Written in English.*

Local organizations, especially the library and the Schuylkill County Council for the Arts, have hosted annual O'Hara meetings, panel discussions, dinners, and original plays based on his stories. A bronze statue of the author was unveiled downtown. As his Eagle Scout project, a local Boy Scout placed signs identifying O'Hara's fictional street names above the actual street names.

Originally published as "John O'Hara Could Go Home Again" in the Philadelphia Inquirer Magazine, May 16, 1982.

The Pottsville Library once banned O'Hara's books. Today it has multiple copies of all 42 of his books and a pleasant John O'Hara Alcove, with reading chairs and a glass case containing handsome, dust-jacketed books by and about O'Hara.

O'Hara's study has been re-created at Pennsylvania State University's Library in State College. Among the items on display is the Remington Noiseless portable typewriter he used to create Appointment in Samarra. *His papers are housed in the university's Special Collections Department.*

Over the past 75 years, although some of the Pottsville sites and locations that inspired O'Hara have vanished, a remarkable number have changed very little. There's a brochure-guided walking tour of the town.

The row house at 606 Mahantongo Street, where the young O'Hara lived, has been placed on the National Register of Historic Places. An official blue and yellow state historic marker reads, "JOHN O'HARA[.] This was the home, from 1916 to 1928, of one of America's best known novelists and short-story writers. Born at Pottsville in 1905, he used this anthracite region as a setting for several of his major works. O'Hara died at Princeton, N.J., in 1970."

It seems that you can go home again.

DOWNTOWN POTTSVILLE, sucked dry by suburban shopping malls, scratches the eyes. The signs of municipal putrescence are everywhere. Along Centre Street, the main and hardened artery, vacant stores beg for tenants with desperate red telephone numbers stenciled on plywood where windows used to be.

Automobiles, peppered by coal trucks and salted by PennDOT, wait impatiently at traffic lights, eager to get out of town. Even the parking meters look cold and penniless. In shot-and-a-beer bars, defeated faces mumble syllables of sorrow and dream into a television set where they're offering a 36-foot sailboat to the contestant who comes closest to guessing its actual retail price. Big signs at the Necho Allen Hotel promise food, spirits, and rooms, but little signs say it's up for sheriff's sale.

Pottsville is renowned for only two reasons: the old red-light district along Minersville Street, where Pearl Bailey sang and danced in the 1940s before she became famous, and John O'Hara, who grew up and caroused in Pottsville before he became a famous writer in the 1930s.

It is not at all certain whether the street or the writer was regarded as the greater evil by the respectable citizens of Pottsville. There may be a clue in the fact that when the city fathers tore down the brothels to make way for public housing, one of the new thoroughfares—a short, dingy cul-de-sac—was named John O'Hara Street. It's the only official remembrance of the novelist in Pottsville, but it often makes the local news because there's a lot of crime there.

O'Hara didn't write about the people on Minersville Street. He wrote about the people on Mahontongo Street, which begins at the Necho Allen and runs uphill for about a mile. It was here that the coal-moneyed smart set of Pottsville roosted a half century ago. They liked the climb of the street because it served as a physical reminder of their social and economic superiority. They say Mahontongo is a Native American word meaning "plenty of meat."

Pottsville sits at the southern end of Pennsylvania's anthracite region. In O'Hara's youth, it was a bustling, prosperous city of 25,000 persons, with nine trains a day to Philadelphia. But Pottsville never got over the Depression. The population dwindled to today's 18,000, and there are no trains to Philadelphia, or anywhere else.

Many writers have dealt with the places where they grew up, but few ever made their hometowns the subject of lifelong literary scrutiny, as O'Hara did. He called Pottsville "Gibbsville" after Wolcott Gibbs, late drama critic of the *New Yorker*, with whom O'Hara was friendly in the 1930s. O'Hara's best works—*Ap-*

pointment in Samarra, Ten North Frederick, From the Terrace,
and dozens of stories—are set in Gibbsville. There is an entire
O'Hara geography that fits the real map skin-tight. Mahontongo
Street is Lantenango Street, North George Street is North Frederick Street, Minersville is Collieryville, Cressona is Fairgrounds,
Tamaqua is Taqua, and Pine Grove is Richterville (because the
novelist Conrad Richter was born there).

But it wasn't just places that O'Hara used in mock disguise.
There were human beings, too. O'Hara peopled his Gibbsville
fiction with murderers, bootleggers, philistines, philanderers, pro-
miscuous women, and unscrupulous businessmen. Many Pottsville
residents, some with considerable justification, saw themselves as
unwitting guests at O'Hara's *bal masqué.* It is not entirely clear
just what O'Hara had against Pottsville. The consensus of his
biographers is that his Irish ancestry kept him off society's upper
crust. He was a doctor's son, and his family lived on Mahontongo
Street, owned five cars and a farm in the country, and even gave its
children dancing and riding lessons. But while the O'Haras made
it in Pottsville economically, they never made it socially. When
Dr. O'Hara died in 1925, he left no will and a series of disastrous
investments that soon impoverished the family.

However obscure the reasons, it is clear that O'Hara loathed
Pottsville. In a letter from New York to a hometown friend in
1935, he advised: "If you're going to get out of that God-awful
town, for God's sake write something that will make you get out
of it. Write something that will automatically sever your connection with the town, that will help you get rid of the bitterness
that you must have stored up against all those patronizing, cheap
bastards in that . . . excrescence on Sharp Mountain."

From the time he published his first Gibbsville novel, in 1934,
until he died, in 1970, Pottsville returned O'Hara's hate. You can
still find some old-timers who will sputter in rage at the mention
of his name. But most of the people O'Hara used as models for
fictional characters have since died, so there is not much hate for

John O'Hara in Pottsville anymore. Something far worse has developed: indifference.

There are no secular bookstores left in downtown Pottsville, but there is a Waldenbooks store in a shopping mall not far away, which has an alphabetized fiction section in which Flannery O'Connor is followed by Alan Paton.

"Do you have any books by John O'Hara?"

"What kind of books did he write?" asks the clerk, a woman of perhaps 25.

Could this be true? Would a bookstore in Paris not have any Balzac? No Dickens in London? It seemed preposterous that one of the nation's leading booksellers, at an outlet near Pottsville, would have not a single copy of any of the 42 published books by John O'Hara—or any of the three O'Hara biographies that have been published since 1973. The store manager tries to explain: "We occasionally get a request for one of his books, but not enough to stock them. Anyway, most of them are out of print."

At the Pottsville Library, the free-literature rack has a brochure hawking bus trips to the casinos in Atlantic City. Most of O'Hara's books are available here, though there is no special section for them, and the library does have several scrapbooks of news stories about Pottsville's most famous, though not its favorite, son. "There's not a whole lot of demand for O'Hara's works," says Nancy Smink, library director. "One of the reasons, I think, is that he's not being assigned by high schools and colleges."

If he suffers today at the hands of Pottsville teachers, he suffered mightily from the critics of his own day. He was a vain, sensitive man, so he fought back without ever developing the tough skin of genius. He lusted unashamedly after the Nobel Prize, and he was never able to forget that he hadn't gone to Yale.

He produced a Niagara of fiction in nearly four decades of writing, and he still holds the record for number of short stories appearing in the *New Yorker*: 225. He had unusual writing habits. He would begin work shortly after midnight and write until at least dawn. He typed quickly and cleanly, made a few pencil changes in his first draft, then mailed the manuscript. He had a flypaper memory, and the salient characteristics of his works are tape-recorder dialogue, precise detail, and an almost total absence of simile and metaphor.

At the height of his popularity, O'Hara was outspoken. Indeed, there was no one who could outspeak him. He behaved like a rooster who thought the sun had risen to hear him crow, and he often seemed more concerned about what was in his wardrobe and garage than what was in his books.

O'Hara's lack of critical approbation and his personal abrasiveness may explain the present low state of his reputation. The jury is still out, however, on where, if anywhere, he belongs in the American literary pantheon.

It is safe to say that he was, at times, a very, very good writer. Few would dispute that *Appointment in Samarra* is among the best novels written by an American in this century. Even Hemingway said so. *Appointment in Samarra* covers the final 48 hours of the social and physical destruction of Julian English, a Gibbsville/Pottsville Cadillac dealer and an individualist weary of family and friends. English reaches a crisis point at which he wants to break all patterns of conventional behavior, and he begins his downfall by throwing a drink in the face of a friend, Harry Reilly, at the Lantenango/Schuylkill Country Club. He drinks heavily, insults servants, flirts with the singer girlfriend of a local racketeer, and provokes a brawl at the staid Gibbsville/Pottsville Club. Unable to break free, Julian English asphyxiates himself in his garage on December 26, 1930.

Throughout the novel, O'Hara listed in great detail the business, brand-name, and bedroom preferences along Lantenango/Mahontongo Street. Many of the town's leading citizens found themselves and their friends among the inebriate, adulterous, greedy, snobbish, hypocritical, and criminal characters in the book. Virtuous bosoms heaved with anger and dismay as the novel was passed up and down Mahontongo Street, and men who remembered young John O'Hara sitting quietly at the country club listening to their gossip rued their candor.

Estelle Powers, a retired reporter who worked with O'Hara in the 1920s on the now defunct *Pottsville Journal*, remembers well the heavy local squalls that followed publication of *Appointment in Samarra* 48 years ago this summer: "It was nothing less than horror! People bought the book, read it, and then hid it. No one had a good word to say about John O'Hara. A game soon developed. Everyone tried to figure out who was who, and in many cases it wasn't too difficult. I don't think the other O'Hara boys admitted they were related to John for a long, long time."

The Pottsville Free Library banned the book for what in those days constituted explicit sexual content. After rare favorable reviews from New York critics and a heavy demand from its patrons, the library broke down and bought several copies. They were kept behind the counter.

Speculation on the identity of the "real" Julian English centered on three men, including the author himself. In a letter written to a friend 28 years later, O'Hara identified his model as William "Birsie" Richards, a local gambling figure who fatally shot himself in Pottsville in 1933. "I took his life, his psychological pattern, and covered him up with Brooks Brothers shirts and a Cadillac dealership and so on," O'Hara wrote, "and the reason the story rings so true is that it is the God's truth, out of life."

There was never any doubt in Pottsville about the identity of Elinor Holloway, who, O'Hara says in the novel, "shinnied halfway up the country club flagpole while five young gentlemen, standing at the foot of the pole, verified the suspicion that Elinor, who had not always lived in Gibbsville, was not naturally, or at least entirely, blond" (*AIS*, 46).[1] Most people in Pottsville knew of

1. For all citation abbreviations in this essay, see the "Key to Sources" at the end of the chapter.

the incident before O'Hara wrote about it, and the real-life Elinor considered a lawsuit but changed her mind. Today some residents say the woman is still alive; others say she died several years ago.

O'Hara wrote about Pottsville and Pottsvillians for the next 36 years, and in a 1961 short story he even made an attempt at self-justification. As the story unfolds, a lawyer and a doctor from Gibbsville are discussing a local boy, Jim Malloy, who went off to New York and wrote about his hometown:

> "He gave the town a black eye."
> "And not one damn thing he wrote about actually hap-pened."
> "That's what I said. But you as a lawyer and I as a physician, we know that things like them happened."
> "Oh, hell, as far as that goes, I know things that if young Malloy ever heard about them. . . ."
> "So do I." (*AIS*, 34)

Other American authors have written gossamery indictments of their hometowns, suffered righteous reprisals from their former neighbors, and come out of it well. Even Thomas Wolfe was finally able to go home again. In *Look Homeward, Angel*, Wolfe wrote about his early life in Asheville, North Carolina, concealing places and people with a few transparent name changes. When it was published in 1929, Asheville was aghast. One matron wrote to Wolfe that although she disapproved of lynching, she would not object if his "big, overgrown karkus" were dragged across the public square and hanged. There were numerous lawsuits, all of which were dropped. Today there is a Thomas Wolfe Memorial in Asheville, and visitors can walk through the boardinghouse that was Wolfe's boyhood home.

Sinclair Lewis was born in Sauk Centre, Minnesota, which was the model for Gopher Prairie in *Main Street*. The locals howled in-dignantly when the novel was published in 1920, but Sauk Centre now proudly celebrates its most famous resident. Signs herald the "Original Main Street," and a banner proclaims, "Sinclair Lewis' Boyhood Home and Museum." If anything, it's gotten a bit gushy. The high school athletic teams are nicknamed the "Mainstreeters," and you can spend the night at the Sinclair Lewis Motel. Like O'Hara, Lewis was a doctor's son, but unlike O'Hara, Lewis went to Yale, and he won the Nobel Prize.

Willa Cather had a love-hate relationship with her hometown of Red Cloud, Nebraska, which she disguised with various aliases in her novels. Today the town is mapped for a Cather pilgrimage, and there is a picturesque "Willa Cather Memorial Prairie" just outside the city limits.

When Sherwood Anderson came out with *Winesburg, Ohio,* in 1919, his hometown friends in Clyde, Ohio, felt they had been slandered, and the book was burned by the local librarian. But now you can borrow the book from Clyde's library and read it under a tree in Sherwood Anderson Memorial Park.

If you want to pay homage to John O'Hara, you can go to Princeton, New Jersey, where he is buried and where Linebrook, the Victorian house in which he lived and wrote for the last 20 years of his life, is a popular literary site. Or you can go to Pennsylvania State University, where his study has been re-created.

There is nothing official in Pottsville the way there is in Asheville, Sauk Centre, Red Cloud, and Clyde. But there is still a lot of O'Hara there, and if you know where to look, you can walk the same streets he did and touch concretely the sources of his literature. Mahontongo Street, cleansed and puddled by a morning rain, is no longer the home of the super-rich, just the more prosperous. Many of the mansions have been mangled into apartments and offices, and an upstart aluminum rancher or split-level has occasionally elbowed its way between the Edwardian and Victorian elders, left to sulk on either side.

Cut Loose Hair Design occupies the first floor of 125 Mahontongo. There is nothing here to inform you that the building was the office and home of Dr. Patrick O'Hara from 1903 to 1916 and that the first of his eight children, John, was born here on January 31, 1905. On the right side two blocks up, at 314, is the site of the Gibbsville/Pottsville Club, "where almost any sufficiently solvent Christian man, who had made his money in a sanctioned enterprise and did not habitually leave his car parked in front of whorehouses, could be reasonably sure of election within two years of proposal and seconding" (*TNF*, 101). The club burned to the ground in 1974 and was relocated at the top of the hill. All that's left at the original site is a lined macadam parking lot: the "Gibbsville Lot," as a small sign proclaims.

At 401 Mahontongo is St. Patrick's Church, where O'Hara served as an altar boy until he got caught drinking the communion wine and where he became a pariah after having created the Cadillac-driving priest of *Appointment in Samarra*. On the left side of the 600 block, yellow-slickered schoolchildren are walking up the steps leading to St. Patrick's School, where O'Hara received most of his elementary education.

A few doors away, on the right side, is 606 Mahontongo, where O'Hara lived from the time he was 11 until, at the age of 23, he put on his raccoon coat and sped off to New York in his Buick roadster.

The three-story dwelling, patterned after a New York City townhouse and built about 1870, was first occupied by D. G. Yuengling, founder of a brewing company. Dr. O'Hara bought the house in 1913. Today it accommodates six apartments, and its present owners have painted the exterior cream with dark green trimming—the way it was when O'Hara lived there.

Landis and Mary Heistand, who live just up the street, bought the building in 1977 with the idea that it had historical significance. The Heistands sought government help in restoring it, but say they became discouraged after Harrisburg and Washington expressed little interest.

"There's nothing exciting about it anymore," Mary Heistand says. "It's just an ordinary old house."

Nonetheless, the Pennsylvania Historical and Museum Commission will place an official marker at 606 Mahontongo next month, and Governor Thornburgh, an avowed O'Hara fan, is scheduled to officiate at the ceremonies. But there are no further plans for the building in whose first-floor dining room John O'Hara made his first halting efforts at creative writing. That is not distressing to an old man who, bent in the shape of the question mark that is on his face, stands in front of 606. He is asked whether he knew John O'Hara.

"Yeah, I knew him, but I never had any use for him. He was a bum, and he wrote a lot of lies about this town." At the top of the hill, on a side street off Mahontongo, is the new Gibbsville/Pottsville Club, reincarnated in a ski lodge that failed to survive several mild winters. Not only the location has changed. There are a few Mercedeses and Cadillacs in the parking lot, but they are surrounded by Chevrolets and Toyotas, and there is even a Ford van. About 10 years ago the club broke a long tradition and began admitting Jews, and today even women are allowed to become members, although, unlike men, they are not given keys—they must ring for admittance.

The Gibbsville/Pottsville Club does an amazing impersonation of a Holiday Inn restaurant. Plastic floral arrangements bedeck each table, and oversize menus carry the club seal and founding date (1853). The taped background music is the kind played on elevators and in dentists' offices, with the clash of silver and china providing a disrhythmic percussion. At one table sit eight women with silver-blue hair who exchange pieces of needlework and "*Mmmmmmmm*" favorably while sipping whiskey sours and munching Fannie Farmer candies.

The club bulletin board announces there's a bridge game tonight in the Gibbsville Room and reveals that the club has a ladies' auxiliary. Several members have been posted for nonpayment, just as several were on December 26, 1930, when, in *Appointment in Samarra*, Julian English started the brawl: "It was no distinction to be posted at the Gibbsville Club; it could mean that you had not paid your bill six days after the bill was presented" (*AIS*, 96).

The Lantenango/Schuylkill Country Club, where English threw the drink in Harry Reilly's face, has not moved from its location, well outside of town (though Elinor Holloway's flagpole is no longer there). It, too, has liberalized its membership policy since O'Hara's time. "The dinner was at the country club, and Jews were not admitted to the club. But the golf course is the same, so neatly shaved that it made him think of a farmer in his Sunday suit surrounded by other farmers in overalls and straw hats" (*AIS*, 39).

Still an imposing site in town is the Lantenango/Schuylkill County Prison, where they hanged the Mollie Maguire terrorists a century ago and where, in O'Hara's time, "the warden . . . believed in permitting his wards to have newspapers, cigarettes, whiskey, assignations, cards—anything, so long as they paid for it" (*AIS*, 24).

Pottsville's Norwegian Street, which O'Hara playfully called Christiana Street after a Queen of Norway, runs up the hill and is only one block away from Mahontongo. In Gibbsville, though, the two streets were worlds apart. "In order to get a ball game going the sons of the Gibbsville rich had to play with the sons of the non-rich. . . . Consequently, from the time he was out of kindergarten until he was ready to go away to prep school, Julian's friends were not all from Lantenango Street. . . . They would go down the hill to Christiana Street, the next street, and join the gang. The gang's members had for fathers a butcher, a motorman, a freight clerk, two bookkeepers for the coal company" (*AIS*, 76).

John O'Hara was the eldest of eight children, and four of his brothers and two sisters are still alive; three of the brothers live in Pottsville. Eugene O'Hara does not talk to strangers, but Martin and James O'Hara, both of whom live on Norwegian Street, more than atone for his silence.

Mart O'Hara, 71, born five years after John, has lived with his wife, Marge, at 913 Norwegian Street in a small brick row house for 30 years. Parking is difficult on Norwegian Street, and Mart has placed a sawhorse in the space in front of his house to reserve it for his interviewer. The house, built in 1895, is neat and clean enough to pass a white-glove military inspection.

For most of his adult life, Mart was a foreman at an aluminum plant, but he also worked as a state policeman, and in the 1930s he was a chauffeur for Governor George Earle in Harrisburg. He has been retired for 10 years, though he still works a few hours a day as a bookkeeper. Mart has been interviewed extensively in recent years by scholars and journalists, and he knows all the questions.

The words tumble from him like coal down a chute.

He tells you about the time John called him in Harrisburg and had him fix a speeding ticket issued to Dorothy Parker on the Pennsylvania Turnpike. He tells you how John shared his first big royalty check with the O'Hara family.

He tells you about how John called after the publication of *Appointment in Samarra* and warned the family to "draw the shades at 606":

One prominent Pottsville lady came up to me and complained about "all that filth your brother wrote." I asked her if she had read it, she said she hadn't, so I asked her how she knew it was filthy. Everybody complained a lot, but anytime they heard that John was coming back to Pottsville, the phone rang off the hook with people who wanted to see him.

Everything in *Appointment in Samarra* is true—every event in the book actually happened. Of course, the characters have been changed, most of them are composites. John was funny about the real identities of people in the book, even with me. I remember once asking him who his model was for Julian English, and he yelled at me, "None of your goddamn business."

Except that he's shorter, Jimmy O'Hara looks very much like his famous brother. He and his wife have lived in a 120-year-old row house at 1305 Norwegian Street for 30 years. Jimmy retired as a railroad clerk two years ago.

"We've been annoyed most of our lives by people who keep asking for identities," he says with bitterness. Jimmy and Mart disagree on several points. Mart says the real-life woman who shinnied up the flagpole is dead; Jimmy says he still sees her on the street.

Mart says the model for the society editor of the local newspaper was delighted when she found herself on the pages of *Appointment in Samarra*; Jimmy says she threatened to sue.

On October 13, 1980, the Pottsville Republican carried this headline: "JOHN O'HARA LIVES AGAIN. POTTSVILLE NATIVE WELCOMED BACK." The story that followed described the Second John O'Hara Conference. The first was held in 1978. Both were attempts by a small group of scholars and O'Hara buffs to revive flagging interest in the man and his works. The headline was something of an exaggeration.

The conferences featured lectures, readings, and tours by local O'Hara fans and the tiny band of national scholars who qualify as O'Hara experts. Vincent D. Balitas, a local boy with a doctorate in American literature, is an O'Hara scholar, though he hastens to add he is not an O'Hara fan. He doesn't believe Pottsville welcomed John O'Hara back at either conference.

"Both of the O'Hara conferences were free," he says. "There was no charge for anything. The first one attracted about 1,000 people, including 200 outsiders. The second drew maybe 600. It included a free bus trip of the O'Hara landmarks. There were three buses that could accommodate a total of 120 people. No more than 40 made the trip. There were eight people on my bus."

An offshoot of the first conference was inauguration of the *John O'Hara Journal*, a literary semiannual devoted to articles about O'Hara and original fiction and poetry by local writers. Balitas, the editor, managed to sell subscriptions to 180 persons and 60 college libraries, including those of Harvard, Chicago, and Southern California—but not Penn State. Local bookstores refused to place it on their magazine racks. The *John O'Hara Journal* is now down to fewer than 100 subscribers, and its next issue will be its last.

David Marshall, until recently the executive director of the Schuylkill County Council for the Arts, helped organize the conferences, but he acknowledges that they were "so noncontroversial they were boring." His successor, Merle D. Walker, says O'Hara will figure in the council's future but adds, "Don't expect a lot of Pottsville people to show up for an O'Hara event."

Someone persuaded the Schuylkill County Commission, the county governing body, to ask the U.S. Postal Service to issue a John O'Hara commemorative stamp, but the petition was rejected earlier this year in Washington. "The people of Pottsville are as wonderful as any in the world," says Balitas.

> They're friendly, courteous and hospitable. They just don't read. Reading is not a big pastime here. Pottsville's indifference to O'Hara is nothing more than the general apathy toward literature everywhere. It's the U.S.A. and reading. I spent some time in Poland recently, and the people would borrow my copies of *Time* and *Newsweek* and have evening parties where they'd all sit around and listen to someone read in translation.
>
> The fact remains that the people of Pottsville ought to read John O'Hara because he has a lot to teach them about themselves and their history.

Steven Kachmar, an attorney with an office on Centre Street in the downtown area, believes there is still a lot of simmering resentment against O'Hara. "The segment of the community that has read his books views them not as great literary works, but as being sordid and offensive because of O'Hara's tendency to categorize people into isolated groups based on religion, nationality, and social class," Kachmar says. "Although these categorizations may have been valid then and to some extent are today, the intensity with which O'Hara defines the social classes in this community has left a bad taste in some peoples' mouths—people who are in a position to generate interest in O'Hara."

The people who used to patronize the small local merchants in downtown Pottsville now park and shop at one of several retail smorgasbords called malls, plazas, or centers—instant cities where nobody lives and everybody consumes. The stores are pasteurized and homogenized, offering the same things at the same prices in Terre Haute, Tallahassee, and Tucson.

Outside the videogames arcade in the Fairlane Village Mall, lines long enough to fill a train wait patiently for the privilege of matching wits with such electronic challengers as Armor Attack, Space Fury, and Drag Race. Inside the darkened arcade, flashing multicolored lights illuminate excited faces, and shouts of joy and defeat punctuate the cacophony of simulated artillery fire, machine guns, and high-compression engines.

No one can say Pottsville is behind the times. You can buy almost anything you want here: diamonds, color-coded keys, home computers, wicker chairs, meerschaum pipes, jogging shoes, fox terriers, frozen yogurt. Almost anything, except a book by John O'Hara.

Key to Sources

AIS: *Appointment in Samarra*. New York: Signet, 1957.
TNF: *Ten North Frederick*. New York: Penguin Classics, 2014.

Drawing the Line

The Surveyors Charles Mason and Jeremiah Dixon
Were Hired in 1763 to Settle a Simple Border Dispute.
They Never Knew Their Work Would Become One of
the Most Famous Boundaries in the World.

Because writing this article whetted my desire to know more, this is the only article that evolved into a book. In bits and pieces over long weekends in 1998 and 1999, I walked a good portion of the 332 miles of the Line, and Walkin' the Line *was published in 2000. It is a travel-essay book about the drawing of the Line between 1763 and 1767 and its subsequent symbolic significance as the dividing line between North and South.*

When Charles Mason and Jeremiah Dixon arrived in Philadelphia from England in 1763, they promptly began working on what four years later would become one of the foremost scientific achievements of the eighteenth century: using the stars to accurately measure more than 300 miles of land.

Their efforts would settle a bloody, three-generation border dispute between the proprietary families of Pennsylvania and Maryland, but when Mason and Dixon left Philadelphia in 1767, their work was soon forgotten. Indeed, the official report of the

Originally published as "Drawing the Line" in the *Philadelphia Inquirer Magazine*, January 2, 1994.

survey didn't even mention their names, and almost certainly nei-ther Charles Mason nor Jeremiah Dixon ever heard or saw the phrase "Mason-Dixon Line."

But a half century later, as the national debate over slavery heated up, the Line would take on a metaphorical meaning—the border between freedom and slavery—and the Mason-Dixon Line would become one of the world's most famous boundaries.

This symbolic fame has overshadowed the fact that at the time it was drawn, the Line was the greatest geodetic survey ever un-dertaken and set a new standard for the precise surveying and mapping of large portions of land.

Using satellite technology, an organization called the Mason and Dixon Line Preservation Partnership has located nearly all of the stones set in place by the Mason-Dixon party two and a half centuries ago and has purchased granite markers to replace a few missing stones. The purpose of the project, begun in 1990 and completed in 2013, was both to locate and to preserve the mark-ers, which over time had been damaged by weather, age, and van-dalism but had survived through the Revolutionary War, the Civil War, the Industrial Revolution, and twentieth-century expansion.

The partnership members were surprised at the accuracy of Mason and Dixon's work. According to Todd Babcock, the lead-er of the group, "What they were able to do is simply amazing, es-pecially considering the instruments that they were using and the conditions they were battling. To be able to mark a continuous line of latitude this precisely gives testament to their brilliance."

To this day, the Mason-Dixon Line remains one of the world's most unusual borders. Most boundaries between states and na-tions, if not determined by tangible factors—such as rivers and the crests of mountains—are at least determined by even parallels of latitude and meridians of longitude. But because a court de-cree required that it begin exactly 15 miles south of southernmost Philadelphia, the east–west portion of the Line conforms to the quirky latitude of 39 degrees 43 minutes and 17.6 seconds north.

Y OU CAN'T REALLY WALK the Mason-Dixon Line. There's the problem of creeks and rivers, including the mile-wide Susquehanna. And much of it is on private property—indeed, sometimes it goes right through people's living rooms. But most of all you can't walk the Mason-Dixon Line because it's invisible, an arbitrary and artificial demarcation, direct and true in longitude and latitude but without breadth or thickness.

Perhaps for these reasons, the Mason-Dixon Line is widely misunderstood. It is merely 332 miles long, and it extends only from the Atlantic Ocean to western Pennsylvania. It is the work of two English surveyors; it was completed before the American Revolution; and it had nothing to do with the Civil War. It simply settled a boundary dispute.

But long after the border war ended, and Charles Mason and Jeremiah Dixon died, their surveying job was figuratively extended across the entire nation and became a catch phrase for a complex series of political and social issues. And to this day, nearly two and a half centuries after it was drawn, the Mason-Dixon Line remains a powerful symbol that separates Yankee from Rebel, oatmeal from grits, North from South.

This metaphorical Mason-Dixon Line, celebrated in music and literature, has obscured the fact that the real Mason-Dixon Line is a stunning achievement of skill and courage. Mason and Dixon— constantly fighting against accidents, hostile Indians, snow-covered mountains, flooded rivers, wild animals, and nit-picking bureaucrats—used crude instruments to plot a boundary that is still accepted by the U.S. Geodetic Survey today.

And while you can't walk the full length of the Mason-Dixon Line, you can go out and talk to the people who live on it or near it. You can follow it through many-steepled towns where people and their deeds are still connected; past volunteer fire companies where men and women perform the nation's most dangerous job free of charge; across fields alive with the lusty odors of earth and cattle; and over tree-tufted mountains. It is a strip of landscape, people, and history. History is the realm of ghosts—and ghosts make good traveling companions.

It begins on Fenwick Island, near the emerald meadows of the Atlantic, marked by a stone just outside the chain-link fence protecting the Fenwick Lighthouse, which has a halo of yawping gulls. A woman in a velour running suit, blond ponytail bobbing, jogs by the Mason-Dixon Motel. To her left is Maryland, and to her right is Delaware, though in 1763 the state was part of the province of Pennsylvania and was called "the three lower counties."

Mason and Dixon were summoned from England that year to settle a dispute between the Penn Family and the Calvert Family over just where each other's provinces began and ended. Because of an inept royal geographer, the king's grants to the Penn and the Calverts overlapped. No one noticed for a long time, but then sea captains arriving in Philadelphia with the latest navigational instruments began informing the Penns that their city was in Maryland. The Quaker Penns were not about to give up their famous city to the Catholic Calverts. An agreement on language defining the boundaries was forged in London in 1760.

But knowing where a boundary is supposed to be is one thing; translating that knowledge from map to terrain, with accuracy and precision every foot of the way, is something else. So well did Mason and Dixon do their job that two centuries later, in 1962, when federal surveyors found five marker stones deviating from the Line, they concluded that someone must have moved them because the two Englishmen obviously could not have made such an error.

Delmar, about 27 miles from the ocean, is the first of many towns strung like beads along the Line with names such as Marydel, Penmar, State Line, Maryland Line, and Lineboro. Most of them, like Delmar, live bi-state existences. State Avenue in Delmar is the Mason-Dixon Line—south of it is Maryland; north of it is Delaware. About seven miles farther west is the precise southwestern corner of Delaware, where Mason and Dixon placed a marker on June 25, 1764, to mark the middle point between the Atlantic and the Chesapeake Bay in accordance with the boundary agreement.

Vandals tried to steal the three-foot marker in 1983, but they succeeded only in breaking it off at the base. It was reset two years later, and today it is protected by iron bars and sits just off Route 54.

Eloise Morison, who has lived most of her life at nearby Maple Lawn Farm, stands in her doorway poised in earnest attentiveness, as though she is about to recommend a laundry detergent or offer a hot meal. "We all have a special feeling for the Mason-Dixon Line," she says. "When I was growing up, my father and my uncle took turns cleaning up around the marker, and that's why it's in such good shape."

At her kitchen table, she spreads out a lifetime collection of newspaper clippings and memorabilia from the Line. Then she points to a map and shows how the Line seems to go off slightly away from true north. "My father always told the story that when Mason and Dixon got here, they celebrated a little too much, and the next morning when they started off, they didn't get the 90 degree angle quite right, and so Delaware got more land than it should have." (As coincidence would have it, the list of supplies that Mason and Dixon brought with them to America begins with these items: "120 gals spirits, 40 gals brandy, 80 gals madeira wine.")

As the Line heads north, Delaware is sprinkled with tiny hamlets called Corners (Coopers Corners, Packing House Corners, Lords Corners, Susan Beach Corners . . . Coldwell, Delaney and Everett Corners) and Crossroads (Wrights, Schultie, Melvin, and Adams), as well as unusual names such as Pepperbox, Slaughter, and Hourglass. An occasional horse and buggy clop-clops down the road carrying Amish people, whose ancestors arrived in Philadelphia just 26 years before Mason and Dixon.

Marydel, Delaware, is right next to Marydel, Maryland. They have the same post office but different zip codes; they have different phone companies and different area codes, and a call to a neighbor a few blocks away can be a toll call; playmates board different school buses in the morning. In the middle of town, Delaware Route 8 suddenly becomes Maryland Route 311. Signs on opposite sides of the route say, "Maryland Welcomes You. Please Drive Gently" and "Welcome to Delaware. Home of Tax-Free Shopping."

A young man at the Marydel Volunteer Fire Company directs me to a Mason-Dixon marker in the middle of town. The stone, pitched and skewed by the frosts of 239 winters, is a crownstone marker, distinguished by carvings of the Calvert and Penn coats of arms, on appropriate sides; these were placed at every fifth mile. Other miles were marked with small stones carved with simply "M" and "P."

Many of the Maryland-Delaware markers fell victim to fortune hunters who believed that Captain Kidd and other pirates had buried treasures near the Chesapeake. Others were removed by builders, who found them handy for incorporating into a wall, or by farmers, who found they damaged their plows. Some were pressed into service as doorstops and curbstones.

About 82 miles north of Eloise Morison's farm, the Line begins moving westward as the Pennsylvania-Maryland border. The arc that forms the northern border of modern Delaware is sometimes considered part of the Mason-Dixon Line, but it actually had been surveyed some 60 years earlier. Jeanne Benin and her family live in a house that is in the Landenberg, Pennsylvania, and the Newark, Delaware, city limits. The arc runs through the living room, hallway, and bedroom, and she has a sign hanging from the ceiling in the hallway that says, "Welcome to Pennsylvania" on one side and . . . well, you get the picture.

Just west of the arc, the three state borders meet, and a resurvey of this area in 1849 resulted in a wedge of land, about 800 acres, being in dispute between Delaware and Pennsylvania. Today a sign put up by the State of Delaware along Route 896 gives you a brief history of the Wedge, but the real scoop comes from Enola Teeter, who runs a nursery and lives across the highway on land that was part of the Wedge.

"The Wedge became a no-man's land that was used for boxing matches, cockfights, and other illegal activities," she says, lowering her watering can. "There were so many cockfights that they nicknamed the University of Delaware athletic teams the Blue Hens. If the Pennsylvania police or tax collectors came to your house, you'd say you lived in Delaware, and if the Delaware authorities came. . . ."

The dispute was not corrected until 1921, when it was agreed to have the area and its 100 or so inhabitants—who technically had never been citizens of any state—formally transferred to Delaware. Thus emboldened, Delaware reopened a suit that had been carried on the U.S. Supreme Court docket for more than 100 years as Case No. 1. Delaware contended that it was entitled to all of the Delaware River up to the low-water mark on the New Jersey shore; the case involved fishing rights, and so it was important. In 1924, the high court granted Delaware's claim, and today the state line does not, as it does on most bodies of water, run down the middle of the channel—it parallels New Jersey's low-water mark.

Mason and Dixon began their work in Philadelphia, setting their feet on the cobblestones of Market Street on November 15, 1763. Hardly anyone noticed; their presence was overshadowed by that of John Penn, who had just returned from England with a commission to be governor of Pennsylvania. Their first task was to find the southernmost point in Philadelphia, which at that time they reckoned to be a hog pen near what is now the intersection of Second and South streets. The 1760 agreement called for a boundary 15 miles south of Philadelphia, but since this would have been a spot in the Delaware River, they decided to move the surveying starting point 31 miles west, where they set up a headquarters on the farm of John Harlan.

From a precise spot that they marked with a piece of quartz, Mason and Dixon made observations of the stars, which they used to determine their precise location. Local farmers who saw the two Englishmen gazing skyward every night nicknamed the quartz the Stargazer's Stone, and it still stands today, along with the original fieldstone farmhouse, along Route 162 near Embreeville in Chester County.

The rose-and-gray stone, surrounded by a low protective wall erected by the Chester County Historical Society, seems to be in the spacious grass yard of a large contemporary private home. Nibbling goats stand next to the farmhouse, but it is surrounded by "No Trespassing" signs. Standing at the stone, one imagines the strange sight of two English scientists looking toward the heavens—perhaps nipping at their brandy supply. From this point of reference, they plotted a direct line 15 miles south; they were now on the required latitude and ready for the long trip west.

The Mason-Dixon Line was and remains to this day one of the world's most unusual boundary lines. It is wholly artificial, wholly non-topographical. Most boundaries between states and nations have been determined by tangible factors—rivers, the crests of mountains—or at least by even parallels of latitude and meridians of longitude. But the Mason-Dixon Line does not follow a creek or the crest of a hill, and it does not mark the limit of ancient farms or the course of ancient trails. As it stretches westward, it conforms to the quirky latitude of 39 degrees 43 minutes 17.6 seconds north, and at no point does it touch any prominent landmark.

Frank Peters is sitting on a folding chair in front of the Union Fire House at Oxford, Pennsylvania, chewing on his cheek, pondering a question. He is the unofficial town historian and has a memory like a microchip. "This town's older than its name. . . . Originally it was called Hood's Crossroads. It would've been here when Mason and Dixon went by. I wasn't, though!" says the 81-year-old Peters with a laugh that could topple an oak tree. "The Mason-Dixon Line was important in the years leading up to the Civil War."

The Brandywine Valley, as well as most of the rest of Pennsylvania, was an important thoroughfare for runaway slaves on the Underground Railroad, that collection of secret escape routes used by blacks seeking freedom in the northern states and in Canada. And the Mason-Dixon Line was the goal of every runaway. Slaves plotting an escape often used coded spirituals to communicate with one another, and when they sang of the River Jordan it meant the Mason-Dixon Line.

In all, several thousand people found their freedom by riding an imaginary railroad across an imaginary line.

It was during acrimonious debates in Congress in the 1820s over the issue of slavery that the Mason-Dixon Line first came to be the symbol of division between the slaveholding South and the free North. To this day, the Line is embedded in the national psyche as an extension of the border between Pennsylvania and Maryland to some vaguely defined point in the Midwest. Never mind that all three states—Pennsylvania, Delaware, and Maryland—were on the Union side in the Civil War.

Mason and Dixon moved westward with a tented army, penetrating the wilderness with a party of guides, axmen, cooks, stewards and, apparently, numerous camp followers. To facilitate marking and telescope sightings, the axmen cut down trees and undergrowth to open an eight-foot vista. Most distances were measured with 66-foot iron chains, each made up of 100 links, and each link measuring 7.92 inches.

Today Mason-Dixon Road in Lancaster County takes you through cornfields and some of the world's richest farmland. There are old stone churches with adjacent cemeteries in case you miss the point of it all. Motorists are advised of a coming revival meeting and admonished to "Prepare to Meet Thy God." Here, a pound of sin weighs 20 ounces. Power lines run across a broad swath that cuts through the landscape like a wound.

A series of ever-narrowing downhill roads leads to the banks of the Susquehanna; a well-maintained Conrail track runs along the bank, then into a tunnel spray-painted with the names of lovers and enemies. Just before the tunnel there is a painted line on the rocks that says "Pa." and "Md." When troop trains crossed the Mason-Dixon Line during World War II, it was the signal for black and white soldiers to be segregated; the black soldiers were ordered to the cars immediately behind the engine, where soot would blow in through open windows.

Mason and Dixon arrived here on May 27, 1765, and immediately set about the task of determining the width of the river. For them, this was child's play; they quickly determined it was 67.68 chains, or 4,466 feet, wide. They crossed the river upstream on a ferry at Peach Bottom.

Down at the Delta Family Restaurant in York County, Pennsylvania, the breakfast crowd is still talking about last week's accident. "It happened right on the Line," explains Scrambled Eggs and Home Fries. "Yeah," offers Hot Cakes and Sausage, "one guy was killed, and they didn't know who had jurisdiction. Maryland and Pennsylvania State Police were both there. It took about six hours; all the while, the guy just lay there."

"They finally decided on Maryland," says Chipped Beef on Toast.

Delta, Pennsylvania, and Cardiff, Maryland, seem like the same place, but they are divided by the Mason-Dixon Line, and the waitresses at the Delta are eager to explain about this form of life on the edge; they leap into each other's pauses: "It's a long-distance call across the street." . . . "Delta uses Cardiff's library." . . . "We have a joint fire department with volunteers from both states." . . . "Neighboring kids go to different schools." . . . "We once had a gas station on the Line, if you pumped regular, you paid Pennsylvania tax, but high-test, you paid Maryland."

The Line is marked by a concrete highway obelisk, which looks rather like an ancient fertility symbol, in front of the Service Feed and Supply Store. Inside, the owner, Marlyn G. Flaharty, hands a customer a bag of bird feed in Maryland and crosses over to the cash register in Pennsylvania to check him out. Then he walks to the front door, hitches up his jeans, and warns: "Don't be fooled by that marker. It's about 10 feet too far south. The previous owner moved it because it was blocking the front door."

West of Delta, a section of Maryland Route 624 runs smack down the Mason-Dixon Line: York County, Pennsylvania, is on one side of the road; Harford County, Maryland, is on the other. In New Freedom, Pennsylvania, which got its name because so many runaway slaves crossed here, the road crosses the Line without any sign. This happens in many places, and the only clue to what state you're in is a slight change in the color of the road surface, or the license plates of cars parked at homes.

The Village Inn in Lineboro, Maryland, has a real shuffleboard table, but the bartender has the temperament of an underfed grizzly bear. Do people in town care much about the Mason-Dixon Line? "Nope." He puts a lid on the conversation and sits on it. Then he wipes the bar with a rag that seems to have been dragged in by the same cat that has hold of his tongue.

As befits a man of 83 with a long list of things to do, Ralph Donnelly has little time for superfluity, superficiality, or supper. A retired civil engineer who has spent most of his life as a surveyor, Donnelly is a Mason-Dixon buff (he has built a replica of their portable observatory). On the porch of his home in Hancock, Maryland, a few miles from the Line, he agrees to find some markers.

"But I've got to stop on the way back," he warns in a voice as stern as a Puritan cleric. "I drank up all my Scotch last night, and I've got to get some more."

Before long he is knee deep in weeds, and then suddenly his eyes flare like a lion who has just spotted a plump zebra. He pulls back a handful of weeds and exposes a milestone, the 122d along the Pennsylvania-Maryland border. There's an "M" on the side of the stone that is in Washington County, Maryland, and a "P" on the side that is in Fulton County, Pennsylvania.

Back on his porch, he taste-tests the new bottle of Chivas Regal and offers a professional opinion of Mason and Dixon's job. "It was a very great achievement because it added tremendously to our knowledge about the size of the earth, and because it was so difficult. Think how difficult it was. They had to draw a straight line, but they had no roads. They had to go through thick forests, over mountains, through swamps, dragging their equipment behind them. As you go along the Line, it stayed a constant distance from the North Pole. In order to do this, you must be changing direction on the surface of the earth or you will gradually swing away from the Pole."

From Donnelly's porch, the bluish hump of the Appalachians looms to the west. From here on, the going gets rough. When Mason and Dixon were here, these mountains were called the Appalachian Barrier, and only a few Europeans had ever been beyond them.

It was near here, at Sideling Hill on the Bedford-Fulton county border, that Mason and Dixon stopped placing the stone markers because the wagons couldn't carry them up the steep grade. Instead, the surveyors erected cairns, piles of stones. In 1906, many of the original stones were gathered up and placed along the Line from Sideling Hill west.

At the Ellerslie, Maryland, Post Office, the postal clerk, Janet Phillips, says she lives on Mason-Dixon View Road. "I can't see the Mason-Dixon Line from my house, but I sure can see Pennsylvania. Folks cross the Line all the time and never even notice it. The only problem I know of is hunters who shoot a deer in Maryland and have to track into Pennsylvania. It causes problems for the game wardens."

In Somerset County, Pennsylvania, the Mason-Dixon Line crosses the Eastern Continental Divide, the range that separates streams whose basins drain into the Atlantic Ocean from those that go to the Gulf of Mexico. It's a sinister area, and it inspired Mason to a rare bit of poetry in his journal. "Laurel Hill (or rather Mountains), is a Wild of Wildes; the Laurel overgrown, the Rocks gaping to swallow up, over whose deep mouths you may step. The whole a deep melancholy appearance out of nature."

Mason kept daily field notes on the expedition; his journal is meticulous on dates and places, but most of it is taken up by whole pages of mathematical computations and references to things like azimuths and nutations.

Mason or his descendants either lost or discarded the original manuscript. In 1860, it mysteriously turned up in Halifax, Nova Scotia, among a pile of papers consigned to a trash heap. It was rescued, purchased by the United States in 1877, and is now in the National Archives.

As the surveyors moved through what is now Fayette County, Pennsylvania, but back then was the wildest of the Wild West, there were increasing encounters with hostile Shawnee and Delaware Indians. Workmen, fearful for their lives, began deserting the surveying party.

On October 9, 1767, Mason and Dixon came upon the Catawba War Path, sometimes called the Iroquois Main Road, which ran from Olean, New York, to the Cheat River in what is now West Virginia. The war path was about 18 inches wide and worn a foot and more deep from generations of moccasined feet. The Indians firmly told the two Englishmen their Line could go no farther. They set their final marker atop Brown's Hill, about 22 miles from the southwestern corner of Pennsylvania and 233 miles from where they started the east–west Line.

It was only October, but winter came early to the Appalachians, and the two surveyors and their remaining party trekked eastward in foot-deep snow. They spent nearly a year tying up loose ends, and then on September 11, 1768—four years and 10 months after their arrival—the Englishmen sailed from New York for Falmouth. When he stepped aboard, Mason signed off his journal: "Thus ends my restless progress in America."

The symbiotic pair—Dixon was a Quaker bachelor; Mason, a married Anglican—soon parted. Dixon continued to work with the Royal Observatory at Greenwich and died in 1779 at

45. Many historians attributed his early death to the hardships endured in America.

Mason declined in both physical and economic health, and in 1786, he, his wife, and his eight children turned up in Philadelphia. He wrote to Benjamin Franklin, whom he had met during the survey, and said he was "ill and confined to bed." A few weeks later, at 58, Mason died embittered and impoverished on the street. He was buried in an unmarked grave at Christ Church Burial Ground on Arch Street, where Franklin himself would be laid to rest three weeks later.

Although their last names would become household words, Mason and Dixon are almost unknown as people. No likeness of either has ever been found. Both died before their achievement acquired its lasting fame. Indeed, the final report on the survey does not even mention their names.

Summer is rusting into autumn, and today there are yard sales on both sides of the Mason-Dixon Line. Pennsylvanians and West Virginians browse among lunch boxes, jelly glasses, 78-rpm records, work shirts, and born-again Christian Diors. Everything is laid out on tables presided over by friendly women who are aproned, kerchiefed, and smocked.

They direct me to a trail running along the ridge of Brown's Hill. They say not many people go up there. It's an old logging trail that fades almost to invisibility, then rallies. The grass is wet. A deer stands at the final marker; its tail shoots straight out, and then it breaks into a run—a marvel of grace and speed—through the slanting shafts of light and shadow.

Gravel has been placed around the marker to hold down vegetation. Green mold is growing on the north side of the stone, the Pennsylvania side. This was the end of the Line for Mason and Dixon. There is no sound except the oceanic roar of freeway traffic on the interstate below.

The Chair of Death

Some Have Been Dragged to It; Others Have Run to It.
They Have Died Crying and Laughing. Many Have Died
as Converts; Others Have Shouted Their Rejections. No
Two Stories Are Alike.

*As it turned out, Elmo Smith, who was executed in 1962 for the
rape and murder of a teenage girl, was the last person to die in
Pennsylvania's electric chair. The U.S. Supreme Court abolished
capital punishment in 1972 but two years later allowed states to
reinstate it.*

*There were no more executions in the electric chair, and in 1990
Pennsylvania prescribed lethal injection as the preferred method.*

*In 1995, Keith Zettlemoyer, 39, became the first person to be
executed in Pennsylvania in 33 years, for the killing of a friend
who planned to testify against him in a robbery trial. Near the
end of a 15-year appeal process, Zettlemoyer fired his lawyers
and begged the courts to let him die. "I see my execution as an
end of suffering to my imprisonment—blessed, merciful release."*

*Three months later, Leon Moser, 52, a former U.S. Army offi-
cer and seminary student, received a fatal injection for the murder*

Originally published as "The Chair of Death" in the *Philadelphia Inquirer
Magazine*, November 17, 1985.

of his ex-wife and two daughters outside a church on Palm Sunday. After pleading guilty, he told the court, "I request the death penalty and that it be carried out as soon as possible." It took 10 years.

In 1999, Gary Michael Heidnik, 55, was executed for the kidnaping, torture, and rape of six women after holding them hostage in the basement of his home. He was killed 11 years after his conviction.

Today the state's execution chamber is in a former field hospital outside the main perimeter of the Rockview State Correctional Institute in Centre County.

The electric chair, "Old Smokey," is in storage at the State Museum of Pennsylvania in Harrisburg. There are no plans to put it on display.

As of this writing, a total of 1,043 people have been executed in Pennsylvania since 1693.

Execution No. 1: John Talap, February 23, 1915

ABOUT 7:00 A.M. the sun chinned itself on the eastern horizon, bathing the new Rockview State Penitentiary in an eerie pink light. Inside the Electrocution Building, Talap was being led by two uniformed guards from his death row cell to the oaken chair, still shiny from its first coat of varnish. He was accompanied by Father Antonio Ulanitizky, a Greek Orthodox priest, who had just heard Talap sob out his confession.

Talap, wearing slippers, a gray shirt, and black trousers with the left leg slit, drew back and hung on to the guards as he saw the chair. Fear splayed on his face. When he turned to face 16 official witnesses, seated on stone benches, his eyes were saturated with tears. Two guards backed him into the chair. He whimpered as straps were applied to his shins, thighs, stomach, wrists, arms, and chest.

Father Ulanitizky knelt on a mat a few feet in front of Talap and raised a crucifix to Talap's lips. Talap kissed the crucifix and said, "God have mercy on me; Christ have mercy on me." He shuddered as the electrodes were attached, one to his left leg and one, inside the mask that was placed on his head and strapped under his chin, to his head. The priest remained on the mat, looking at Talap with a childlike smile.

Zephyrs of tension swept through the room at 7:16 when a deputy warden flicked a white handkerchief at the executioner, standing in dim light behind the chair. The executioner applied 2,300 volts furnished by the State-Centre Electric Company. There was a whip-crack sound as Talap's body surged against the straps, as though it had been struck a tremendous blow from behind. The cords of his neck stood out like steel bands. There was a slight sizzling sound as Talap's body temperature rose to about 240 degrees.

The current was applied for one minute, turned off for 15 seconds, and then reapplied twice more for 15 seconds each. A tiny corkscrew of blue smoke arose from Talap's left leg and was quickly sucked away by an overhead exhaust vent. His fingers doubled back and turned chalk-white. Urine gushed on the floor beneath the chair. There was an odor of burning flesh, urine, feces, and vomit. Father Ulanitizky wordlessly stepped back to the witness area. At 7:21, R. J. Campbell, the prison physician, tore open Talap's shirt and thrust a stethoscope to the heart area of his chest. He turned to the witnesses and said, "I officially pronounce this man dead."

Talap, who had killed his wife in a fit of jealousy at their home near Pottstown, was a native of Hungary and had no relatives in the United States. His lawyer had written to a brother in Hungary after Talap was sentenced to death, but he received no reply. The unclaimed body was buried in a nearby Catholic cemetery.

Death, the king of terrors, is the ultimate collection tool for debts to society. The wrung-out legal battle over capital punishment has subsided, and once again throughout America, men and women are being electrocuted, shot, gassed, and injected. Between

1915 and 1962, judicial homicide in Pennsylvania was accomplished by having convicted murderers die seated, masked, and strapped to a high-backed wooden chair with electrical contacts fastened to the head and left leg.

John Talap was the first of 348 men and two women to sit condemned in the stout, businesslike chair at Rockview. None ever got up. The spark of life is no match for 2,300 volts. There's a telephone linked to the Governor's Office in Harrisburg during an execution in case of a last-minute reprieve. It has rung only once, and that was a wrong number. The condemned have used guns, hatchets, ice picks, meat cleavers, screwdrivers, arsenic, bare hands, and an umbrella to kill wives, sweethearts, sons, daughters, fathers, mothers, and strangers. Whether it's patricide, matricide, uxoricide, infanticide, or homicide, the state's answer has been electricide.

But within this mass of similarity, there are 350 different tales. Some have been dragged to the chair; others have run to it. They have died crying and laughing. Many have died as new converts to the faith; others have shouted their rejections. The chair either melts faith or bakes it hard. There is a kind of electrical version of gallows humor—corn on the macabre. No two stories are the same, like broken shards of the pot at rainbow's end.

Execution No. 8: Mike Louissa, April 10, 1916

Louissa died for killing his wife with an umbrella in Schuylkill County. The executioner was a student at Pennsylvania State University, six miles from Rockview.

The late nineteenth century was a period of rapid electrification in the United States, and a fierce competition developed between companies promoting direct current, led by Thomas Edison, and those promoting alternating current, led by George Westinghouse. Westinghouse argued that AC would permit higher voltages, but Edison contended this was dangerous, and to prove his point he arranged for a demonstration. First a cat was led to contact with an AC current and electrocuted. Then a dog. Finally a horse. The demonstration had little effect on the AC-DC wars, but it showed penologists that a human being could be killed by electricity.

Interest ran especially high in New York State, where a number of recent hangings had been botched, leaving the victims to die of slow strangulation. The big question was how much voltage was required to kill a human being. There were obvious problems with experimentation. Nevertheless, the legislature agreed to designate electrocution as the official state capital punishment. But then another obstacle arose. The electric companies opposed the idea because it would make the public fear and avoid electricity. Westinghouse refused to sell the necessary generators to the state, which finally managed to obtain them by ordering them through a dummy firm in Rio de Janeiro.

The world's first judicial electrocution was held in the Auburn, New York, Prison on August 6, 1890. The victim was a convicted ax murderer named William Kemmler, who couldn't sleep the night before because workmen were still sawing and hammering, preparing the death room. They weren't even finished when he arrived for his execution, so he sat down in one of the witness chairs and watched the final preparations. The execution itself took nearly an hour, as the state experimented with various voltages. The district attorney who had prosecuted Kemmler fainted in the witness area. Westinghouse was furious and said the job "could have been done better with an ax." Edison urged that the process be called something other than electrocution. He first suggested "ampermort," but then he was advised that the guillotine had been named for its inventor, a French physician, whereupon Edison suggested that the process be called "Westinghousing."

Execution No. 20: John Nelson, July 10, 1917

John Nelson was a black man who inadvertently killed a white man on Halloween in Wyoming County, Pennsylvania. Nelson had been hitchhiking when he was accosted by some children who began teasing him and asking whether he was wearing a mask. When Nelson drew a knife, he was approached by a man named John Sickler, who attempted to calm the children but frightened Nelson, who stabbed and killed him. Many people doubted that the murder was in the first degree, but Nelson said nothing about himself or his motives at his trial, and he was convicted and sentenced to death. While awaiting execution, Nelson read constantly from classic literature. The local newspaper ran this headline on the day of his execution: "Gorilla-like Black Man Leaped out of Darkness from Nowhere and Stabbed to Death Victim He Had Never Seen before Goes to Electric Chair without Revealing Secret of His Life."

Execution No. 142: Tony Burchanti, June 1, 1925

Tony Burchanti and a co-defendant, John Torti, were condemned for shooting a passenger in a train holdup near Scranton. Burchanti ran the 40 feet from his cell to the chair and sat down smiling. Minutes later, Torti walked to the chair slowly. Both gave instructions that no clergyman should visit them, and they were buried without ceremony at the prison cemetery in wooden caskets made by Rockview prisoners.

Because of the botched Kemmler execution, there was no rush among the states to join New York in having an electric chair. But as executions got smoother and became almost routine at Auburn, six eastern states began considering electricide. In Pennsylvania, the legislature replaced hanging with the electric chair in 1913 and appropriated $50,000 for the construction of an Electrocution Building at the new Rockview Prison, situated almost in the geographical center of the state. The architect was John J. Windrim of Philadelphia. About 50 prisoners worked on the construction project, but the Buchanan Electric Company of Philadelphia built and installed the chair, thereby avoiding the unfortunate experience in Ohio. There, the electric chair was built in 1903 by a prisoner whose armed robbery sentence was shortened for his efforts. Several years after his release, he was convicted of murder and became the 38th man to die in the chair he built, becoming, in a sense, his own executioner, as had Dr. Joseph Guillotine in France a century earlier.

Execution No. 154: Michael Weiss, October 26, 1925

Michael Weiss was electrocuted for killing a gas station attendant in Sharon, Pennsylvania. His mother boarded ship in Romania to bid her son good-bye, but it was delayed, and she didn't arrive in New York until two days after the execution.

At first, the execution in Pennsylvania varied from one "sitting" to the next. Talap's executioner had been the chief engineer for the electric company that installed the chair. An official of the construction project remembers that he later died in a railroad accident, and this was but the first of a number of Pennsylvania executioners to come under malevolent stars.

About 1920, there developed a tradition of itinerant executioners, traveling from one jurisdiction to another, like the old circuit judges. Pennsylvania's first regular executioner was Sylvester Mc-Neal, who died of a heart attack in the warden's office after an execution in Ohio, where he also worked. Next was Edward S. Davis, who resigned after about a year and lived the rest of his life as a recluse. The executioner John Hulbert shot and killed himself in 1926.

Hulbert was succeeded by a man who was perhaps America's best-known executioner, Robert Elliott, who served Pennsylvania, New York, New Jersey, Massachusetts, Connecticut, and Vermont between 1926 and 1939, executing 370 people. Elliott was a grandfather who lived on Long Island, but he looked his part: tall, gaunt, slit-eyed. The columnist Damon Runyon saw Elliott at work several times and wrote about him when he died: "He was as methodical as a man digging a well. We often watched his hands. They were white and quick. When he reached for something, he never fumbled the object. They were sure hands."

It was Elliott who executed Bruno Richard Hauptmann, the convicted Lindbergh kidnapper, at Trenton while the nation sat glued to the radio. Elliott executed Ruth Snyder and Judd Gray for the murder of Snyder's husband. He executed Nicola Sacco and Bartolomeo Vanzetti—and shortly afterward, his home was bombed. Elliott, his wife, and his two children were thrown from their beds by the blast, but no one was hurt. The State of New York paid $2,000 to repair the house. Elliott would die in bed of a heart attack in 1939.

Execution No. 174: Jerry Weeks, November 21, 1927

Jerry Weeks was convicted, on the basis of circumstantial evidence, of killing his sister-in-law and her three children. A Salvation Army chaplain, Fred Goddard, became interested in Weeks's case and was convinced of his innocence. He obtained permission from the warden to question Weeks after he was strapped in the chair.

"Jerry, you only have a few more seconds of this life to live," Goddard said. "What you say now cannot help you. No earthly power can save you now. But I have been your friend. With your last breath, I want you to tell me the truth. Are you guilty of this murder for which you are about to die?" Weeks looked straight in Goddard's eyes and said, "You are my friend. I would not lie to you. In the name of my mother in heaven, I am innocent."

Goddard bowed his head and stepped back. The electrodes were applied, the mask placed over Weeks's head, and Elliott threw the switch. In the last days of his life, Elliott became a firm opponent of capital punishment, and he pointed to Weeks's execution as the principal reason.

Execution No. 191: Paul A. Jawarski, January 21, 1929

Paul Jawarski, the confessed slayer of seven men in Pittsburgh, was calm as he walked to the chair. His only complaint was that he had been reading a serial in a magazine and the final installment was not due until February. "Gee, it's tough not to know how that thing ended," he said.

Execution No. 205: James Flori, July 8, 1930

A Philadelphia underworld figure known as "Dapper Jimmy," James Flori was convicted of killing a rival bootlegger. But three weeks before his execution, seven members of the jury that convicted him petitioned the state Board of Pardons to commute his sentence to life. The jurors said they had had second thoughts about the death sentence. The Pardons Board denied their petition, and Flori walked jauntily from his cell to the chair. As the mask was placed over his head, he addressed his last words to his wife: "Think of me, Mabel. I love you."

Execution No. 208: Irene Schroeder, February 23, 1931

She was the first woman to be electrocuted at Rockview, and prison officials were besieged by requests for witness seats—including one from a minister who said it would be an educational experience that would help him in his work. Dubbed "Iron Irene" by the press, Irene Schroeder and her boyfriend, Glenn Dague, killed a state trooper as they were fleeing a burglary in Butler. Her four-year-old son, Donnie, was beside her as she fired the fatal shot.

On the morning of the executions, Schroeder told the matron who brought her breakfast, "Please be sure to tell them in the kitchen to fry Glenn's eggs on both sides. He likes them that way." She walked to the death room smiling pleasantly, sat down, and closed her eyes. Elliott said she was the most composed person he ever executed. Several days later, Elliott received an unsigned letter that said, "Your daughter will die just like you killed Irene Schroeder."

Execution No. 233: Anthony Tretosky, January 8, 1934

At the precise instant that Elliott threw the switch on the 19-year-old Luzerne County man, the telephone rang about four feet from him. Elliott experienced intense anxiety for several seconds until the prison operator explained that she had dialed the wrong number.

Execution No. 238: Richard C. Bach, April 9, 1934

Richard "Slim" Bach, convicted of stoning a 19-year-old Philadelphia girl to death, was six-foot-seven and the tallest person ever to die at Rockview. Elliott said he had difficulty getting the mask, which was attached to the chair, to reach Bach's head.

Execution No. 239: Charles Walker, May 21, 1934

Charles Walker, a Philadelphian who slashed his sweetheart with a razor, was the first to die under an enlightened Rockview policy. The first 238 electrocutions had been held at 7:00 A.M., but since few of the condemned men were able to sleep through the night, the time was changed to 12:30 A.M. for Walker's execution. In 1955, the time was changed to 9:00 P.M. because it was more convenient for the witnesses and the prison staff.

Execution No. 242: Robert Allen Edwards, May 6, 1935

Robert Allen Edwards died for killing his girlfriend with a blackjack after a swim at a lake in the Poconos. The case attracted great attention because it paralleled Theodore Dreiser's 10-year-old novel *An American Tragedy*, and a mob of 4,000 people staged a near-riot at Rockview's gates in an effort to witness the execution.

Execution No. 274: Paul Ferry, October 23, 1939

Paul Ferry was convicted of killing his wife with an ax in 1936, but he was granted 13 stays under two governors and committed to Farview State Prison for the Criminally Insane. After two years, the Farview warden said Ferry was feigning insanity, but when Ferry was informed that he would be executed in three days, he refused to believe it and complained that the prison doctor owed him money.

Elliott had retired a few months earlier, and Pennsylvania hired its own executioner: Frankie Lee Wilson, an electrical contractor from Pittsburgh. Wilson's identity was withheld until the night of the Ferry execution, when he was introduced to reporters at a dinner in the home of Warden Stanley P. Ashe. "He is the best-qualified man we knew," Ashe said. "I wanted a man of high reputation who knows electricity from beginning to end."

But Wilson had his timing wrong for Ferry. He held the rheostat at 2,300 volts for 30 seconds instead of the prescribed 20 seconds. Ferry had a frail body, and smoke curled from his head, and blisters were raised over his entire body from the intense heat. There were two other executions that same night, and these went more smoothly as Wilson studied his watch carefully after flipping the rheostat to full. The season's first snowstorm whined a requiem in the death house after the third execution. Wilson lit a cigarette. He had dispatched all three men in 14.5 minutes and was paid $450—$250 for the first, and $100 each for the second and third. "Mr. Wilson did a swell job," said Warden Ashe.

When Elliott retired, about 20 people had submitted applications to the state for the job, including one John Van Steen, an employee of the Works Progress Administration, who said he would "do anything to get off WPA." Mrs. Van Steen chipped in that her husband was "awfully handy at fixing up electric light fixtures."

But Wilson had the inside track because he had installed a power plant at the Western State Penitentiary in Pittsburgh. He was frail and blue-eyed, married and the father of two children, and he considered himself a public servant. He had studied electrical engineering at Carnegie Tech night school for seven years and then opened his own contracting business.

Wilson served as the Pennsylvania executioner until 1953, electrocuting 55 men and one woman. He resigned after a court ordered him to pay $145 a month in support to his estranged wife, who testified at the hearing that Wilson had once punched her across a room, knocking out a tooth, because she doubled his bid during a bridge game. Wilson became an alcoholic and died impoverished.

Execution No. 285: Paul Petrillo, March 31, 1941

Paul Petrillo and his brother, Herman, who was executed six months later, were leaders of the most bizarre mass-murder plot in Pennsylvania history: Philadelphia's Arsenic Murder Ring. Paul ran a tailor shop in South Philadelphia, and he developed an idea for making more money than he could by pressing trousers. He found that a great number of married women in the city were dissatisfied with their husbands and had acceptable replacements waiting, so to speak, in the wings. Petrillo offered to get rid of the husbands, plus make the women some money on insurance, for fees ranging from $300 to $500. Petrillo discovered a tasteless, odorless, and lethal "miracle drug"—arsenic—that could be given to the husbands in small doses by the wives. The victims would die of pneumonia, a heart attack, or gastroenteritis. It was believed the ring was responsible for 55 deaths before being broken when investigators began exhuming bodies. Arsenic's one drawback is that it doesn't decompose.

The Petrillo brothers were sentenced to death, and 21 other people, including eight women, were given life sentences. Paul resisted being seated in the electric chair, and he had to be forcibly strapped in by guards.

There is no death row, as such, in Pennsylvania. Condemned prisoners are kept in other maximum-security penitentiaries until a few days before their scheduled executions and then brought to Rockview and housed in one of six cells directly across a corridor from the electric chair.

When the prisoner arrives at Rockview, the warden gives the escort party a receipt and reads the death warrant to the condemned. This happened 384 times—34 of the prisoners had their sentences commuted after they reached Rockview. The prisoner is fingerprinted to verify his identity.

Execution No. 294: George Gatling, September 25, 1944

George Gatling strangled a five-year-old Philadelphia girl and was executed less than three months after his conviction. He sat down in the chair and said, "Well, that's life, I guess."

Execution No. 299: Corinne Sykes, October 14, 1946

Corinne Sykes, the only other woman to die at Rockview, was a diminutive 22-year-old maid who murdered her employer in the bathroom of the woman's Olney home. She told the victim the seams of her stockings were crooked, and when the woman bent over to straighten them, Sykes pushed her into the bathtub, stabbed her with a butcher knife, and tore two diamond rings from her fingers.

Two guards and a chaplain accompanied Sykes to the chair, but she rejected physical and spiritual assistance and instead sat unassisted and sullen.

When Wilson threw the switch, small wisps of smoke rose from her head and her leg. Then a kind of gray fog enveloped her body. She looked like a child sitting in an adult chair.

Once at Rockview, the prisoner is as guarded as a crown prince. Any meat served with meals is deboned and cut into small pieces, and until the advent of plastic spoons and forks, all meals were served without silverware. On the last night, the condemned is given the normal prison menu for dinner, but special requests are granted if they are reasonable and available. The most frequent special request is for ice cream.

Execution No. 306: Joshua E. Beatty, September 29, 1947

Joshua Beatty, who murdered his estranged wife in Harrisburg, slept well the night before and ate a big breakfast. He had convinced himself he would not die. He walked to the chair calmly, looked at the telephone, and said, "I have nothing to worry about. I know the governor will give me a reprieve." He died four minutes later.

To prepare the prisoner for execution, the head is shaven to expose the scalp to the first electrode, and the outside seam of the left trouser leg is ripped open to place the second. Coral sponges are immersed in a saline solution—five pounds of salt to three gallons of water—and placed on the electrodes to ensure good contact.

Moments before the execution, the executioner plugs the two electrode cables into a five-foot-long board holding 10 light bulbs. If the bulbs light up, he informs the prison officials, "The apparatus has been tested and is in proper working order." A telephone line is opened from the death room to the warden's office, where another line is opened to the Governor's Office in Harrisburg. After the condemned is seated, a prison official signals the executioner, who causes 2,300 volts to pass through the victim's body. Most executioners prefer a series of shocks to one long jolt, which can burn the body severely. When the doctor has declared the condemned dead, the governor is informed.

Execution No. 314: Daniel P. Taranow, November 8, 1948

Daniel Taranow, a New York City resident, shot and killed a man who gave him a ride in Delaware County. Three days before his execution, he was allowed to marry Sheila Noto of Brooklyn, who had given birth to a daughter fathered by Taranow. The ceremony was held in the warden's office, and the nine-month-old daughter was present. The newlyweds were allowed to hold hands for several hours before Taranow was returned to his cell. He strutted to the chair, and his last request was directed to a guard: "Make that strap tighter, will you?"

Execution No. 318: Edward DiPofi, January 9, 1950

Edward DiPofi shot and killed a Pittsburgh policeman who caught him in a burglary. His last request was that he be allowed to see his three-year-old daughter, Carol. The warden resisted, saying death row was no place for a child, but DiPofi persisted, and the girl was brought to Rockview to see her father a few hours before he was executed.

Execution No. 321: Alexander L. Niemi, September 25, 1950

After Alexander Niemi was executed for killing a Chester tavern owner, his mother tried to collect on a $5,000 life insurance policy that named her the beneficiary. The insurance company refused and was upheld in the courts.

Execution No. 331: Charles E. Homeyer, May 18, 1953

Charles Homeyer, convicted of killing and dismembering his sixth wife in Wyoming County, planned and paid for his own funeral before his execution.

There are two schools of thought on the humaneness of the electric chair. One says electrocution is totally painless; the other maintains there is an instant of excruciating torture. The debate is rendered somewhat sterile by the absence of firsthand testimony.

The human body is a bag of salt water, and an admirable conductor. The body itself—the heart, the brain, and all tissue—use minuscule electrical currents to function, and the introduction of a massive electrical jolt overrides this biological circuitry. When the current hits the body, the body temperature is raised about 140 degrees. Electrocution stops the heart and all brain activity. Indeed, the heat causes the brain to coagulate. Death is not instantaneous, but the first shock renders the victim unconscious. The bowels and bladder empty, and vomit, then blood, spills from the mouth. The lips quickly turn red, then blue. Last year, Nebraska tested its electric chair by placing a barrel of water in it. The water quickly came to a boil.

Execution No. 332: Ollie M. Carey, May 18, 1953

Ollie Carey was convicted of killing an Abington Township policeman, but he maintained his innocence even as he was strapped into the chair. "I have no confession to make because I have nothing to confess," he shouted at the chaplain. Three years earlier, after he had been condemned in Montgomery County Court, he conveyed his fate to his deaf father, who was in the courtroom, by suddenly sitting erect in a chair, stiffening, and then falling back as though electrocuted.

Execution No. 334: William Patskin, April 5, 1954

William Patskin was convicted of killing his wife with a hatchet, but after his trial a court-appointed commission found him insane. However, the Lackawanna County Court, in a 2–1 decision, refused to accept the sanity commission's report. Two days before

Patskin's execution, the warden presented him with an early birthday cake. As the mask was placed over his head, Patskin smiled. It was his 46th birthday.

The requirement of an autopsy was imposed because several men showed signs of life hours after their executions in New York State. The legislator who sponsored the bill noted that no one shows signs of life after an autopsy. At Rockview, the corpses are removed on a litter and taken to a nearby autopsy room. All 350 autopsies have shown that the victims died of electrocution. The body is then wrapped in sheets and placed in a refrigerated, slide-out tray to await funeral arrangements.

Execution No. 335: Joseph Bibalo, May 17, 1954

Joseph Bibalo, convicted of killing a fellow deer hunter, originally was scheduled to be executed in March, but he was granted a stay because a sanity commission said it needed more time for further tests. Patrick Manley, warden at the Lackawanna County Prison, went to Bibalo's cell and said, "Joe, I've got good news for you. They've granted you a stay." Bibalo, 22, hung his head. "What's the matter? Aren't you glad?" asked the warden. "No!" shouted Bibalo. He walked to his cot and put his head in his hands. Three weeks later, the commission pronounced Bibalo sane, and he was executed.

Execution No. 344: Harry Gossard, June 4, 1956

Harry Gossard, convicted of killing a six-year-old Cambria County girl on Halloween, directed that his body be sent to the Hospital of the University of Pennsylvania for medical research.

Execution No. 345: Lester Graves, April 13, 1959

Lester Graves, 23, murdered his four-year-old daughter because she wouldn't eat her dinner. Two psychiatric examinations showed

Graves to be mentally retarded, with an IQ of 66. He walked to the chair seemingly unaware of what was happening and died wordlessly.

Execution No. 346: Cleveland Thompson, May 4, 1959

Cleveland Thompson killed a Pittsburgh bartender in 1949, but his attorneys managed to delay his execution for nearly 10 years. U.S. Circuit Judge William H. Hastie severely criticized Pennsylvania law for allowing Thompson's jury to hear evidence of prior criminal convictions and said that if he were Governor David L. Lawrence, he would commute the sentence to life imprisonment. Lawrence declined. Thompson had to be dragged to the chair and strapped in.

Execution No. 348: Arthur G. Schuck, October 23, 1961

Arthur Schuck, who ambushed and killed two women in Beaver County, died in the chair with his wrists bandaged. He had tried to commit suicide two days earlier.

Execution No. 350: Elmo Smith, April 2, 1962

Elmo Smith had been jailed in the 1950s for a series of savage sexual assaults on women, and psychiatrists called him a "caveman." Over the strenuous objections of Montgomery County law enforcement authorities, Smith was released before serving a minimum term, and less than a year later he raped and sadistically killed a 16-year-old girl. It was said that if any man ever deserved to be executed, it was Elmo Smith. He died quietly, walking to the chair while the chaplain intoned the 23d Psalm: "Yea, though I walk through the valley of the shadow of death."

Smith was executed by Jerry Kramer of Pittsburgh, who succeeded Frankie Lee Wilson in 1954. Kramer, an electrical engineer, wore a charcoal business suit on duty. Soon after Smith's execution, he resigned, saying he didn't "want to be a part of this anymore."

As it turned out, the state didn't need Kramer's services. Opponents of capital punishment mounted a successful legal battle throughout the nation in the 1960s, and the chair at Rockview went unused. In 1971, State Attorney-General Fred Speaker ordered the chair dismantled and placed in storage. The chair was covered with two sheets, placed in a padlocked cage, and locked in a solitary confinement cell.

But in 1978, the Pennsylvania General Assembly enacted a death penalty law that passed constitutional muster, and today about 50 men have been sentenced to die in the chair. Governor Dick Thornburgh signed death warrants for three of them on August 1, and that same day the chair was returned to the death room.

Since the chair was first used, America has fought four wars, conquered polio, split the atom, and landed men on the moon. There have been changes at Rockview, too. It is no longer a penitentiary; it's a state correctional institution. And it's no longer run by a warden; he's a superintendent. The Electrocution Building is now the Deputy Warden's Building. The walls in the execution room have been painted aqua instead of gray, and witnesses will sit on folding chairs rather than on stone benches. A new executioner has been hired, and as part of his contract his name will not be revealed; the state is not even saying how much he will be paid. Executions will be held on Tuesdays instead of on Mondays, at 10:00 P.M. rather than at 9:00 P.M. There's a new telephone to take the call that has never come.

The argument over capital punishment, as Old as the Old Testament, rages on. But the 70-year-old chair is ready for Execution No. 351.

Why Would a Nice Town like Jim Thorpe Want to Be Mauch Chunk—Again?

How a Pennsylvania Town Came to Be Called
Jim Thorpe—even though the Famous Native American
Athlete Never Set Foot in It

*In the years after this article appeared, I was contacted sever-
al times by Jim Thorpe's sons and daughters, who were seeking
to have their father's remains returned to a burial ground near
Shawnee, Oklahoma, where the great athlete's own father and
many other relatives are buried.*

*For most of that time, Thorpe's adult children sought to con-
vince the people of Jim Thorpe, Pennsylvania, that it was the right
thing to do.*

*"According to Sac and Fox tradition, Dad's soul will never be
at peace until his body is laid to rest, after an appropriate ceremony, back here in his home," Jack Thorpe, the athlete's youngest
son, told me. "Until then, his soul is doomed to wander. We must
have him back."*

Originally published as "Why Would a Nice Town like Jim Thorpe Want to
Be Mauch Chunk—Again?" in the *Philadelphia Inquirer Magazine*, August
8, 1982.

But local officials were adamantly opposed. They credit the presence of Thorpe's body with the restoration of the community from a dying coal town to a modest tourist mecca crowded with visitors on most weekends.

The reality, however, is that most of the visitors do not come to see the rectangular red granite mausoleum that bears images of Jim Thorpe's life carved in relief.

Most of them head for the Asa Packer Mansion, a stunning 18-room Victorian home that was built by a nineteenth-century coal and rail baron and is now a National Historic Landmark. Some are content just to stroll the narrow streets and admire the architecture. In addition, the town is the starting point for hikers, cyclists, and rafters heading to the nearby Lehigh Gorge State Park.

In 2009, Thorpe's offspring filed a suit in federal court claiming that Jim Thorpe Borough was obligated to surrender the remains under the 1990 Native American Graves Protection and Repatriation Act. The law requires federal agencies and institutions that receive federal funds to return Native American cultural items and human remains to their respective peoples.

A federal district court rejected the suit, and in 2015 the U.S. Supreme Court refused to hear the family's appeal.

This apparently brought to an end one of the most bizarre of all American sports stories.

THE WOOD-FRAME BUILDING was constructed in 1844 for the International Order of Odd Fellows, and the window bears the name "Hotel Switzerland" from another of the structure's incarnations. But the locals in Jim Thorpe, Pennsylvania, know it only as Weiksner's bar.

Weiksner's, which is right across from the county courthouse, looks a little rundown from the outside, but inside it's downright dingy. The pressed tin ceiling is jaundiced by years of tobacco smoke wafting up from the mahogany bar. The men's room seldom has paper towels but features an abundance of telephone numbers written on the walls, some followed by promises of various activities worthy of study by Masters and Johnson.

A gallon jar on the bar, labeled "hot bologna," contains liverish hunks suspended in brackish fluid. There are also bouillon cubes and cans of chili con carne to oblige the gastronomically intrepid, but mostly people come to Weiksner's to drink. They dine on nostalgia. About half the conversations begin with, "Remember the time . . . ?"

For example, "Pickles" Pry, a regular at Weiksner's, was recently swizzling a shot of 50 cent whiskey and recalling the day he came back from World War II: "I got off the train at the station, kissed the platform, and promised I'd never leave again."

Jim Thorpe, Pennsylvania, is, indeed, the kind of town people love—a place of substance and of tightly woven social fabric, where nicknames, conferred for some early particularity, are carried to the grave and etched on gravestones between quotation marks. Most people who are born here choose to live here, propagate here, die here. Life chases its own tail.

But although everyone loves it, not everyone loves its name. The town that Pickles Pry came home to was called Mauch Chunk. But for the past 28 years it's been called Jim Thorpe because the legendary Native American athlete, against his expressed wishes—not to mention the current wishes of at least some of the residents (and a clear majority of the patrons at Weiksner's)—is buried here.

Because a lot of people feel their town has been robbed of its good name, there is a sort of municipal split personality here in which the Mauch Chunk Trust Company vies for depositors with the Jim Thorpe National Bank and local hunters belong to the Mauch Chunk Rod and Gun Club and the Jim Thorpe Sportsman Club. There are Thorpers and Chunkers, and one man has resolved a connubial division on the issue by placing a plate on front of his car that says, "Jim Chunk."

Actually, the Chunkers and the Thorpers are both outnumbered by The Indifferent. The younger generation, which has always lived in a town called Jim Thorpe, would like to forget about the whole thing. And there is no current drive, as there was twice in the early 1960s, to have the name changed back to Mauch Chunk by referendum.

However, a new element has entered the picture: Thorpe's seven children have decided they want their father's remains moved to a Native American burial ground in Oklahoma. One of them is Jack Thorpe, 44, who is now chief of the Sac and Fox Tribe in Stroud, Oklahoma, and who wants his father's remains placed in the family burial plot near Shawnee with his brothers and sisters. "Tribal tradition is that when you die, you have to be buried within three days, between sunrise and noon, with your head facing east," he says. "Your soul goes to the west. If you're not buried properly, your spirit continues to roam." His stepmother, he says, removed his father's body "before the ceremony was completed in 1953, and his spirit has not returned."

There are some difficult legal questions involved in the children's effort, which is still in its preliminary stages, but if they succeed, there will be no reason whatsoever to call the town Jim Thorpe.

The story of how Mauch Chunk came to be Jim Thorpe and might come to be Mauch Chunk again teeters between comedy and tragedy. Though the story is fascinating, it is, frankly, doubtful that it is all that instructive. But probably nothing like it will ever happen again.

One thing needs to be clear right from the start: Jim Thorpe, the man, never set foot in Jim Thorpe, the town, while alive. As far as can be determined, the closest he ever got was probably Bethlehem, about 40 miles southeast, where on a leafy afternoon in 1912 he scored four touchdowns in the Carlisle Indian School's 34–20 victory over Lehigh University.

Even the briefest biography of Jim Thorpe, though, must begin with the caveat that his life is encrusted by myth. His accomplishments predate the videotape era, and the truth has been alloyed by Hollywood and several fawning biographies. But at the same time, the accomplishments speak eloquently for themselves.

It is certain that Jim Thorpe was born on a Sac and Fox Indian reservation near Shawnee, Oklahoma, 94 years ago. He came to the federal government's Indian Institute at Carlisle, Pennsylvania, and in 1911 and 1912 was the star of the football team. It is said that he could casually punt a football 70 yards and consistently kick 50-yard field goals. But mainly he was a swift, powerful runner.

Thorpe and his Carlisle teammates defeated Pitt, Penn, Harvard, and Syracuse, and in a 27–6 victory over Army in 1912, some accounts, possibly apocryphal, have him running over a young cadet halfback named Dwight David Eisenhower. He went to the 1912 Olympic Games in Stockholm, where he won gold medals in the pentathlon and decathlon. No one had ever done that before, and King Gustav of Sweden called him "the greatest athlete in the world."

But Thorpe was stripped of his Olympic medals when it was discovered that two years before participating in the Olympics he had played semi-professional baseball in North Carolina for $60 a month. It was a common practice among college athletes of the day, but the rulers of the Olympics decreed that it was unconscionable professionalism.

Thorpe subsequently played professional football and baseball for 16 years, and in 1950 he was chosen as the greatest athlete of the half century in a poll by the Associated Press.

Thorpe's athletic prowess won him fame but no fortune, and two years after he retired from football in 1929 he was working with a pick and shovel for $4 a day. A stream of short-lived jobs followed—nightclub bouncer, movie extra, night watchman, and seaman. A weakness for liquor cost him two marriages.

Thorpe eventually fell into obscurity save for an occasional poignant appearance in the press. He was photographed digging ditches at a Los Angeles construction site; he was fined for drunken driving and reminded by the judge that he was "a legend to our youth." At the age of 51, the world's greatest athlete had to be pulled from the Pacific surf by lifeguards while auditioning for a bit part in a movie.

In 1945 he took a third wife, Patricia, who prodded him into making paid appearances. He was on tour with the Jim Thorpe Show, a Native American dance troupe, in Philadelphia in 1951 when he noticed a sore on his lip. It was diagnosed as cancer and removed at Lankenau Hospital. He had no money to pay for the operation and was treated as a charity case.

That same year Warner Brothers released Jim Thorpe All-American, with Burt Lancaster in the title role, but the movie didn't help Thorpe's finances. He had sold the movie rights to his life years before for $1,500. He died of a heart attack on March 28, 1953, in a house trailer in Lomita, Calif.

Patricia Thorpe was determined to establish some permanent memorial to her husband. The city fathers of Shawnee, Oklahoma, paid to have Thorpe's body shipped from California, and Native American and Roman Catholic services were held near his boyhood home. A few months later, when the rent on the crypt became overdue, Patricia Thorpe moved his body to Tulsa.

About that time, the Oklahoma Legislature appropriated $25,000 to build a memorial, but the bill was unexpectedly vetoed by the governor—apparently because a member of the newly formed Jim Thorpe Memorial Commission had become entangled in an unrelated scandal.

In the fall of 1953, Thorpe's widow set out in earnest to find a final resting place for her husband. Specifically, she wanted him to be buried in a town that would change its name to Jim Thorpe in his honor. Carlisle, Pennsylvania, seemed singularly appropriate, but borough officials politely declined. She continued eastward to Philadelphia, hoping to get help from Bert Bell, then commissioner of the National Football League and a longtime friend of Jim's.

Watching the 6 o'clock news in her room at the Bellevue Stratford during her stay in Philadelphia, she heard that a small town 90 miles northwest of Philadelphia named Mauch Chunk was creating an industrial development fund by having each of its residents pledge a nickel a week for five years. Mrs. Thorpe wondered whether perhaps a town with that much innovative determination might be interested in her proposition.

Although it's not one of those names that ice skates off your tongue, like Nesquehoning and Catawissa, Mauch Chunk (pronounced "MOCK Chunk") is a Native American name that means "bear mountain" (though at Weiksner's bar some say it means "sleeping bear"). And the town had a rather impressive history of its own long before Mrs. Thorpe heard of it on the evening news.

The barons of the Lehigh Coal and Navigation Company chose it as their principal town in 1818, and it soon became the site of the world's first gravity-powered railway, called the Switchback Railroad. Empty cars were hauled up a coal-fat mountain ridge, loaded, and sent coasting down to waiting barges. By the middle of the nineteenth century, 13 millionaires called Mauch Chunk home—more per capita, it was said, than any other community in the United States.

The most famous person ever to live in Mauch Chunk was Asa Packer, whose genius was to recognize that coal was better transported by rail than by barge. He built the Lehigh Valley Railroad and ran the company and town until he died in 1879. Packer was a Democrat who served as a judge, a state legislator, and a member of Congress. He ran for governor in 1869 and lost by fewer than 5,000 votes, and at the 1868 Democratic National Convention he was the Pennsylvania delegation's favorite-son candidate for president.

Packer's principal legacy to the state is Lehigh University, which he founded in 1862. He supposedly intended to establish the school in Mauch Chunk but changed his mind and built it in Bethlehem. Some think he spurned his hometown because he was defeated in an election for burgess. (At Weiksner's, however, they say Packer was talked out of locating the college in Mauch Chunk by a friend who had several nubile daughters and worried about an influx of young men in the community.)

While it was prospering as a coal and rail center, Mauch Chunk also developed into one of the East's most voguish resorts. It was known as the "Switzerland of America." This was a slight oversell of its admittedly handsome but clearly subalpine mountains, but trains pulled into Mauch Chunk from Philadelphia, Baltimore, and New York.

By the early 1900s, five U.S. presidents—Grant, Garfield, Cleveland, McKinley, and Teddy Roosevelt—had checked into the leading hotel, the Mansion House. When the last of the coal was scraped and gouged from the mountain, the Switchback Railroad was converted to a sightseeing vehicle.

Mauch Chunk's bubbly prosperity began turning to vinegar during the adolescence of the twentieth century. Fickle industry abandoned coal and embraced petroleum. Fickle tourists with their new automobiles preferred places they couldn't get to before by train. The only gold in sight was the rust on the rails. The Mansion House was condemned by the state and razed in 1933. The Switchback Railroad was sold as scrap metal to the Japanese in 1937. ("We got it back at Pearl Harbor," they say at Weiksner's.)

There were actually two towns at this time: Mauch Chunk and East Mauch Chunk. They were separated, and alienated, by a deep gorge through which ran the Lehigh River and, on either bank, the now weedy tracks of the Central Railroad of New Jersey and the Lehigh Valley Railroad. Only a single bridge linked the two communities, each of which had about 3,000 residents, along with its own churches, schools, municipal services, and community pride.

Joe Boyle, the editor of the *Mauch Chunk Times-News*, was convinced that the first step in economic renaissance of the area was the merger of the two Chunks. He promoted the idea in his newspaper, but there was always one big barrier: What to name the new community? There was no way East Mauch Chunkers were going to live in a town called Mauch Chunk. And it was silly to call it East Mauch Chunk if there was no West Mauch Chunk.

Only one attempt at transpontine cooperation had enjoyed even temporary success. In the 1930s, finding that neither town's high school had enough able-bodied boys to field a football team, the schools combined for gridiron purposes only. The team was called "Inter-Chunk."

So Boyle placed his dream of a Greater Chunk on the back burner and organized the Nickel-a-Week Drive to build an industrial development fund in 1953. The idea was unusual enough to be picked up by the wire services, and Pat Thorpe heard it broadcast in her hotel room.

In late September 1953, the widow appeared at the Mauch Chunk National Bank carrying a Pekinese dog. (At Weiksner's, Knappy Knappenberger says she had two Pekineses.) She asked a teller where she could find Joe Boyle, who, as it happened, was standing at the next window. She made Boyle her offer: name change for body. She added that she had arranged for the National Fraternal Order of Eagles, a group Thorpe had belonged to most of his adult life, to finance a suitable memorial.

Boyle at first thought the idea preposterous, but it grew on him. The clincher was that the name change could break the stalemate over merging the two Chunks. By November, the two towns and Mrs. Thorpe were making plans. As part of the deal, it was reported, the Jim Thorpe Memorial Heart and Cancer Foundation, headed by Bert Bell, might build a hospital in the town. There would be a Jim Thorpe Museum, and Bell would work toward establishing the National Football Hall of Fame in the town. On her own, Mrs. Thorpe had plans for a motel to house some of the hordes of tourists. It would be called Jim Thorpe's Teepees.

To show her good faith, Mrs. Thorpe had the body of her husband disinterred in Tulsa and brought to Mauch Chunk even before the name change (and merger) were approved by voters in the two boroughs. Thorpe's body arrived by train in Allentown, where it was transferred to a hearse and brought by motorcade to Mauch Chunk. Children, given the day off from school, and adults lined the streets of both towns to watch the procession to Evergreen Cemetery, where the body was placed in a temporary crypt.

It was February 9, 1954. Jim Thorpe had been dead 11 months.

The following May, the voters of Mauch Chunk and East Mauch Chunk, by a 10–1 ratio, approved the merger of their communities under the name of Jim Thorpe Borough. When the results were announced, church bells reverberated between the mountains.

The next day Mrs. Thorpe and five officials of the new town signed a remarkable contract in which the only real property was a corpse. It provided that so long as the town shall be named Jim Thorpe, the body of Jim Thorpe shall remain in the town. It also required the borough to provide a permanent memorial to its namesake within three years.

But the thorns in this conceptual bed of roses bared themselves almost immediately. The National Fraternal Order of Eagles backed out on the plan to build a memorial. Mrs. Thorpe began asking the town for money. (Boyle says she never got a penny, but at Weiksner's they're not so sure.) Mrs. Thorpe then dropped out of sight for a time, and in a letter to a friend during this period she said, "I regret from the bottom of my heart ever having allowed Jim to be removed from California."

Then a nasty rumor began creeping through the town that Jim Thorpe's body wasn't really up there in Evergreen Cemetery. It was based on the report of one of the pallbearers, who said the coffin was so heavy it could only have been filled with rocks. Boyle heard the rumors and made arrangements with two local morticians to squelch it. "We opened up the casket," he recalls with distaste. "There was a plastic bag over the head. We removed it. There was no doubt it was Jim." (Even at Weiksner's, they're certain that the body buried in Jim Thorpe's tomb is Jim Thorpe's.)

When the three-year deadline approached, the borough used $17,000 from the accumulated nickels in the industrial development fund to purchase a 10 ton, red marble memorial. The dedication was held on May 28, 1957, nine days beyond the deadline. President

Eisenhower, Thorpe's old gridiron antagonist, was invited to attend but declined. Bert Bell was too ill to be there. But Thorpe's three daughters and many of his Carlisle teammates were present.

Four years and two months after he died, Jim Thorpe was laid to rest.

But the controversy over Thorpe's posthumous presence was becoming increasingly lively. Many townspeople were seething over the use of the industrial fund for a mausoleum. ("We gave all those damn nickels for a factory, not a tombstone," they still complain at Weiksner's.)

The Jim Thorpe Foundation collapsed after Bert Bell died during an Eagles-Steelers game at Franklin Field in 1959. Moreover, it was becoming clear that there was going to be neither a hospital nor a museum. And the Football Hall of Fame went to Canton, Ohio, where, coincidentally, Thorpe had played for a pro football team.

Back in Jim Thorpe, Pennsylvania, there were no tourists. There was no economic deliverance. After all was said and done, far more was said than done. In 1963, somebody attacked Thorpe's mausoleum with a ball-peen hammer, and it had to be repaired.

One of the angriest residents was Johnny Otto, a railroad man. Aided by Jocko Williams and Waxie Gassner, he mounted a drive in 1964 to have the town's name changed back to Mauch Chunk. There were lathered emotions in the weeks before the election, and a dogged rumor was that a millionaire from California had offered to set up a $1 million college scholarship fund for the town's youth if the name were changed, though no such offer was ever officially made public. But when the polls closed on November 3, 1964, there were 1,392 votes for Jim Thorpe and 1,032 votes for Mauch Chunk. A second effort in 1965 lost by a slightly wider margin.

Joe Boyle, for one, thinks it was all for the best that the town remained Jim Thorpe. Today he is a youthful 67 with snowy hair and an undiminished love for his hometown. He has retired from newspapering but still works with the area Chamber of Commerce and says that if he had the chance, he'd do it all over again the same way.

"I resent it when they say that all we got is a dead Indian. We got the world's greatest athlete, and without him we'd all be back where we were 30 years ago," he says. "The merger was the big thing. It saves us money every day and makes us more efficient in dealing with our problems. Without Jim it would still be Mauch Chunk and East Mauch Chunk fighting each other and wasting money on duplicate services. This town's coming back. I can really see it starting to take off."

Out at Mike's Barber Shop, Mayor (and proprietor) Michael Hichok is giving a customer a crew cut and agreeing with Boyle's sentiments so emphatically that he seems to be about to snip off a piece of ear lobe. "You talk to the kids who were born in Jim Thorpe, and there's no way they want to go back to Mauch Chunk, with the exception of a few, who I call radicals," he says. "This town is moving again."

Sure enough, the town is moving again. Part of the reason is the very fact that the town never did recover after its heyday in the nineteenth century. Everything is as it was 75 years ago. Colonel Sanders and Ronald McDonald never showed up here. What's more, the town's architectural heritage is being retained by a project financed through the National Trust for Historic Preservation.

In addition, an arts-and-crafts center opened this summer, and the Opera House is being rebuilt. The refurbished Jersey Central Station houses a railroad museum and the Carbon County Tourist Promotion Agency. A good way to start a day in Jim Thorpe, in fact, is with the slide presentation at the railroad station. It outlines the town's attractions, and near the end there's a five-second segment suggesting, almost as an afterthought, a visit to Jim Thorpe's mausoleum.

Many visitors do show up at the tourist center asking to see "where Jim Thorpe lived," and some of them are no doubt disappointed, but there are plenty of other things to do. Jim Thorpe River Adventures offers white-water rafting, there are daily tours of Asa Packer's Mansion, and the view from the park atop Flag-staff Mountain is impressive.

At Weiksner's, the walls are covered with Mauch Chunk memorabilia: an arrow-shaped sign for Flagstaff Park; a Switchback Railroad schedule; a portrait of Asa Packer; a poster from the 1964 counter-referendum that says, "Vote Yes! Bring Back Mauch Chunk. The Switzerland of America." You know you're in Chunker territory.

Al Weiksner started tending bar here for his father at age 16 in 1923, and he's looking forward to his 50th year of continuous community service next year. His T-shirt says, "I conquered the Lehigh River," which seems doubtful, for his complexion reflects thousands of summer afternoons spent tending bar. Al is all gray except his hair, which is white. Only his citrus green suspenders, which hang uselessly to the knees of amorphous khaki trousers, relieve his monochromatic drabness.

Strangers are guilty until proved innocent at Weiksner's, and its takes a while before he'll tell you that he voted in favor of changing the town's name back to Mauch Chunk in 1964 and 1965. "And we'd of won if the election was held a year earlier," he says. "By '64 too many of the old-timers had died off."

Weiksner uses Mauch Chunk, Pennsylvania, as his return address, and he says he always gets his mail on time. Behind the bar, he keeps a running list of new enterprises in town that use Mauch Chunk in their name. "We just got the Mauch Chunk Medical Center," he says authoritatively. "Every new operation coming into town is going by Mauch Chunk."

Weiksner says Johnny Otto, leader of the Chunkers' 1964 counter-revolution, is still around and in the phone book. Otto answers the third ring in a voice loud enough to eliminate the need for the telephone. "Yeah! All we got is a dead Indian! A man named McGinley said he'd give the town a million bucks for scholarships if we'd change back to Mauch Chunk. I'll show you the letter. No, don't come over here. I've got a dog, and he's a mean son of a bitch. I'll meet you at Weiksner's."

Johnny Otto, hunter-capped and unshaven, walks through the doorway, his head snapping like a turtle's. Weiksner, rummaging through his magician's hat behind the bar, pulls out a photograph of four men presenting petitions to have the town's name revert to Mauch Chunk in 1964. Otto examines the photograph, but he doesn't recognize himself in it. At 76, he is thinner and shorter.

With Weiksner bobbing his head in affirmation from behind the bar, Otto tells a story of how Butch McGinley, a native Chunker who went to California and made a fortune in oil, wrote a letter to Otto in 1964 promising to set up a $1 million scholarship fund if the town would take back its old name. Only McGinley wouldn't allow his letter to be made public. From the hat behind the bar Weiksner has pulled a handwritten letter, which he lays on the bar. "This is it. I have it right here. That's what it says. That's his signature."

At this moment, Joe Boyle steps in. He is greeted teasingly, but warmly, by the assemblage. Pickles Pry says Joe is OK. "I used to write letters to his paper, and he'd print them just as they were. Never even corrected the pronunciation or anything." Weiksner is explaining about Butch McGinley's letter. "He'd have donated the million, but he wouldn't let us publish it, so it didn't do us any good."

Boyle orders a ginger ale and says it's not true. "Doc Dougherty called McGinley in L.A., and McGinley denied he ever made any such promise."

Weiksner alleges, in so many words, that the late Doc Dougherty was laden with excrement. He and Boyle go outside and, with a parking meter serving as referee, stand facing each other on the sidewalk. Weiksner shows Boyle the letter. Boyle agrees that it bears McGinley's signature because he remembers seeing it on correspondence from him. Boyle walks away. Weiksner returns to the bar, fighting back a smile.

Every four years Jim Thorpe's name comes back to the sports pages as attempts are made to have the International Olympic

Committee restore the gold medals he won in 1912 and lost in 1913. Several groups, plus his children, are lobbying to accomplish this in time for the 1984 Games in Los Angeles. But his four sons and three daughters have a second goal—the return of his remains to Oklahoma. It's not just Jack Thorpe. They are all in on it.

When you dial Charlotte Thorpe's telephone in Phoenix, Arizona, you get a recording: "Hello, this is Charlotte Thorpe. I'm still pushing my Jim Thorpe projects, writing a book, and trying to get his medals back. I'm also into metaphysics. If you'll leave your name and number, I'll get back to you." Fifteen minutes later, Charlotte Thorpe, 62, is on the line giving her version of why her father is buried in Pennsylvania.

"Dad's third wife, Pat, my stepmother, hated Oklahoma. And when she got to the people in the town in Pennsylvania, she promised them the sky. The children were opposed. We wanted him in Oklahoma. But Oklahoma didn't seem to want him. In order to have Dad buried someplace, we went along. Whenever I go to Oklahoma, I can feel Dad's spirit very strongly. Indians believe that unless they are buried in their own tribal ground, their spirits won't rest. Dad's spirit is not at rest. It's time for him to come home to Oklahoma."

Grace Thorpe, 64, lives in Tahlequah, Oklahoma, with her sister, Gayle, 60. "What we hope to do is have the State of Oklahoma appropriate enough money to compensate the people in Pennsylvania for the expenses they incurred in burying Dad. Their heart was in the right place, and I wouldn't have it any other way. . . . Gayle says she agrees with everything I've just said."

Carl Thorpe, 55, is a retired Army lieutenant-colonel who works for the Bureau of Indian Affairs in Washington. "Pat was a real opportunist. None of us had much to do with her. I think she was trying to figure out some way she could make more money on him. It was his wish, expressed to me several times, that he be buried in Oklahoma. When the time comes, we will certainly take into account the feelings of the people in Pennsylvania and do it the right way. But the family is united in the belief that our father belongs in Oklahoma, and we assume that the people of Jim Thorpe will take our feelings into account."

But the Thorpe clan can guess again on that score. "No way," says Mayor Mike Hichok, who is razoring a sideburn when the Thorpe family's desires are mentioned. "They can't take the body back. The contract says that as long as this town is named Jim Thorpe, the body stays here. That's all there is to it."

"Amen," says Joe Boyle. "We picked the man up when nobody else wanted him. The State of Oklahoma had its chance, and it turned its back on Jim Thorpe."

On a summer day in downtown Jim Thorpe, the old Jersey Central Station is jungled with tourists, who keep getting into each other's snapshots. They have sampled the Victorian charm of Old Mauch Chunk. There's no one at Jim Thorpe's mausoleum, which is several miles away on Route 903.

A hundred yards or so before you reach the grave, the Olympian Drive-In Restaurant is closed, and newspapers cover its windows. A bank, the Mauch Chunk Trust Company, sits on the other side of the two-lane highway, insolent and busy.

A sign in front of the granite-grim mausoleum tells you, perhaps inaccurately, that this is the "Final Resting Place of J m Thorpe—All American." The "I" is missing from "Jim," but otherwise the site is properly pampered by the Jim Thorpe Lions Club.

Across the road, just out of Thorpe's field goal range, there is a row of split-level and ranch homes, their backyards to the highway sprouting aluminum clothes trees and children's swing sets. An under-mufflered car turns into the grave site's semicircular drive, makes a U-turn, spits gravel, and roars back toward the town.

A cathedral hush settles over the memorial, save for a meek breeze that wimples the grass and carries the aroma of mountain laurel and sadness.

Pennsylvania's Deer-Hunting Season

The Largest Participatory Recreation Event in the World?

Deer hunting is still a big business in Pennsylvania and an important part of the state's culture. And with more than a million licensed-firearm deer hunters, more than in any other state, Pennsylvania's annual deer season is still, arguably, "the largest participatory recreation event in the world."

But today the most dangerous wild animal in Pennsylvania is causing deaths and serious injuries. It also carries an often debilitating and sometimes fatal disease.

The same menacing creature is ruining crops; destroying valuable timber; stripping the woods of seedlings; changing the very nature of forests; killing nursery stock; and ravaging the lawns, gardens, and golf courses of suburban Pennsylvania.

It's not the bobcat, black bear, wild boar, or rattlesnake. It's Odocoileus virginianus. *The white-tailed deer. The Official State Animal. Bambi.*

Originally published as "Does Bambi Have It Coming?" in the *Philadelphia Inquirer Magazine*, November 27, 1983.

Wildlife experts and other scientists say Pennsylvania's deer population is out of control.

Not only are deer starving by the thousands; they're laying waste to forest ecosystems. There may be as many as 1.5 million white-tails roaming around not just the forests of northern counties but also places like Fairmont Park, Valley Forge National Park, and the grounds of Graterford Prison.

As a deer-slayer in Pennsylvania, the motor vehicle is second only to the rifle. There are about 40,000 documented deer highway deaths in Pennsylvania every year, but these do not account for animals who are fatally wounded but die away from the scene of the accident. Bob Frye, author of the definitive 2006 book Deer Wars: Science, Tradition, and the Battle over Managing White-tails in Pennsylvania, *says the annual carnage may reach 100,000. Hunters, by comparison, take about 300,000 a year.*

Deer also carry the ticks that transmit Lyme disease, which is an emerging infectious affliction that causes headache, fever, fatigue, and depression and, if untreated, can lead to more severe problems and even death.

When the Pennsylvania Game Commission combined the buck season with the doe season in 2001, it changed the name to "fire-arms deer season"; still, most people call it buck season. Whatever the name, it's an unofficial state holiday.

FORGET THE WORLD SERIES, the Super Bowl, the Stanley Cup, the NBA playoffs. Tomorrow is the big sporting event. Color it orange. Not rusty, autumnal orange, but fluorescent safety orange. Orange vests, orange jackets, orange caps. Tomorrow is Opening Day in Pennsylvania. The Opening Day: the first day of the annual two-week period when it is legal to hunt male deer. Buck season begins one-half hour before sunrise (at 6:32 A.M. in eastern Pennsylvania, at 6:52 A.M. in western Pennsylvania). Clockwork orange. There will be a million hunters, give or take a few thousand, in the woods at dawn. They will be spread over a legal hunting area big enough to swallow New Jersey. Though Guinness has yet to arbitrate the matter, the first day of buck season in Pennsylvania appears to rank as the largest participatory recreation event in the world.

The best guess of the game biologists is that there are 225,000 bucks out there who are legal candidates for—to borrow the official euphemism—harvesting. If all goes according to plan, as it usually does, 70,000 of them will die before the smoke clears on December 10; 45,000 of these will die tomorrow, and 25,000 of these will die before 9:00 A.M. tomorrow. The deer aren't aware that the season begins tomorrow, but they learn fast. In the next fortnight, a million hunters will seek a buck in Pennsylvania. Only one in 12 will succeed.

Opening Day is to Pennsylvania as the Mardi Gras is to New Orleans. And perhaps more. Pennsylvania has more deer hunters than any other state. Most public schools in rural Pennsylvania will be closed tomorrow, and those that aren't will experience the adolescent version of the "blue flu." The state legislature is not scheduled to be in session (during the 1977 budget crisis, with the state running out of money, the lawmakers still took off for Opening Day). Many labor contracts have clauses designating Opening Day a paid holiday. Telephone companies will have additional personnel on duty to handle the high volume of calls later in the day as hunters check in at home. In hunting areas, farmers will carry dishpans into the fields and beat them with sticks so hunters don't mistake them for deer and, for similar reasons, housewives will wear orange when they hang out the wash. Court trials will be postponed because key witnesses are off in the woods, and generally manpower will be less available everywhere. In 1975 a house in Clearfield County burned slowly to the ground because all the volunteer firemen were in the woods. The owner of the house was deer hunting, too.

In the history of American wildlife, which is marked by terrible excesses against the buffalo and the eagle, the white-tailed deer is a notable success story. Though they were nearly extinct in Pennsylvania and the rest of the United States in 1900, more deer are here today than there were when European colonization began. And the principal reason is a management program inspired and financed by hunters. That the hunter should turn out to be the deer's best friend is difficult for non-hunters and anti-hunters to accept. It is easier if the deer and the hunter are viewed as species rather than individuals. Seen collectively, the deer becomes less noble, though certainly not ignoble; the hunter becomes less ignoble, though certainly not noble.

Pennsylvania is splendid country for *Odocoileus virginianus*, the white-tailed deer, that marvel of grace and speed that is the nation's most plentiful, popular, protected, and sought-after big game animal. By act of the Pennsylvania General Assembly, October 2, 1959, it is the official state animal. It is far from an endangered species. There are, in fact, too many deer in Pennsylvania right now—perhaps a million. But for every deer in Pennsylvania, there is a deer hunter. And for many non-hunting Pennsylvanians, that ratio forms the antlers of a dilemma. For if you love deer, you must wish the hunters well.

———

There is a rhythm to the forest, and man fits in poorly at best. Alone among the animals, man beds down when he is not tired and arises when he is. The forest is on nature's time, and there are nocturnal and diurnal shifts, clocked only by the wind and the weather and the cycles of the sun and the moon. Only man thinks in terms of tomorrow. The hunter, therefore, must take extraordinary steps to outwit the deer.

The expert hunter will shave carefully on the morning of the hunt, for the rubbing of stubble against wool is enough to scare a deer off. By law and by prudence, he must wear a fluorescent orange uniform, for man, unlike the deer, fears his own species. The expert's rifle will be sighted, and he will wedge tissues into both ends of the scope to prevent fogging when he carries the rifle from the warmth of his house to the cold of the woods. He will empty his pockets of change and tape his keys together to avoid a jingle that would betray his presence. Studies by the U.S. Fish and Wildlife Service show that most American hunters receive their first rifle before they are 16 years old. As teenagers, many spend hours poring over books, magazines, and catalogs on guns. Their fascination with guns is lifelong, and they are likely to pass it on to their male children. Not surprisingly, many hunters drive rugged pickups and off-road vehicles with stickers that proclaim, "Register Communists, Not Guns!"

Biologically, deer can live for 20 years, but few make it to 10—and these are usually does. Bucks rarely reach five years of age in Pennsylvania. Most deer spend their entire lives within the same square mile of forest. By the time buck season arrives, the hormonal tides of the rut, which a few weeks earlier were an obsession, have largely ebbed. By late November, the deer's reddish brown coat has completed its annual shift to cinnamon gray, providing good camouflage in the wintry brush. The deer has extraordinary sight and hearing, and his sense of smell is so keen that he can detect an acorn under two feet of snow.

Acorns, his favorite food, become scarce as winter approaches.

————

HUNTING IS AN ISSUE on which reasonable men and women differ, but seldom reasonably. And more than any other American animal, the white-tailed deer, with its soft brown eyes, slender limbs, and gentle ways, convinces people that it is either wrong to hunt or wrong not to hunt. To anti-hunters, the hunter is the embodiment of evil—a festering, marble-hearted anachronism; to the hunter, the anti-hunter is an un-American, effeminate bleeding heart. There are, however, a few accurate generalizations about both groups.

Most Pennsylvania hunters—92 percent, according to the 1980 census—are men. Most Pennsylvania hunters—70 percent by the census—live in rural areas. Or, to put it another way, one in every six rural Pennsylvanians hunts; one in 25 urban Pennsylvanians hunts. Anti-hunters seem to fall into two broad categories: those who are disturbed by what happens to the animals, and those who are disturbed by what happens to the hunter. The first type tends to view animals as individuals rather than species and to see nature as an idyllic preserve where animals suffer only when man intrudes. The second type believes that the hunter is barbarized by the killing process.

Hunting with weapons predates man, for scientists have evidence that man-like creatures used specialized killing equipment to take the lives of other animals, and of one another, more than a million years ago. The desire and necessity to destroy life has been with man from the beginning. People have been taking sides over the hunting issue ever since Jacob and Esau of Genesis fame, but it is safe to say that the controversy has never been more intense than in the past 50 years. Two people, more than any others, are responsible: Walt Disney and Lee Harvey Oswald.

Felix Salten, an Austrian naturalist, wrote a book called *A Life History of the Woods*. It was translated into English in 1927 by a brilliant young student, Whittaker Chambers, who would later make history before the House Un-American Activities Committee. Disney purchased the rights to the book and produced an animated film that elevated the main character, Bambi, to a kind of Jesus White-tailed Superstar. Bambi has kept tears flowing in movie theaters for 41 years. It is possibly the greatest children's film ever made. It is indisputably the greatest anti-hunting tract ever made.

When Oswald fired from the sixth-floor window of the Texas School Book Depository in Dallas on November 22, 1963, he fired a 6.5 mm Mannlicher-Carcano rifle that was used in World War II by the Italians, confiscated by the Americans, and later sold as a deer rifle. His shot started a war over the right to bear arms that continues to this day. In the 20 years since, Americans have lived through terrible experiences involving guns—war, murder, assassinations, and hijackings. Rightly or wrongly, guns are perceived as evil; the tools of assassins and hijackers, the crutches of robbers, the muscle of bullying nations.

Today, the hunter, as the most visible user of the hated gun, is under a steady fire from a growing band of critics that is both vocal and articulate. Across the nation, anti-hunting groups have taken to walking through the woods during hunting season playing Sousa marches on portable stereo tape players, buying human hair in barbershops and strewing it through the hunting lands so the deer will be frightened by the human scent, buying up specialized hunting licenses subject to quotas and then not using them, and renting helicopters to fly over game lands to frighten animals out of the range of hunters' rifles.

Many anti-hunters are able to talk of their reverence for life as they dine on the flesh of a domesticated animal that was killed with a blunt instrument and bled and gutted in a slaughterhouse. Is meat purified when it is placed on cardboard and wrapped in cellophane? Most eaters of venison have at least watched the deer die. Surely the meat business would drop if customers had to watch the animals die. The same goes for the fur business. And what of the cosmetics industry, which tests its products by dabbing them in the eyes of laboratory rabbits and blinding them? Where does one draw the line in reverence for life? Flies quivering on a sticky tape?

Whatever the answer, the hunter, once the idol of his village and the hero of sagas, is today the object of widespread scorn and derision. Much of it is his own doing. The truth is that among Pennsylvania's million hunters there are a significant number whose manner is boorish, whose skills are barely existent, and whose kinship with the animals they hunt is nonexistent.

Few who venture into the woods tomorrow will hunt deer in the classic manner, which is to move through the woods alone, matching one's own stamina and senses against those of the deer. Rather, they will lurk in tree stands, clown-like in fluorescent orange, waiting for a deer to chance by so they can shoot it. Or groups of them will move noisily through the deer habitat, yelping and howling, terrifying the deer in the direction of waiting confederates. Those who kill will return home triumphantly, their glassy-eyed carcass dripping red, to stand for photographs next to their deer, proud as Olympic gold medalists. They will use a geometrically expanding array of equipment designed to make the predator-prey contest even more lopsided—scopes, sights, binoculars, hand and foot warmers, tree stands, and scents (a company called the Buck Stop in Stanton, Michigan, offers the original Doe-in-Heat-Scent that is "so powerful its natural, musky, sexy odor brings 'em on the run!"). Daniel A. Poole, president of the Wildlife Management Institute, was moved to inquire, "Has anyone stopped to ask what new technological developments the good Lord has hung on deer in these past decades to better equip them to cope with the technically augmented sportsman?"

Peter S. Duncan, the executive director of the Pennsylvania Game Commission, complains that there are not enough real hunters in the woods. "The major element of the hunt is the chase, and many of our Pennsylvania hunters don't even bother with this. A popular way to hunt deer today is from a tree stand. In my opinion, a real sportsman wouldn't hunt from a stand. He'd stalk and track the animal. A real hunter eats everything he kills, or gives it to someone who will, and gets his prey from the field to the freezer with a minimum of public display."

Duncan is the overseer of 135 state game protectors, who regularly see the ugly side of the Pennsylvania hunter: fields littered with beer cans and ammunition boxes, cows and other farm animals shot by mistake, deer wounded and left to die. Less typically, there is the practice of jacklighting. Cars or trucks roam through game lands at night shining spotlights in the woods. When the light finds a deer, the animal will freeze momentarily—and become an easy shot. A newer poaching technique is to chase deer with snowmobiles until, terrified and exhausted, they drop and

wait for the poacher's bullet. In 1976 the Game Commission prosecuted two Indiana, Pennsylvania, men for stalking and shooting
a deer from a helicopter.

————

WHILE THE INDIVIDUAL PENNSYLVANIA HUNTER may not be impressive, Pennsylvania hunters collectively are a pretty formidable
species. Through their license fees (they shelled out $17 million
this year), they are the major force for conservation in the state.
The hunters' lead role in bringing the white-tailed deer back from
near-extinction in Pennsylvania is history.

No one knows how many deer were in Pennsylvania when
William Penn landed in 1682, but venison and buckskin were sta-
ples of the colony's economy. Bounties were placed on the deer's
principal predators, the wolf and the mountain lion, in 1683.
As the settlers cleared ever more land, nature provided excellent
browse—the small trees and bushes that deer thrive on. Pennsylvania, once marginal white-tail country, became prime white-tail
country. Wildlife in general was plentiful and seemed inexhaust-
ible. In 1760, in Snyder County, two hunters recorded a bag of
41 mountain lions, 114 bobcats, 109 wolves, 122 foxes, 17 black
bear, one albino bear, two wapiti, 111 bison, one otter, 12 wolver-
ines, three beaver, 98 deer, and 500 smaller animals. After taking
a few tongues and hides, these sportsmen covered some 1,100
carcasses with pine boughs and set them afire. It is not recorded
that anyone objected to their excess.

The white-tailed deer quickly went from a provider of subsis-
tence and warmth to the target of commercial enterprise. Professional deer-slayers used guns, dogs, steel traps, and wire snares.
Pennsylvania deer hides were shipped by the boatload to Europe,
where they were prized for gloves. In the 1850s, Philadelphia's better saloons featured venison on their free lunch counters. But by
1880, a few pioneer conservationists were expressing fear for the
declining white-tail population. By 1890 the federal government

estimated that the total white-tail population of the United States and Canada was no more than 3,000. And by 1900, *Odocoileus virginianus* had all but disappeared in Pennsylvania. Indeed, there were so few deer at the turn of the century that dozens of hunters publicly took credit for shooting "the last deer in Pennsylvania."

The Pennsylvania Game Commission was established in 1895. Over the next decade it secured legislative approval of laws against the use of salt licks, hounds, and buckshot to kill deer. These laws were aimed at the commercial hunter, and the driving force behind them was the sport hunter. In 1906, the commission imported 50 white-tailed deer from Michigan and began an annual stocking program. Logging operations became extensive in many areas of Pennsylvania, and the huge trees felled by the loggers were being replaced by young forests of hardwoods and conifers—the ideal deer habitat.

The response of the deer to these changes was astonishing, beyond Malthus's wildest dreams. By 1920, herds of up to 100 deer could be seen along country roads at twilight. Evening strollers near Philadelphia often were startled by the appearance of a disoriented deer. In rural Pennsylvania, the deer invaded cornfields, orchards, and even barns. By 1930, the Pennsylvania white-tailed herd numbered more than a million. It was a joyous time of behind-every-bush hunting in Pennsylvania.

But the wildlife roller-coaster was on its way down again. The trees left by the logging operations were maturing. There was less food, and the deer were still multiplying. There were massive starvation losses. The winter of 1926 was especially harsh, and starving deer huddled together in "yards" to die. How many died will never be known, but one scientist counted more than 1,000 starved deer in just four townships of northern Pennsylvania. Game Commission biologists noticed a deterioration in body size and antler development.

There was a Hegelian synthesis at the Game Commission. Neither too many nor too few deer was desirable, and the size of the deer herd had to be regulated by an ongoing program of management. The policies would be set by the commission. The policies would be carried out by the hunters. But for a time the commission was literally a voice in the wilderness. The key to controlling the herd was does, but when the commission declared the first antlerless does and young bucks deer season in 1923, there was violent opposition from hunters who wanted as many deer as possible in the woods for them to shoot at. Indeed, many hunters who return empty-handed tomorrow night will blame their failure on the fact that there are not enough deer because the Game Commission allows the hunting of does. The early antlerless seasons were somewhat ineffective because the law allowed hunters in each county to petition to close the season in that county. It happened often until 1951 when the legislature repealed the loophole, and the commission began annual statewide antlerless seasons in 1957.

———

According to the Game Commission, the most popular way to hunt on the first day of deer season is from a tree stand, which can either be purchased for about $100 or built by the hunter for a few dollars. The expert hunter will be in his stand before dawn, and the tree will be carefully chosen. It will be downwind from where he hopes to see the deer, and it will be facing northward, so there will be no sun in his eyes. If possible, there will also be a complex background of branches to break up his silhouette.

Among the many findings of the Deer Research Center at Pennsylvania State University is that deer instinctively will move along the crest of a ridge so they can jump quickly to escape danger from either side. The deer is a super-athlete that can sprint 100 yards in five seconds in bounds of 20 feet and easily jump an eight-foot fence. The deer's air-filled coat hairs make it an excellent swimmer, and fishermen have seen deer gliding five miles out in the ocean. A deer's antlers begin growing in early spring—at the rate of several inches per week—and reach full size in about five months. Sometime in late winter, deer shed their antlers, which are quickly eaten up by squirrels and other rodents that prize them for their high mineral content. Big antlers give a deer a dominant position in the herd during the rutting season. They are the measure of both the deer and the hunter.

———

THE PENNSYLVANIA GAME COMMISSION operates out of a sprawling headquarters off an obscure road between Harrisburg and Hershey. In the weeks leading up to the buck season, it is athrob with purpose. The audience in the lobby includes a 22-point deer head, a huge elk head with the notation that it was killed illegally, a taxidermic bald eagle, and a bust of Theodore Roosevelt. The deer and the elk look bored, the eagle looks angry, and T.R. looks pompous.

The rental on the building, the salaries of everyone who works here and in the field—indeed, all of the expenses of the commission—are paid by hunters through license fees and other expenditures. There is about $5 million a year in federal aid for wildlife restoration, but the commission does not use any state tax dollars. For the past nine months, the daily business of the agency has been conducted by Peter S. Duncan.

"Although our official estimate is that there are 860,000 white-tailed deer in Pennsylvania this fall, it's a conservative estimate, and our biologists will tell you off the record that there's more likely a million deer out there right now," Duncan says. "That's too many, and one way or another, the population adjustments are going to be made."

Few deer die of old age. Duncan ticks off white-tail mortality statistics:

Last year, there were 24,667 reported killed by vehicles on highways, and the actual figure is much higher. Wild dogs got about 1,750 deer. Another 1,476 were shot by farmers for crop damage. Poachers got about 5,000 illegal deer, and perhaps 2,700 died of malnutrition.

Wild dogs are not a pretty sight. They usually chase the deer until it collapses and then eat the hindquarters first so it can't run but is still alive. Starvation is not nice either, and a starving deer would probably welcome a hunter's bullet.

"That's garbage," says I. B. Sinclair, a lawyer in Media, Pennsylvania, who is a board member of the Defenders of Wildlife and eastern U.S. chairman of the Sierra Club. To his way of thinking, the use of hunting to control population among deer is something like using a guillotine to cure dandruff. "The position of the Pennsylvania Game Commission is to breed deer to be killed by hunters, and in doing so, to perpetuate its own bureaucratic existence. The commission is not managing our wildlife either for the benefit of the people or the wildlife. People who just want to watch deer in the wild have rights, too. Hunting as the only means of population control is just pure garbage. There are deer in Florida, called the Key Deer, in an area that has never been hunted. They have basic internal biological controls that force the does to stop ovulating under population pressure."

But it's not just the Pennsylvania Game Commission that supports hunting as a means of wildlife management. The National Wildlife Federation, hardly a group of insensitive fascists, neither encourages nor discourages hunting among its 4.1 million members, but it has this to say on the issue: "The federal government, all 50 state governments, all of the nation's major conservation organizations and reputable wildlife biologists recognize regulated hunting as an efficient means of reducing surplus wildlife populations. There is no biological question whether surplus animals will die, only how. With songbirds, nature takes the entire surplus. With game animals, man takes part of it. But the surplus must die." Indeed, Sinclair's own Sierra Club has an official policy in favor of "regulated periodic hunting" to "promote optimum diversity and numbers in wildlife."

The buck season is only one, and the less important, of two major deer-hunting seasons. The second, which Duncan calls the linchpin of game management, is the two-day antlerless season (December 12 and 13 in 1983) in which does and young bucks are fair game. The commission estimates the deer population in each of Pennsylvania's 67 counties and issues the number of "doe licenses" in each county it reckons is needed to level the population. The desired population is determined by the extent and condition of the deer habitat in each county. This year, the commission has approved a statewide allocation of 536,000 antlerless licenses, which is designed to reduce the total doe population by 79,000. Why have a buck season at all?

Because, says Duncan, "we have to maintain the male-female sex ratio. If we have too many bucks for the does, there would be a dramatic decrease in reproduction."

———

NOT FAR FROM BEAVER STADIUM, where, during the autumn, representatives of Pennsylvania State University engage representatives from other colleges in a game involving a pig's bladder, there is a large, fenced wooded area. A sign at the entrance reads: "DEER RESEARCH CENTER. POSITIVELY NO DOGS!"

Inside, behind an eight-foot fence, deer with red ear tags munch on alfalfa. Penn State's Deer Research Center was established in 1958 and is the leading such facility in the world. A captive herd of white-tails, numbering about 100 at any given time, is maintained on 20 acres in wooded paddocks and holding pens. According to Dr. Robert L. Cowan, the founder and professor emeritus of the center, nutrition is the main area of research. But first he wants to discuss Bambi.

Bambi reaches a thicket and says, "We made it mother, we . . ." A gunshot shatters the stillness. A tear courses down Bambi's beautiful face.

"There is little concept of maternity among deer or any other animals. I've done some farming, and I butcher my beef. I have butchered a calf with the mother of the animal watching, and there are no signs of grief or regret. Just curiosity. Does will drive their own fawns away from food until they themselves have had enough to eat."

Bambi's father tries to console his offspring over the death of the mother.

"This one's really way out. There is absolutely no concept of paternity among deer. The buck mates with the doe and then takes off for the next doe. No fawn ever knew who its father was. The male deer is not monogamous and does not maintain a harem."

The father saves Bambi's life in a forest fire.

"The problem with all of this is that they tried to make a human being out of Bambi, just as a lot of anti-hunters tend to view all wildlife anthropomorphically. Too many people think of the cute little squirrels helping Snow White clean her house without knowing anything about real squirrel ecology. I have a great affection for deer. They're nice to be around. They are beautiful to look at. But I hunt them, too, because I see the need to control the herd. I like to see a lot of deer when I hunt and reassure myself that the herd is healthy. But . . . when I shoot . . . I want a clean kill. I don't want to wound a deer. I never have."

In one sense, the white-tailed deer is its own worst enemy. Its voracious appetites—sexual (a buck can impregnate four does in a single hour) and gastronomic (it takes 10–12 pounds of food a day to satisfy a normal adult)—lead to the classic Malthusian dilemma of diminished food supply from producing too many of its own kind.

November is the peak breeding time in Pennsylvania and the one time the white-tailed buck discards his intrinsic caution and dignity and comes close to making a fool of himself. He becomes extremely belligerent and will slash at trees and bushes with his antlers. When rutting bucks meet, they will cough and wheeze at each other, circle slowly watching for an opening, and suddenly slam their antlered heads together. Thus engaged, they will push at each other until one weakens and retreats. There are isolated cases of bucks being gored, and even rarer instances of the rivals becoming antler-locked and starving to death. But most of the time no one gets hurt. By the end of November, the lovesickness has largely abated.

For those white-tails that survive the hunting seasons, winter is the critical season. The most important influence on Pennsylvania's deer habitat has been commercial lumbering, because it provided low-lying vegetation. Deer food must be within six feet of the ground, and in mature forests the interlaced crowns and limbs of big trees check the development of lush undergrowth. Height is more important to a deer than to a basketball player, and most of the deer who starve in the winter are fawns.

What would happen if there were no hunting seasons? "It's quite simple," says Cowan. "So many deer out there are going to die this year, but not enough if we let nature take its course. If not enough deer are killed by hunters, they will overpopulate and eventually starve or die of disease before they starve. It's all very nice to say we should let nature take its course, but nature is very cruel, for one thing, and for another thing, man has intruded. We can't go back to the way things were 200 years ago in Pennsylvania. Mountain lions and wolves are now extinct, and bobcats are very rare. In the ecological scheme of things, the predator-prey system is very important, and the hunter is the deer's main predator."

What about birth control? It was tried by the National Park Service in 1968 after unhunted deer within Kentucky's Mammoth Cave National Park were near starvation and showing signs of dwarfism. Park rangers tried to administer oral contraceptives but found it impossible to catch most of the deer. Those that were caught developed an aversion to the chemicals. Next they tried trapping the deer and equipping them with an intrauterine ring, but it didn't work. Neither did hormone injections. The birth control experiment was abandoned in 1975.

Cowan also rejects one of the anti-hunters' most frequent objections: that by seeking out the biggest and the best buck, hunters interfere with the natural selection process. Alice Herrington, president of Friends of Animals Inc., has made this claim: "In Pennsylvania, they don't have deer anymore. They have oversized bunny rabbits with spike antlers."

"That one's really nonsense," says Cowan. "We've had animals brought in here from all over for 25 years, and I have yet to see any evidence of a genetic weakening of the species. The genetic argument doesn't hold because the hunting season follows the rutting season, and by the time the hunter arrives on the scene, the superbuck has already reproduced. Many times, I might add."

———

Instinct is as dangerous to the hunter as it is important to the deer. The expert hunter will be certain that he wants to kill what he is about to shoot at. He shouldn't shoot if it's too far away, or if it's moving too quickly, or if there's too much intervening brush. Unless the antlers are absolutely visible, he shouldn't fire.

The woods at this time of year are magical and mysterious, and for many hunters it is precisely this opportunity to become intimate with nature that makes hunting so appealing. Before dawn, the forest is a wonderland of gray silhouettes. Then the sun elbows its way onto the horizon, illuminating pine trees that stand like pencils. As the wind picks up, branches rattle above and schooners of cloud cruise across the sky. The warming sun turns the frost crystals into droplets that soak the sere leaves, but it is still cold. And cold is the major enemy of the tree-stand hunter, for it can cut through even thick layers of wool and chamois, numbing his body and eroding his patience.

The deer has no such worries. A deer's coat is so effective as an insulator that it can lie in snow all day without melting a flake.

The deer is a vegetarian but primarily a browser rather than a grazer. He's an avid acorn consumer in autumn, but most of the year he subsists on the tender tips of trees and shrubs. His favorite foods are acorns, dogwoods, maples, and birches. Red oaks and hickories also are favored. Starvation foods are mountain laurel and rhododendron. The vegetation must be within his reach, which is no more than six feet. He is a ruminant, which means he has a four-chambered stomach and chews his cud like a cow. When food is plentiful, it can be stored in the first stomach and digested slowly as it passes through the other three. When a deer is aroused, the tarsal glands on the inside of his hocks spray the air with a strong scent that all deer downwind recognize.

———

THE U.S. FISH AND WILDLIFE SERVICE reported that Pennsylvania's 1.1 million licensed hunters spent $264.9 million on equipment, transportation, food, lodging, and licenses in 1980; the average annual expenditure per hunter was $224, making hunting Pennsylvania's most expensive form of recreation. By comparison, each golfer spent $194; each skier, $175.

About 60 percent of the total, or $168.7 million, was spent by deer hunters. Seldom are so many bucks spent in pursuit of so few. If Pennsylvania is the deer-hunting capital of the world, then the deer-hunting capital of Pennsylvania is Potter County, a pentagonal block of happy hunting ground in the middle of the state's northern tier. By self-proclamation, shouted from bumper stickers and T-shirts, Potter County is God's Country. Maybe so, but about half of the county belongs to the people of Pennsylvania in the form of state forest and game lands, and 50 weeks out of the year the deer outnumber the 18,000 human residents by better than 2–1.

Beginning tomorrow, however, and continuing for the next fortnight, the county's population will swell by an additional 50,000 people, nearly all of them male. And when the buck season closes, there will be about 5,000 fewer deer. Potter County has about 4,500 deer camps, a term denoting everything from a well-appointed lodge to a rudimentary shack. There are a few motel rooms, and many sportsmen will arrive in those modern-day Conestogas, the motor home. All the émigrés will have rifles, and at least half of them will have a pouch of Red Man stuffed in their hip pockets. The streets of places like Coudersport and Galeton will look like Center City Philadelphia, and merchants will be hard pressed to keep up with demands for gloves, boots, bacon, gasoline, and a favorite local anesthetic, gin and Squirt. The merchants of Potter County do 20 percent of their annual business during the next two weeks, and a few will feel compelled to hire armed guards to prevent shoplifting. Restaurants and churches will offer special pre-dawn "hunter's breakfasts," and at night the bars will be filled with raucous men who will tell the truth only when their whiskeyed imaginations wane.

Among the 50,000 human carnivores in Potter County, there will be some, a significant minority, who might be called real hunters. They will live in organized camps, make their beds, clean their dishes, obey the game laws, and go to bed early. In many cases, these groups will include three generations of one family— grandfather, father, and son.

———

THE FORMPAC DIVISION of W. R. Grace and Company is just off a sooty stretch of industrialized highway north of Reading. A guard stops you at the gate and asks your business, and if you have an appointment, he has you sign in and gives you a visitor's badge. They have made a valiant effort to make it look like something other than an industrial site by surrounding the low-lying building with arborvitae, maples, and grass. But the overall impression on the outside is one of drums and valves and tanks surrounded by cyclone fence. The six-foot-three-inch, 220-pound presence of Larry Balsbaugh, the plant engineer, materializes in the doorway of the waiting room and extends a viselike grip. A hallway of yellow brick and blue heavy-duty carpet leads to his office. On the wall is a picture of his son, a West Point cadet, in uniform; a management award from the YMCA; and a framed quotation that begins, "We need to re-establish our American philosophy of self-reliant, self-responsible individuals."

"We manufacture those plastic trays that they put meat on in supermarkets," Balsbaugh explains. "They come in four colors— white, yellow, blue, and green. The white is for red meat, but poultry doesn't look so good on white, so they use yellow. The green and the blue are for seafood."

Balsbaugh has been going to Potter County on Thanksgiving weekend since 1952, when his father took him on his first deer hunt at 13. He missed only two of the next 30 buck seasons— once because he had a high school basketball game, once because he was in Korea with the Army Signal Corps. In his 29-season deer-hunting career, he has shot 12 bucks. He planned to be there this week with his 67-year-old father and his 16-year-old son:

> We go for the whole week, and I would never want to miss it. We have a camp that is well organized. There'll be 14 of us this year, plus we hire a cook from the Reading area. Each day, we have a captain of the hunt. All the venison taken by the camp is split up equally. There are bigger deer right here in Berks County, but we go to Potter because we have the camp, because there are a lot more deer up there, and because you don't see a hunter every 100 yards. Buck season has always been an important part of my life.
>
> I don't consider myself a killer. I don't like to kill. Yesterday I picked up a daddy longlegs from the floor in here and carried it outside. People who oppose hunting should go up to Potter County in the spring during trout season and smell the stench from the carcasses of deer who starved over the winter. I see hunting as a sport and a challenge. It's

the outdoors and the companionship . . . and a lot of other things. I guess that's the best way I can explain it to you.

Few hunters are able to articulate why they hunt. Many reasons are given, and perhaps the least convincing is that hunting is a public service to wildlife. To say that man hunts to spare animals the agony of starvation is to say that man copulates to propagate his species. Consider that nearly half of the hunters who kill deer ignore the law requiring that they report the kill to the Game Commission, and these reports are crucial in the commission's efforts to manage the size of the deer herd.

Scholars have been pursuing the question of hunters' motivation for a number of years, and the most common threads are love of the outdoors, the adrenal high of the chase, and the communal camaraderie of the hunt. But remove the element of the actual kill, and one can still have all these things. Probably, hunting is a mosaic of many motivations, with roots too deep and dark to be examined objectively.

Like the history of all hunting, the history of deer hunting is less than inspirational. In eighteenth-century Europe, a common "sporting" practice was to herd deer down canvas chutes so that noblemen and their guests, standing under canopies, could shoot them gallery-style as they passed by. Hirelings ran behind the deer, setting off firecrackers to keep them moving. Until very recently it was common for New Zealand hunters to place a bushel of apples in an open field, wait for a herd of deer to appear, and then rake them with submachine guns.

Public opinion would never allow this to happen in Pennsylvania today, but I. B. Sinclair, the avid anti-hunter; Larry Balsbaugh, the avid hunter; and Peter Duncan, the wildlife bureaucrat, all agree on a single point: There are a lot of ugly hunters in Pennsylvania today.

Sinclair: "Hunters are lazy. They sit up in the trees and wait for the deer to come to their bait. They want to park their cars in a paved lot, walk a couple of yards, and wait for a deer to show up accidentally. They're real sports."

Balsbaugh: "About one in every four out there are real hunters. The rest of them are slobs. And they're on the increase. I have a feeling it's part of the general breakdown in the family. My father taught me how to hunt the right way, and I've taught my sons. You don't get much of that anymore. I see the same thing happening out on the golf course, where the gentlemen are getting fewer and fewer."

Duncan: "Many Pennsylvania hunters have gotten spoiled and don't want to bother with the challenge. They want to park their car, walk into the woods, sit down, and shoot something. If we can't clean up our own act, there's going to be organized, intense opposition to sport hunting in Pennsylvania in the next few years."

———

The slightest alien sound, as that of a hunter flicking the safety off his rifle, will cause a deer to become hyped up by his own glandular system. When he senses danger, the deer's tail stops wagging and shoots straight out. For the hunter, it is a powerful moment, too. As he eases his finger around the icy trigger, the hunter may feel his heart rattle in his rib cage. For a frozen instant, the hunter and the deer may look at each other, mammal to mammal. As the shot is fired, the deer's ears will drop and often he will emit a shrill, nasally whistle, as he breaks into a wild run.

The zenith of American industrial genius is in the manufacture and embellishment of the gun. The hunter, by exerting no more than five pounds of pressure with one finger at the trigger, starts perhaps 100 grains of chemical burning rapidly. About 50,000 pounds of pressure build up in the breech of his rifle. A small projectile weighing 200 grains moves forward in a perfectly controlled flight at a speed of 3,000 feet per second. The projectile hits a deer with about 6,000 foot-pounds of energy, expanding in an ever-increasing diameter as it tears through tissue and bone.

Not all living things feel pain. The nervous systems of plants probably are too rudimentary to register pain. But fish and fowl will struggle to escape pain and death. It is reasonable to assume that large mammals, including men and deer, experience pain similarly. A real hunter will track the deer he has shot. If he has hit the deer in the chest—the preferred location—he shouldn't have more than 100 yards to go, following the scarlet blotches of the deer's blood. If the deer has been shot in the chest cavity, the slug probably will destroy the heart and open veins and arteries. Most of the blood will have been pumped from the deer's body in the final flight. According to veterinarians and wildlife biologists, a deer dies with his tail down in death panic. The muscles twitch violently; there is choking and a gasp. The brown eyes remain open but no longer see.

In its instructions to hunters, the Game Commission is explicit on the procedures for field dressing a deer. The hunter should unload his gun and set it aside, roll the deer on its back, and slit open the abdomen. Next, cut out the bladder, being careful not to spill the urine and thereby contaminate the meat. The gullet should be severed in front of the stomach to remove the contents of the abdomen. The innards will be warm, almost hot, and they usually steam in the cold air.

Tales of the Pennsylvania Turnpike

The Pennsylvania Turnpike Is, in a Very Real Sense, America's Highway—a Fenced City, 470 Miles Long and 200 Yards Wide, with a Heterogeneous and Resurgent Stream of Mobile Citizens. And Every Mile Has a Story.

Now well into its eighth decade, the Pennsylvania Turnpike is showing its age, and it has been criticized by safety experts and professional drivers.

In 2010, Reader's Digest *conducted a poll of truck drivers, traffic reporters, and road safety experts and named it "one of the seven worst roads in America," citing short entrance ramps, narrow lanes, and too many hills and curves.*

In 2014, Cardinal Logistics Management Corporation, a leading provider of organizational planning for trucking companies, identified the turnpike as one of "the worst highways in America," adding, "Narrow lanes and sharp curves make this highway extremely dangerous. To boot, it's been under construction for decades."

The Pennsylvania Turnpike has always been criticized by editorialists and good-government groups. The governing commis-

Originally published as "Tales of the Pennsylvania Turnpike" in the *Philadelphia Inquirer Magazine*, September 9, 1984.

sion has been continually peopled by stalwarts of the Democratic and Republican parties, and the odor of scandal has never been far away. The turnpike has also been a cash cow for politicians. Turnpike employees and contractors have always been tapped for contributions to the parties.

And the turnpike is criticized by motorists for ever-rising tolls. Because of a 2007 law that requires the Turnpike Commission to share a portion of its toll revenues for use on other state transportation projects, tolls have risen nearly every year for the past decade. It has been predicted that if this continues, by 2021 drivers will have to pay $50 for the privilege of crossing the state on the turnpike.

Nearly forgotten is the promise that when the original construction bonds were paid off in 1956, the toll booths would come down. Clearly, that's not going to happen.

FOR TWO GENERATIONS OF AMERICANS, the Pennsylvania Turnpike has been a route to the Liberty Bell, Valley Forge, and the Gettysburg Battlefield. Now there is another historic treasure along the way: the Pennsylvania Turnpike itself. Last year, one of the original turnpike tollbooths was carted off to the Smithsonian Institution, and 1984 is a year of important anniversaries for the first of America's superhighways. It was 100 years ago that its tunnels were bored by railroad builders, and it was 50 years ago that the idea of using those tunnels for the World's Greatest Highway was born.

It was built by freewheeling, fearless men who ignored angry landowners with shotguns and skeptical Wall Street investors with myopia to transform a 50-year-old abandoned railroad bed into a superhighway that soared across and occasionally through the Appalachian Mountains. They inspired their successors to drain "bottomless" marshes for the New Jersey Turnpike, move entire rivers to make way for the New York State Thruway, and bridge commuter rail lines in Connecticut that were so busy that the maximum workday was 60 minutes.

The Pennsylvania Turnpike has never used a penny of state tax money, never lost money and never knowingly given anyone a free ride. Its obituary has been written several times, but today the turnpike, which is 14 years older than the Schuylkill Expressway, is the very best road Pennsylvania has.

The Pennsylvania Turnpike is, in a very real sense, America's highway—a fenced city, 470 miles long and 200 yards wide, with a heterogeneous and resurgent stream of mobile citizens. And every mile has a story.

MILEPOST 0: Today the Pennsylvania Turnpike begins in the west at the state line, where it links with the Ohio Turnpike. This is an extension of the original road, and when it opened in 1951, it ended in a cornfield because the Ohio Legislature was still debating over that state's toll road. A special access road was built to the nearest town, Petersburg, Ohio, which was ill-prepared for the sudden surge of westbound traffic from Pennsylvania. It had neither a traffic light nor a policeman, and on the day the Pennsylvania extension opened, George E. Knesal, president of the Petersburg Booster Club, complained that it took him eight minutes to get across the street.

The 67-mile extension cuts a southeastern diagonal around Pittsburgh, then turns directly east toward the Appalachians. In colonial Pennsylvania, the Appalachians were called the Endless Mountains, and they were a formidable barrier to westward expansion. The approximate route of the Pennsylvania Turnpike across the Appalachians was first traveled by bison and elk; later, it was the original Native American trail from the Atlantic seaboard to the Ohio Valley. The first survey of this route was made in 1837 by John Augustus Roebling, a young engineering apprentice who many years later would help his son design and build the Brooklyn Bridge.

But it took an old-fashioned, greed-inspired business war between the Pennsylvania and New York Central Railroads for a final route. William H. Vanderbilt, son of Cornelius "Commodore" Vanderbilt, ordered the construction of a New York Central line to compete with the Pennsylvania Railroad's Main Line in 1882. The Main Line followed the meandering water route through the Appalachians, and Vanderbilt's idea was to breach the barrier with a straight line by going under the mountains.

Vanderbilt sent representatives to Italy to recruit laborers experienced in boring tunnels through the Alps, and by 1884, 3,000 workers had poured into Pennsylvania to work on the New York Central's South Penn Railroad. By 1885, bridge piers studded the rivers, long cuts had been gashed into smaller mountains, and the towering peaks of the Alleghenies had been pierced by nine tunnels.

But a rising young financier named J. P. Morgan saw the rate war as bad for American business and persuaded Vanderbilt to drop his project. When the railroad was abandoned in 1885, it was 60 percent completed at a cost of $10 million and the lives of 27 tunnel workers. The South Penn Railroad came to be called "Vanderbilt's Folly," but the route is still considered the most exhaustive topographical survey ever to precede the building of an American railroad.

MILEPOST 56: It was here, at the Pleasant Valley Service Plaza near the Pittsburgh Interchange, that Governor Milton J. Shapp stopped in 1972 to answer the call that waits for neither commoner nor king. Shapp discovered that five of the toilets had a 10 cent admission charge, and he felt that this was carrying the turnpike's pay-as-you-go policy too far. When he got to Harrisburg, he summoned the press and declared that he wouldn't stand for it. Thereupon, the commission ordered Howard Johnson's, the concessionaire, to remove the locks on all turnpike toilets.

After Vanderbilt abandoned his railroad project, the forest reclaimed the roadbed and the tunnels filled up with water from mountain springs. Meanwhile, three highways were built across the Appalachian Barrier: the Lincoln (Route 30), the William Penn (Route 22), and the National (Route 40). All had steep grades that posed a real challenge to the low-powered autos of the 1920s and 1930s and made for treacherous winter driving. Trucks had to transfer their loads to specially geared, high-powered vehicles for the trip.

Then along came Victor Lecoq, an obscure employee of the state Planning Board—an agency then under pressure from the New Dealers in Washington to come up with public projects to provide employment. Lecoq opened discussions late in 1934 with the Pennsylvania Motor Truck Association, which liked the idea of an all-weather superhighway across the Appalachians.

It took nearly three years to convince the Pennsylvania Legislature, which even then was a hotbed of cold feet, to approve the project. Opponents dubbed it "pie-in-the-sky" and predicted that it would bankrupt the state treasury. But on May 21, 1937, legislation was approved authorizing the construction of a 160-mile toll road from a point near Carlisle to a point near Irwin and creating the Pennsylvania Turnpike Commission to oversee the project.

Survey parties worked for more than two years to find a better path for the turnpike, but in the end they found that they could not improve on the one established by Vanderbilt's engineers 50 years before. The route of 1884 was adopted almost in its entirety by the turnpike commission. The turnpike would breach the Appalachian barrier with seven tunnels, six of them original South Penn tunnels. Three other Vanderbilt tunnels were abandoned in favor of deep mountain cuts.

The new commission was having trouble raising the $60 million needed to build the highway. Bankers in Philadelphia and New York laughed the commissioners out of their offices. But President Franklin D. Roosevelt was interested in the project for military reasons, the Reconstruction Finance Corporation agreed to underwrite a $35 million bond issue, and the Works Progress Administration came through with a $26 million grant. At Roosevelt's insistence, the federal money carried the stipulation that the road be "substantially completed" by July 1, 1940. The commission spent nearly a year in final design and contractor bidding, and when FDR released the federal dollars on October 26, 1938, the commission had not taken title to a single right-of-way. But the following day, contractors rushed out to a Cumberland County farm, received permission from the owner to proceed, and brought in their equipment to clear the land. Thus did the builders of the Pennsylvania Turnpike begin. They had 20 months to finish.

MILEPOST 65: It was here on July 25, 1953, that State Police found the body of a truck driver who had been shot and killed as he slept in the cab of his vehicle parked at a rest area. Three days later, another truck driver was slain in identical fashion 30 miles east. The nation's newspapers were filled with headlines such as "Reign of Terror" and "Turnpike Phantom." The drivers began bunching at service plazas and taking turns standing guard over sleeping colleagues. The Teamsters union and the Pennsylvania Motor Truck Association each offered a $5,000 reward for the killer.

On July 30, a third sleeping trucker was shot just off the turnpike on Route 30; he survived. A week later, a 24-year-old farmhand from Fayette County, Pennsylvania, named John Wesley Wable was arrested on a minor assault charge in Uniontown and confessed to police that he was the Turnpike Phantom. They dismissed him as a "screwball" and let him go. A week later, the wounded driver's stolen pocket watch turned up in a Cleveland pawnshop, and police traced it to a rooming house where they found the German pistol used in the three shootings and a woman who said she was John Wesley Wable's girlfriend. A nationwide manhunt ensued, and Wable was arrested on October 13 near Albuquerque, New Mexico. He admitted owning the pistol used in the killings, but he said he had given it to a man in Pittsburgh before the killings.

Wable stuck to his story at his trial in Greensburg, Pennsylvania, but he was convicted by overwhelming circumstantial evidence. He was electrocuted at Rockview State Penitentiary on

September 26, 1955—the seventh person to be executed in Pennsylvania that year.

In this day of almost routine space travel, it is difficult to realize how the construction of the Pennsylvania Turnpike captured the imagination of a Depression-weary nation. In those days, few people owned an automobile, and even the best roads of the day were high-crowned, weak-shouldered two-lane affairs that even had some unpaved sections. Route 1, the East Coast's main north–south route, went through the downtowns of Boston, New York, Philadelphia, and Washington, and you had to wait hours to cross the Hudson and Delaware rivers on ferries. Coast-to-coast driving was achieved by taking Route 30 into the center of Chicago, where you picked up Route 66.

The builders of the Pennsylvania Turnpike were talking about a road across mountains that was two-thirds straightaway and permitted you to go 160 miles without shifting gears! It would be the marvel of the Motor Age: no intersections, no railroad grade crossings, no traffic lights. The cloverleaf, that ubiquitous concrete pretzel of today, was new. The project was compared to the Great Wall of China, the Pyramids of Egypt, and France's Maginot Line, which would crumble a few weeks before the opening of the turnpike.

MILEPOST 85: On October 19, 1940, three weeks after the turnpike opened, Arthur B. Turner, 66, of Bethlehem, was killed when his car skidded and overturned between the Irwin and Donegal interchanges. It was the first traffic fatality on the new superhighway.

Scientific American magazine called the turnpike the greatest road-building project ever attempted because "never before have highway builders tried to tunnel a roadway through such a mountainous region." It was designed so that no grade would be more than 3 percent—a three-foot rise to every 100 feet of length. Sections of the William Penn and Lincoln highways had 9 percent grades. Crossing the Appalachians on either existing highway involved a cumulative ascent of 13,000 feet; the total climb on the turnpike would be 4,000 feet. Most of the road was on the southern and western exposures of the hills and mountains, meaning that the sun would aid in the clearing of snow and ice. The entire 160-mile roadway would be enclosed by a fence that, according to contract specifications, was to be "horse-high, bull-strong and hog-tight."

About 18,000 men worked on the turnpike for an average hourly wage of 75 cents. Contractors were required to give men on relief preference in hiring for the common laborer jobs, but there were many experienced workers from the Boulder Dam and New York City subway projects. As Hitler grew bolder in Europe, Roosevelt prodded the commission to hurry the construction work. Using floodlights, the men worked in three seven-hour shifts, with the hour between shifts used for equipment maintenance.

Residents unhappy with property settlements or the construction work turned out with shotguns along the right-of-way. Workers were pelted with garbage and rocks, and some were beaten. Existing restaurants, fearing that the new road would ruin their businesses, put up signs in their windows, "No Turnpike Workers!" As the road neared completion, the *New York Times* gushed, "The Pennsylvania Turnpike is a road such as has been hitherto seen only in miniature at the Futurama of the World's Fair—superspeed, supersafe, the longest route of homogenous design in the country." The workers kept up their half of the federal bargain: The turnpike was "substantially completed" by July. During construction of the original turnpike, 19 workers lost their lives; all but one died in the tunnels. Tunnel workers were paid an extra 15 cents an hour.

MILEPOST 107: A giant 350-year-old oak tree, which President Zachary Taylor had visited in 1848 and suggested was "a symbol of democracy," was chopped down on June 21, 1939, to make way for the turnpike.

MILEPOST 110: Hundreds of thrifty, God-fearing, all-American farmers lived along the planned route of the turnpike. Most of the land had been owned by the same family for more than a century. For them, the land had no price. It was theirs. About 800 farms were taken over by the turnpike for its fenced right-of-way, and in fewer than 100 cases was the settlement amicable.

Initial plans were to dedicate the turnpike on July 4, 1940, with President Roosevelt heading the list of honored guests. But FDR was running for reelection at the time, and the Republicans on the commission tried to delay the opening until after the November election. A Labor Day ceremony was canceled, and by this time the road was ready for use. Finally, it was decided that there would be no ceremony, and on October 1, 1940—two years to the day after the commission asked for bids from contractors—the World's Greatest Highway was opened to traffic.

Drivers lined up at the tollbooths for 10 hours before the opening, and the first car through was driven by Homer D. Romberger, a Carlisle feed and tallow dealer. The toll for a full 160 miles of the turnpike was $1.50 for passenger cars, and the biggest trucks paid $10. The first Sunday was a balmy Indian summer day, and 27,000 vehicles got on the turnpike. There was an eight-hour traffic jam near Somerset. It was compounded by confusion over the cloverleafs (people lost their sense of direction), the tollbooths (they didn't know they had to stop for a ticket), and the tolls (they didn't bring any money). Tollbooths at several interchanges ran out of tickets.

Early traffic use surpassed all estimates, but in the fourteenth month of the turnpike's operation, America went to war, and between Pearl Harbor and V-J Day it was essentially a military highway. The turnpike was an important link in the transport of steel from mills in the Pittsburgh area to the East Coast, and it was used in the vast movement of men and materiel to Europe, Africa, and the Pacific. General Lucius Clay said after V-J Day that the Pennsylvania Turnpike had hastened the end of the war.

MILEPOST 129: The only break in the turnpike's right-of-way fence occurs here, between the Bedford and Somerset interchanges. Steps lead from the edge of the turnpike to St. John the Baptist Catholic Church. Some motorists stop to worship here. No one knows how the church retained its direct access to the otherwise restricted highway.

MILEPOST 139: Trooper Manley Stampler was on routine patrol on July 5, 1953, when he noticed a black Chrysler with Missouri plates twice cut in front of vehicles trying to pass it. He pulled the driver over, strode up to the car, and found himself looking at Harry and Bess Truman. Stampler issued a warning to the man who had been president of the United States six months before and pocketed a story for his grandchildren. "He was very nice about it and promised to be more careful," Stampler said later.

MILEPOST 147: It was here at the Midway Service Plaza near Bedford that John H. Dent, the Democratic leader of the State Senate, stopped for lunch on his way to a legislative session in April 1947. He didn't like his lunch, and so he wrote a letter to Governor James Duff complaining that his cheese sandwich had been so thin "you could read a newspaper through it." Had Dent bothered to do this, he would have discovered that Duff was already complaining that an ice cream cone cost 20 cents on the turnpike and had ordered an investigation. The only concrete result of the controversy was that Howard Johnson's lowered its cone to a dime—after reducing the amount of ice cream in each cone. But it was the beginning of a continuing stream of criticism against services on the turnpike.

While the Turnpike Commission was getting a cold shoulder from Wall Street in 1938 in its attempt to line up financing for the World's Greatest Highway, the son of a Massachusetts cigar salesman had established the first link in a chain of restaurant franchises. His name was Howard Dearing Johnson.

Two years and 28 flavors later, Johnson was contacted by Standard Oil Company, which had just won the contract to operate the service plazas on the Pennsylvania Turnpike. The contracts included the operation of restaurants, but Esso wanted to sell petroleum, not potatoes, and was looking for a subcontractor. Johnson gambled that the turnpike would succeed, and partly because of the exclusive right to the captive turnpike market, survived the lean war years and became king of the roadside restaurant trade.

There were five service plazas for eastbound motorists and five for westbound motorists on the original 160-mile turnpike. An eleventh here at Midway was at the halfway point and served all traffic. Midway featured indoor and outdoor restaurants, a barber shop, and, for truckers, a 38-bed dormitory, showers, a lounge, a game room, and valet service.

Throughout the decades of controversy over the restaurants, the commission's position has been that the turnpike plazas are placed there as a convenience, not a bargain. Moreover, because of the subcontracting arrangement, the commission had no direct control over the restaurants. Howard Johnson himself weathered the storm from homes in Milton, Massachusetts, New York, and Miami; frequented New York nightspots; bought a 60-foot yacht and an art collection; and married four times. He died in 1972. The Howard Johnson monopoly on the Pennsylvania Turnpike was broken when the original oil company contracts expired in 1978 and the commission chose ARA Services to operate the restaurants at Brandywine and Valley Forge. Howard Johnson's retained rights at six other plazas; Burger King has three. The new agreements placed the restaurant operators directly under the control of the commission.

MILEPOST 148: Just east of Midway, on the north side of the turnpike, is a small mountain from which sand was taken in 1936 and fused to create a 200-inch mirror for the world's largest telescope at the Mount Palomar Observatory in California.

MILEPOST 154: On August 18, 1939, two weeks before Hitler invaded Poland and World War II began, laborers found 21 sticks of dynamite under a small bridge here that was almost completely constructed over Snake Spring Valley Run. The dynamite had been capped, fused, and lighted, but the fuse burned out before it reached the explosives. An extensive investigation failed to find the culprits, but it was widely supposed to be the work of German saboteurs.

MILEPOST 163: For the first 25 years of the turnpike's existence, Breezewood, Pennsylvania, was a somnolent town of fewer than 200 people on the old Lincoln Highway. There was no road connecting the town and the turnpike. Land was selling for $50 an acre for the few people who wanted to buy it. But as fate and the federal government would have it, Interstate 70, bringing traffic north from Baltimore and Washington, intersected the toll road near the town in 1965. Soon, three million vehicles were passing through Breezewood each year, and a huge service area sprang up between the turnpike and the interstate. Today, there is a strip of 50 motels, restaurants, and service stations, and when the sun sets on Breezewood, thousands of tractor-trailers lumber into the parking lots, like herds of buffalo coming to a water hole, and family station wagons bring in children teetering perilously at the ends of their parents' patience. A prime acre in this "City of Motels" sells for $50,000 and up.

MILEPOST 180: From the beginning of the air age, the Appalachian Mountains of Pennsylvania were dreaded by aviators because of their height, treacherous fogs, and drafts and winter storms. The turnpike became a favorite of flyers because the white ribbon of concrete was an infallible navigation guide and a good place to land in a pinch. In the first 10 years of the turnpike's operation, there were more than 100 emergency landings on the highway, and the state in 1952 began building a series of emergency airstrips adjacent to the right-of-way. The first was here at Fort Littleton. The fields were abandoned in the early 1960s when advances in navigational and deicing systems made them obsolete.

By 1960, it had become clear that the original two-lane tunnels would no longer do. Because they abruptly narrowed traffic to two lanes, they were the sites of regular weekend traffic jams. And despite the best efforts of turnpike maintenance workers to wash the tile tunnel walls and repaint the road lines, the continued exposure to exhaust fumes quickly begrimed them, reducing visibility for drivers. The commission decided that for four of the tunnels there would be parallel two-lane tunnels built, while the turnpike would bypass the Ray's Hill, Sideling Hill, and Laurel Hill tunnels with deep cuts that would maintain the sacred 3 percent grade restriction. All work was completed by October 1968, and for the first time the entire east–west turnpike had four continuous lanes.

MILEPOST 225: West of Carlisle, there is a 13-mile, rolling straightaway section of the turnpike, and on June 3, 1940, the National Broadcasting Company took television movies here of a car going 100 miles per hour (mph). The film was shown over the company's network of more than 4,000 televisions in New York City.

MILEPOST 226: Truck weight limits on the turnpike had been suspended during World War II, and in the postwar years they were not enforced until 1948. In protest against the restrictions, truckers blocked the road beginning here for 12 miles and moved out only after Governor James Duff threatened to send in bulldozers to remove them. Six major trucking companies banded together and offered to buy the whole turnpike for $100 million, but the commission, far from thinking about getting rid of the highway, was plotting a massive expansion program.

MILEPOST 247: Since 1956, the commission has operated out of a modern headquarters building just off the Harrisburg East Interchange. While most of the day-to-day work is handled by a professional, full-time staff, the commission itself is composed of five part-time members—some of whom give bigger parts of themselves than others. One of the members is always the state transportation secretary, and the other four traditionally have been appointed on the basis of political pedigree. Since 1940, five of the appointed commissioners have been convicted of official crimes. Two of them had their convictions overturned on appeal; three went to jail.

MILEPOST 262: July 31, 1960, was a sunny, clear day four miles west of the Lebanon-Lancaster interchange. At 3:35 P.M., an eastbound car went out of control, crossed the 10-foot grass strip and crashed into two westbound cars. The driver of the eastbound vehicle was killed along with a couple and their three children in one of the other cars. It was at that time the worst accident in turnpike history, but its real significance was that it ended years of debate within the commission over whether to install guardrails in the dividing strip. Larry Keighley, a freelance photographer, happened by right after the accident, and his graphic, gruesome photos appeared in newspapers and newsmagazines and, later, in the "Face of America" feature of the *Saturday Evening Post.* Nine days after the accident, the commission announced plans to erect guardrails along the middle of the entire turnpike.

The designers of the turnpike claimed before it opened that 90 percent of the causes of accidents had been eliminated, and as part of its pre-opening hype in 1940 the commission issued press releases stating that turnpike curves could be safely negotiated at 100 mph and that on the straightaways, 120 mph could be achieved in safety. There was no speed limit on the turnpike in the beginning, and in early 1941 the *Ford Times* advised its subscribers that "the closest the average American comes to breaching the sonic barrier is when he eases himself behind the wheel of the family car and has a go at the Pennsylvania Turnpike."

MILEPOST 265: Here, on January 23, 1976, a State Police radar unit clocked a white Lincoln Continental tearing along the dotted line at 90 mph. Trooper R. William Keller pulled the car over and found that it was driven by a plainclothes colleague, Trooper Anthony Diguglielmo. In the back seat was Governor Milton J. Shapp. Keller did not issue a citation, but he reported the incident on his radio, and the broadcast was picked up by a ham radio operator. It all came out in the papers the next day. Shapp explained that he was late for a news conference and had ordered Diguglielmo to speed. The governor paid a fine of $105 for himself and $105 for the driver and was assessed five points on his driving record. Keller explained that he had not written a ticket because he assumed that there was an emergency. Shapp confessed that he was on his way to a news conference to announce a contest to come up with a new state slogan.

The 100-mile turnpike extension began where the original turnpike ended near Carlisle, ran eastward through the rectilinear fields of some of the world's richest farmland, and ended at a point near a tiny hamlet in Montgomery County that took its name from a Revolutionary War tavern called the King of Prussia. The extension opened on November 20, 1950. It cost $87 million, but by now the money-earning record of the turnpike had been well established, and the commission had no trouble selling its bonds.

There was strident opposition to the building of the turnpike near Valley Forge, where historical groups complained about the desecration of General Washington's encampment. But the commission stuck by its plans and instead prepared an elaborate diorama of the Valley Forge area that it displayed at public sites in the Philadelphia area. The historical types were unmoved by it and gleefully pointed out that the diorama placed the Memorial Arch of Valley Forge on the wrong side of the Schuylkill.

MILEPOST 288: It was here on April 5, 1969, that Donald Lambright, the 30-year-old militant son of Stepin Fetchit, the old-time black screen comedian, began a shooting spree along the turnpike. Lambright's .30-caliber rifle killed a Philadelphia couple on their way to Penn State to visit their son on Easter Sunday and wounded 17 other motorists. Lambright pulled over near Milepost 264, shot and killed his wife, placed the muzzle in his mouth, and killed himself. Friends described him as "paranoiac" over the problems of race relations in America.

MILEPOST 305: It snowed all day and night on March 20, 1958, and when spring arrived the following morning, there were 46 inches of snow on the ground. It was a wet snow, and conventional snowplows couldn't clear the turnpike. Motorists and bus passengers were marooned between the Morgantown and Down-ingtown interchanges, and they were picked up by helicopter and brought to the Brandywine Service Plaza here. More than 800 persons—men, women, children, and babes-in-arms—spent the next 36 hours in the heatless, lightless Howard Johnson's restaurant. One man died as he tried to wade through the drifts to the restaurant, but luck was with the others. Among the stranded were a doctor, who treated shock and frostbite; a truck driver who provided 144 blankets from his rig; and another truck driver who maneuvered his milk truck into the parking lot. Entertainment was provided by Frankie Avalon, Danny and the Juniors, and the Storey Sisters—all of whom were trapped by the storm.

MILEPOST 310: The worst accident in the history of the turn-pike occurred near the Downingtown interchange here when a car carrying the Regis Allen family of Philadelphia was struck broadside by another auto. Killed were Allen, his wife, and six of their children and the driver of the second car. State Police said the Allens were en route to Reading to visit relatives for Thanksgiving when they attempted to make an illegal U-turn.

MILEPOST 325: Despite vehement protests, a barn once used by Lafayette was razed here to make way for the eastern extension in 1949. The commission dismissed the complaints of historic sac-rilege by saying the structure was dilapidated.

MILEPOST 343: The turnpike's 33-mile extension to the Del-aware River was opened on August 22, 1954, and Commission Chairman Tommy John Evans, his Cadillac lapping contentedly, headed a line of 150 cars at the new Willow Grove interchange, waiting ceremoniously to become the first on the new extension. Suddenly a car roared down the virgin concrete and pulled into the interchange. The perplexed driver explained that he had gotten lost and found himself on the Pennsylvania Turnpike. Evans took his fare, waved him through the tollbooth, and everyone went home.

Work on the Delaware River Extension suffered many interrup-tions from unhappy property owners in Montgomery and Bucks

Counties. In May 1952, U.S. Army General James B. Newman, stressing the strategic importance of linking the Pennsylvania Turnpike with the New Jersey Turnpike, decried the "obstinate people of the Philadelphia area" for delaying the project. It cost $65 million to build the 33-mile stretch—nearly the same as the cost of the entire original 160 miles. And although the Pennsylvania Turnpike now ran from border to border, there was no bridge across the Delaware River, and it was a two-hour driving struggle through Philadelphia and its suburbs to get to New Jersey.

MILEPOST 351: Toll collectors at the Philadelphia interchange in Bucks County led a rebellion in 1962 against strong-arm tactics by local Republican leaders seeking political contributions. The collectors entertained organization efforts by several unions, and in 1971 turnpike toll collectors became members of the Teamsters union.

MILEPOST 354: Anna M. Werner forced contractors and engineers off her condemned property in Bensalem Township, Bucks County, on May 7, 1952, and sent her dogs after them. The dogs bit three of the turnpike builders. Then she put away her shotgun, called off her dogs, and hired a lawyer. The lawyer was not as effective.

MILEPOST 357: A 22-year-old woman was fired on November 29, 1972, four days after a superior said she caught her making love to a truck driver at 4:00 A.M. in the tollbooth at the Delaware Valley interchange, where she was retained by the commission to collect tolls. Teamsters Local 77 appealed her dismissal and she was reinstated, but a court refused her demand for back pay.

MILEPOST 359: While interstate traffic struggled through the Philadelphia area to get from the Pennsylvania Turnpike to the New Jersey Turnpike, the governors of the two states struggled with the legal problems of crossing the Delaware on a jointly financed bridge. Finally, on May 26, 1956, Governor George Leader of Pennsylvania drove eastward from Edgely, Pennsylvania, and

Governor Robert Meyner drove west from Florence, New Jersey, and met on the middle of the 6,571-foot Delaware Memorial Bridge to snip a ribbon and reduce the driving time in the Philadelphia area by an hour and 15 minutes. On a larger scale, the bridge opening made it possible to drive from Maine to Indiana without encountering a stoplight.

It now costs $8.70 to drive a passenger car across Pennsylvania on the turnpike. The biggest trucks pay $61.75 for the same privilege. The original cost of the entire trip was $3.60 for a passenger car. There have been only two toll increases in the 44-year history of the turnpike—once in 1969 and again in 1978. It took the commission from 1940 to 1973 to collect its first $1 billion in tolls. The second $1 billion came along only 10 years later. Last year alone, the turnpike toll collectors took in $123.5 million from 73.5 million vehicles.

When the turnpike opened in 1940, the promise was that it would become a toll-free segment of the regular state highway system when the construction bonds were paid off in about 1956. That never happened, and it almost certainly never will happen. Several governors have found the populist notion of a toll-free turnpike irresistible, but in the end they have backed away because the state can't afford to maintain the turnpike. The commission is likely to sell more bonds in the near future to finance improvements, thereby extending the tolls beyond the millennium.

There is another section of the turnpike, running perpendicularly north from the main east–west route to form a "T." The 110-mile Northeast Extension from Norristown to Scranton was a chronic financial loser from the time it opened in 1957, and only since the 1978 toll increases has it begun to pay for itself. Its lesson is that even a superhighway cannot generate traffic where none existed before.

But in 1954, Governor John S. Fine saw the Northeast Extension as the economic salvation of his native anthracite area. It turned out to be the turnpike's monumental shame. During construction, a major multimillion-dollar scandal was uncovered, involving a company that was supposed to be filling old mine shafts under the turnpike's right-of-way. Ultimately, five persons were convicted on conspiracy charges, including former Turnpike Commission Chairman Tommy John Evans.

Evans's fall from grace coincided closely with the demise of the Turnpike Era in America. The carefully nurtured myth that the success of the Pennsylvania Turnpike was the result of efficient management and financial acumen was destroyed forever. Moreover, Congress had authorized the construction of the 44,000-mile Interstate Highway System that would cost $76 billion and be toll-free. It was the biggest public works project in American history, and for the next 25 years nobody even talked about toll roads.

But now, a half century after the idea was born, the Pennsylvania Turnpike and the 61 U.S. toll roads that followed it are experiencing a new surge in popularity. The interstates are in dreadful shape, and the cost of repairing them is estimated at $60 billion. The growing disparity between tax revenues and the need to maintain existing highways has brought America to the brink of a New Turnpike Era. The Governor's Toll Road Task Force has recommended expanding the Pennsylvania Turnpike and converting all of Interstate 80 and part of Interstate 70 into toll roads. Turnpikes are an idea whose time has come and gone and returned.

Updike Is Home

The Author Vowed to Leave His Pennsylvania
Home Behind, but He Never Quite Escaped—
in His Work or His Life.

*This article had a very interesting repercussion. Indeed, I briefly
became John Updike's muse.*

*In the spring of 1983, I successfully pitched an idea about
the relationship between Updike's fiction and the geography of
Berks County, Pennsylvania. I made a pro forma contact with his
publisher, Knopf, asking for an interview, but I did not receive a
response—nor did I expect one.*

*I decided to do the article without Updike, and the follow-
ing week I went to his original hometown of Shillington. When
I asked the reference librarian at the Shillington Public Library
whether she had any information on Updike, I felt an insistent
tug at my sleeve. I turned to face a pair of granny-rimmed,
bleached-denim eyes. "I know all about him," the woman said.
"He's my son."*

Originally published as "Updike Is Home" in the *Philadelphia Inquirer
Magazine*, June 12, 1983.

Linda Hoyer Updike and I went to lunch, and then she took me to the family farm in Plowville, where I interviewed her for about four hours and amassed information beyond my dreams.

Delighted with my good fortune, I went home and began writing the article. Four days later, I got the phone call from Mrs. Updike. "Chonny will be here tomorrow. He's coming to put in my screens. He does it every year. Why don't you stop by?"

I appeared at the Updike farm the next day—May 3, 1983— at 10:00 A.M. As I stepped from my car, Updike—wearing blue sneakers, faded tan corduroy trousers, a charcoal sweater, and a dark blue watch cap—poked his head outside the kitchen door. "Let's go," he said. "I'll drive so you can take notes."

He was reluctant at first, but then he warmed to the situation. We spent the entire day driving around Berks County and didn't get back to the farm until after dark. I had a great piece, and the magazine displayed it prominently.

About six months later, Art Carey, who edited the article, called me and asked whether I had seen the latest New Yorker *magazine. I hadn't, and he urged me to get it immediately. What I found was a short story by John Updike entitled "One More Interview." It was about a famous actor who comes back to his hometown to be interviewed by a young journalist.*

At one point, the actor-protagonist exclaims, "I can't stand interviews!"—but by story's end he's demanding that his interviewer write down every single detail and name that the actor can recall from his childhood.

The fascinating part for me was that many of the situations are exactly as they occurred in the real interview, and some of the dialogue is taken virtually word for word from our conversations. It felt eerie for a while, but after a few years I came to like the story, telling my kids and friends how I once served as muse to one of the greatest of all American writers.

This incident, by the way, is recounted in the opening of Adam Begley's 2014 biography, Updike.

THE ISOLATED FARMHOUSE where John Updike spent his adolescence is as easy to find as elegant metaphors in his novels, stories, and poems. Leaving the Pennsylvania Turnpike at Morgantown, you head north on the old highway for about five miles and make a turn where **a pink triangle of sandstone stared through the bare treetops** (FFP, 69).[1] It's less than a mile to the 171-year-old farmhouse, **set square to the compass and slightly tall for its breadth, as if the attic windows were straining to see over the trees** (TA, 176). Cornfields escort the final stretch of macadam to a lane, **eroded to its bones of sandstone, up to the barn door** (*OTF*, 3).

There are greetings, genial as the morning sunshine, first from Prince, a collie, and seconds later from Linda Hoyer Updike, 79, who is on her way to replenish a bird feeder. "John is still upstairs, and he's a bit grumpy, but he often gets that way when he visits." A laugh crinkles her eyes, and she looks like the dust-jacket photographs of her son. "Go in and sit down. I'll be in in a minute."

The house, small-roomed and steep-staired, is dominated by **the smutty little fireplace that provided their only heat** (PF, 13). Its stone dissolves into a white bookcase that has nearly two of its shelves filled with volumes by John Updike. "He told me when he left for Harvard that someday he was going to fill those shelves," says Mrs. Updike, who has returned without removing her coat and scarf. "There's only room for one or two more."

"The house hasn't changed that much since John lived here," she says. "We put in a bathroom upstairs. You know, my father died right upstairs in the bedroom."

My grandmother sat on the edge of the bed, dazed, smiling to greet me. She was confused, like a craftsman who looks

---

1. For all citation abbreviations in this essay, see the "Key to Sources" at the end of the chapter.

up after a long period of concentration. The sanest of old
men, my grandfather had on his last day lost his mind.
He had bellowed; she had struggled to restrain him. He
thought the bed was on fire and sprang from it; she clung to
him and in their fall to the floor he died. (TBM, 93)

More than other contemporary fiction writers, John Updike
has made his life the subject of his work. He has insistently translated his own family and his own geography into the universalities
of literature. In his early novels *The Centaur* and *Of the Farm*,
and in dozens of jewel-like stories about his youth, he has made
himself, through different voices and physiognomies, his own
chief character. As an adult at his full literary powers, Updike
has drawn on a store of laid-up memories and transformed the
mundane into dazzling lyricism. In his exact observation of the
small triumphs and disasters of ordinary life, Updike has made his
readers intimately familiar with his parents and his two boyhood
homes. Shillington, where he lived until he was 12, is Olinger
(long "O," hard "g": "Oh, linger") in Updike's fiction; Plowville,
his adolescent farm home, is Firetown; and Reading, the closest
metropolis, is Alton.

In the preface to a collection of short stories about his youth,
Updike explained his use of geography: **The locality is that of
Olinger, Pennsylvania . . . audibly a shadow of "Shillington," the
real name of my hometown, yet the two towns, however similar,
are not at all the same. Shillington is a place on the map and belongs to the world; Olinger is a state of mind, of my mind, and
belongs entirely to me** (PF, 7).

The locale is less precise in Updike's trilogy—*Rabbit, Run,
Rabbit Redux*, and *Rabbit Is Rich*—and the life of the title character, from high school basketball star to paunchy new-car salesman, is hardly autobiographical. But the sense of place is there,
and the questions of guilt and salvation that haunt Rabbit Angstrom also trouble John Updike.

Growing up in the Shillington area gave Updike a feeling of security and order. Two-thirds of his kindergarten classmates graduated from high school with him. Updike is aware that a sense of place is not as common as it used to be, and though he has lived elsewhere since he left home for Harvard in 1950, Updike comes back to Shillington regularly—in his life and his fiction. He never misses a high school class reunion, and though he has announced several times that he is finished with southeastern Pennsylvania as a setting, he has broken that vow repeatedly.

Updike appears, as if summoned. He is wearing blue sneakers, faded tan corduroy trousers, a charcoal sweater, and a dark blue watch cap. There is a scab on his nose from a fall on the ski slopes. He pokes his head outside the kitchen door, as though toe-testing the temperature, then removes his hat and shrugs on a light denim jacket. "Let's go," he says. "I have a lot of other things to do today."

Outside is the barn, wearing a new coat of brown paint, where the 14-year-old Updike, at his mother's request, shot resident pigeons who were fouling furniture stored there. He used the incident for one of his best-known stories, "Pigeon Feathers." **A barn, in day, is a small night. The splinters of light between the dry shingles pierce the high roof like stars, and the rafters and cross-beams and built-in ladders seem, until your eyes adjust, as mysterious as the branches of a haunted forest** (PF, 29).

"I'll drive so you can take notes, but I want to drive your car," he says. He lollops over to the waiting vehicle, opens the door on the driver's side, and says, "I've never driven a Rabbit before." His eyes flare puckishly. We rattle down toward the macadam, past the field where Joey, in *Of the Farm*, plowed. **I could see the individual teeth of the treads swinging upward like the blank heads of an advancing army. The farm recedes through the rear window, barn and house, like cow and calf** (OTF, 42).

Updike makes a right turn onto Route 10 and heads north toward Shillington. "This is the way my father and I used to go to Shillington High School. He was a mathematics teacher. We had no indoor plumbing at the farm in those days, and we'd take our showers at school." On the right is the Plowville Lutheran Church, now called the Robeson Lutheran Church. **My grandfather had helped build that steeple; he had pushed the breast stones in a wheelbarrow up a narrow path of bending planks** (*CEN*, 75). It was here that adolescent Updike briefly lost his faith during a catechetical class **in a threadbare basement that smelled of stale hay** (PF, 131).

Updike apologizes for the difficulty he is having with the five-speed transmission and comes to a gravelly stop off the highway. "That view hasn't changed too much since I was a boy." **About halfway down, the embankment foliage fell away, and a wonderful view opened up. I saw across a little valley like the background of a Durer** (*CEN*, 75). Updike says a collection of his early writing for the "Talk of the Town" section of the *New Yorker* is scheduled to be published this fall. "I guess that will be my book for this year. I'm working on a novel that I expect to have to the publisher in a few months." He raises his right hand defensively and says: "I don't like to talk about my novels before they're published." He closes the subject and sits on the lid.

In a literary career spanning nearly three decades, Updike has published 30 books—novels, story collections, poetry, essays, and three children's volumes. *Rabbit Is Rich* won the 1982 Pulitzer Prize, an American Book Award, and a commendation from the National Book Critics Circle. At 51, Updike still exhibits traces of the twin thorns of his childhood: stuttering and psoriasis. **Psoriasis. The very name of the allergy, so foreign, so twisty in the mouth, so apt to prompt stammering, intensified the humiliation** (*CEN*, 52). Time and success have rounded his angular, stork-like body, and Massachusetts is crowding Pennsylvania out of his speech. He has recovered from a painful estrangement and divorce in the mid-1970s and now lives with his second wife in a small town north of Boston.

Not trusting the side-view mirror, Updike thrusts his head out the window before pulling back onto the two-lane highway. Passing through the small community of Green Hills, he says, "My father used to stop at the little store there on the way home from school": **Item by item, as if he were a druggist filling a prescription, my father went around the shelves gathering bread and sliced peaches and Ritz crackers and Shredded Wheat, piling them up on the counter** (*CEN*, 282). The hills and curves of Route 10 disappear, and Updike accelerates to 55. **After the tiny town of Galilee, the road like a cat flattening its ears went into a straightaway where my father always speeded** (*CEN*, 79). "I guess it's really grown up a lot, but when I was a boy, I thought we lived at the end of the world": **From where we lived not a highway, not a tower, not even a telephone pole was visible** (HIP, 176). "It's been so long that now I notice the things that haven't changed rather than the things that have."

After passing under the bridge of the interstate carrying purposeful traffic to Reading, Route 10 slices between two red embankments where, in *The Centaur*, his father picked up a hitchhiker. **The road then knifed between two high gashed embankments of eroding red earth. Here a hitchhiker waited between a little pile of stones. Some force of mystery or weather had scrubbed his white face down to the veins; broken bits of purple hatched on his face like infant snakes** (*CEN*, 79). "My father thought it was Christian and American to stop for hitchhikers, and he'd go out of his way to take them where they wanted to go. It used to make me furious, but now I think it was a beautifully moral thing to do. I still feel guilty today when I see one and don't stop."

Wesley Updike—**Mr. Downdike of high school hilarity** (DG, 70)—is remembered as a generous, eccentric man who **indulged himself in self-denial as other men are sensualists** (*OTF*, 99). *The Centaur* is Updike's tribute to his father. Shortly after the publication of the novel in 1963, father and son were standing outside the Plowville Church on a Sunday morning when an adolescent approached the novelist and criticized his portrayal of his father. "My father said to the girl, 'No, the kid caught me exactly,'" Updike recalls.

Linda Updike, on the other hand, said it was painful for her to read *The Centaur*. "It reminds me that I was supposed to be a teacher but failed, and so my poor husband had to be the teacher." *Of the Farm*, published in 1965, was in a sense Updike's tribute to his mother. She has a first edition of the novel with this inscription: "To my parents with much love, this little fantasy containing bits of familiar landscape—Johnny." Though the portrait is not a wholly flattering one, Linda Updike says, "He portrayed me as he saw me, and I respect his vision."

Linda Updike is an educated, ambitious woman who took correspondence courses on writing during her son's adolescent attempts at creativity. **Underneath the scratching of my sweaty pencil ran the intermittent mutter of my mother's typewriter** (DG, 181). "Johnny knew it was possible to be a writer because he saw me trying," she says. "I only had a little gift, but it was the only one I got." Under her maiden name of Linda Grace Hoyer, she has published several stories in the *New Yorker* and a novel.

Eberly Hill begins with a yellow warning from PennDOT—"1 Mile Hill"—and at the bottom Route 10 is joined perpendicularly by Route 724. A left turn takes you toward Shillington. On the right, high on a hill, is Kesher Zion Cemetery—the Jewish Cemetery, **where Abe Cohen, Alton's famous Prohibition gangster, lies buried** (*CEN*, 258). Updike drives another mile in silence before he pulls off the road and stops near a small section of sandstone wall that is crumbling from malign neglect. This is the remnant of a huge wall that surrounded the Berks County Poorhouse, which served as the model for Updike's first novel, *The Poorhouse Fair*. Behind the wall now are garden apartments and suburban homes reached by winding streets. The Rotary and the Lions have planted signs near the wall welcoming everyone to Shillington. **The wall, its height slightly waving, like a box hedge, enclosed four**

and a fourth acres. There was a hell of a big yellow house back
from the wall. Old people were crawling around like bugs on a
lawn (PER, 11).

Updike turns off the motor and applies the hand brake. Getting
out of the car, he sidesteps a Styrofoam Big Mac container and a
Mountain Dew can, jumps up on the wall, and begins walking
along the top. "The drop doesn't look as big as it did when I used to
walk along here as a kid": **A dreadful pit of space congruent with
the pit of time into which the old people (who could be seen cir-
cling silently in the shade of the trees whose very tops were below
my feet) had been plunged by some mystery that would never touch
me** (PER, 14). "It's still a beautiful wall," he says, jumping down.
"I don't know why they had to tear down the rest of it."

Wesley Updike and Linda Grace Hoyer were married shortly
after they graduated from Ursinus College in 1923. After several job setbacks in the early stages of the Depression, Wesley Updike was forced to move into his father-in-law's large white house
in Shillington, and in 1932, the Updikes' only child was born at
Reading Hospital. The parents and grandparents planted a pink
dogwood tree in the side yard of the house at 117 Philadelphia
Avenue to commemorate the birth. **This tree, I learned quite early,
was exactly my age, was, in a sense, me** (DG, 151).

A doctor now lives in the house at 117 Philadelphia Avenue, and
he has added a wing on the left side to accommodate his patients.
The dogwood tree, on the right side of the house, is now 51 years
old, like the man sitting behind the wheel of the Rabbit at the curb.
The big white house seems alone and aloof on a street dominated
by more modest row houses. **Our neighbors / Live higher than we,
in gaunt / two-family houses glaring toward our arbor** (MID, 38).
"My piano teacher used to live there . . . or maybe it was the next
one," Updike volunteers, aiming a long, thin finger. "And right
there is where Mrs. Lutz lived. She was famous during the war
because she was a five-star mother. It's a happy story, too, because
all five boys came back."

Grandfather Hoyer had bought the house on Philadelphia Avenue **before I was born and his stocks went bad, which happened in the same year** (THIB, 69). It was a close family in which **everything was examined for God's fingerprints** (DG, 181), but Wesley Updike's $1,740-a-year teaching salary was not enough to support a family of five. Poverty bred despair; despair bred tension in the household. **Tigers of temper lurked beneath our furniture, and shadows of despair followed my father to the door and flattened themselves against the windows as he walked down the shaded street alone** (DG, 176). In 1945, the farmhouse where Updike's mother had been born went up for sale, and the family of five moved to Plowville, about 10 miles to the south. On the farm, Linda Updike found what she wanted. **Every week is different, every day is a surprise. New faces in the fields, the birds say different things, and nothing repeats** (OTF, 181). Moreover, though her son continued to attend Shillington schools, she did not want him to live there, believing him to be in danger of **becoming an Olinger know-nothing, a type of humanity that must be seen to be believed. You can't believe it but the people of that town with absolute seriousness consider it the center of the universe. They don't want to go anywhere. They don't want to know anything, they don't want to do anything except sit and admire each other. I didn't want my child to be an Olingerite** (OTF, 22). But for Wesley Updike, the move began an unhappiness that would last the rest of his life—**a thankless land of hers, eighty acres on his shoulders, land, dead, cold land—his blood sank like rain into that thankless land** (CEN, 198). Updike, who was 13 when the family moved to Plowville, always considered Shillington his home. **We have one home, the first, and leave that one. / The having and the leaving go on together** (SH, 15).

Dr. John Hunter had just returned from the war when he bought the house on Philadelphia Avenue. Now, 38 years later, he and his wife, Grace, say they have a "special feeling" about the house and its relationship to an American literary giant. The

Hunters also have warm memories of Wesley Updike, who taught their son math.

"The best story I know about Wesley Updike is that one winter day he was teaching our son's class about decimal points."

> **This girl in the back of the class said she couldn't see the decimal point. He went to the window and scooped some snow off the sill and made a ball . . . and threw it hard as hell at the f— blackboard.**
> **"Now can you see it?" he said.**
> **Christ, what a character.**
> **You've got a great father there, Peter.** (*CEN*, 122)

The Hunters nurture the dogwood tree. "It's not as full as it once was," he says. "Time has taken its toll. We've had to prune it a couple of times, and we've lost a couple of branches to storms. I talked to a nursery about it, and they said they can live for a long time—maybe even a hundred years. But eventually it will start to go back, and then that's it."

At a dangerous five-way intersection he used to try to avoid on his way home from elementary school, Updike turns right onto Lancaster Avenue, where too-big trucks rumble through the narrow center of town carrying the latest outmoded fashions to the Reading outlets. He parks the Rabbit, hazardously, near an old building housing a firm that sells masonry products.

"This used to be Stephen's Luncheonette, where the high school gang hung out and where I often came to wait for my father after school. I don't remember there were only three steps, but those are the original steps, so there must have been only three. It was a double building then—the post office was on the right, the luncheonette on the left." **It shared a brick building with the Olinger Post Office. There were two plate-glass windows side by side; behind one of them sat Miss Passify, the postmistress, who, surrounded by wanted posters and lists of postal regulations, doled out stamps** and money orders; behind the other, wreathed in adolescent smoke and laughter, Minor Kretz, also fat, scooped ice cream and concocted lemon Pepsis (*CEN*, 114). "I used to spend a lot of my time playing the pinball machines in the back," Updike says, waiting for an opening in a long necklace of traffic. From the rear a chorus of cheers rhythmically rose as the pinball machine, gonging in protest, gave up one free game after another (*CEN*, 122).

Two doors down is a Turkey Hill Minit Market on the site of Becker's Garage—Hummel's Garage in *The Centaur*, where Wesley Updike often took his wheezing 1936 Buick for enough repairs to make the return trip to Plowville. Here the pavement was stained with little maps of dropped oil, islands and archipelagos and continents undiscovered on this globe (*CEN*, 114).

"Each time I come back to Shillington I notice something that is gone," says Updike, whose gear shifting is getting smoother. "After *Of the Farm*, I thought I'd said my Pennsylvania thing. But I came back to it in the Rabbit books, and I recently wrote a little story about the Shillington trolleys in the *New Yorker*. In a way, the longer I'm away from here, the more I find certain things here that I can grab ahold of and make something of." He became a child again in this town, where life was a distant adventure, a rumor, an always imminent joy (PER, 90).

The Shillington School District was gobbled up 20 years ago by the consolidated Governor Mifflin School District, and the Shillington High School, where Wesley Updike taught and John Updike nurtured his genius—the smells of tablet paper and wet shoes and varnish and face powder pierced him with a vivid sense of possession (SN, 41)—is now a tiny, salmon-colored core of the district's junior high school. Updike drives past the new high school, which sprawls across land that used to belong to the poorhouse, without a glance.

The academic records of John Updike are preserved in a vault in the office of Governor Mifflin High School. But school district officials are obliging in sharing the information with someone who wants to write about their most famous graduate. Young Updike had straight As from the seventh through the 12th grade, but so did two classmates with whom he shared valedictory honors at graduation. On the equivalent of today's Scholastic Aptitude Test, Updike scored 711 on the aptitude section and 717 in English, placing him among the top 1 percent of those who took the test in January 1950. A personality test given Updike in his senior year concluded he was responsible, purposeful, actively creative, and genuinely concerned for others.

Also stored in the school vault are issues of the *Chatterbox*, Shillington High School's newspaper during Updike's day.

As a ninth-grader, Updike wrote a series of detective stories for the *Chatterbox*, involving Sing Loo, "a strange Chinese detective." Much of Updike's adolescent writing is imitative of the *New Yorker*, which he was reading weekly throughout high school and where he would work after college. In a periodic verse feature called "The Mags," Updike poked fun at *Time*, *Collier's*, *Esquire*, *National Geographic*, and others, but when he got around to assessing the *New Yorker*, he wrote: "It would be pointless interjection / To list the merits of perfection." Senior Updike also wrote editorials, and in one entitled "The Movies" he complained: "Hollywood has sat down before the greatest piano ever made, in front of the biggest audience ever assembled, and plays chopsticks."

Barry Nelson is a member of the Shillington High School Class of 1950 who now teaches at the consolidated school. He remembers that when Updike was a junior, he wrote "An Ode to Seniors" that appeared to be a gushing tribute to the Class of 1949. But the first letter of each line, read vertically, spelled out "SENIOR CLASS STINKS." The *Chatterbox* faculty adviser caught on and ordered Updike to write an apology for the next issue. Updike complied with sugary contrition, but the first letters of each line spelled "NUTS."

"John used to take us for some pretty hairy rides in his father's old Buick," Nelson says. "He liked to slam on the brakes and spin the car around. One time we were driving to Reading, and I looked in the back seat and he had all his old *New Yorker*s with him. He said he was taking them to a bookbinder to have them bound. I asked him why, and he said, 'Because someday I'm going to write for the *New Yorker*.'"

Past the new high school is land that used to be farmed by the poorhouse residents. It has been covered with macadam, renamed the Shillington Shopping Center, and now supports a varied crop offering Green Stamps, geegaws, modern inconveniences, and one-stop banking. **They felt the poorhouse would always be there, exempt from time. That some residents died, and others came, did not occur to them** (PF, 132). At this point, Shillington dissolves into the mercantile sprawl of Reading . . . **marketable goods / On all sides crowd the good remembered town** (SH, 15). Updike carefully steers his way among the nervous neon of car dealerships, muffler shops, bowling alleys, and restaurants specializing in "Dutch cooking." **Trying to sell what in the old days couldn't be helped. Making a tourist attraction out of fat-fried food and a diet of dough that would give a pig pimples** (*RAB*, 83).

Updike turns around in a Hardee's parking lot redolent of charcoaled beef and returns toward Shillington. He makes a right turn onto a residential street near the old high school and skillfully downshifts his way to the top of a hill. "Here's where Joan Zug used to live," he says. "She and another Joan, Joan Venne, were my real close friends when I was growing up."

Joan Zug George lives only a few blocks from her childhood home in Shillington, and she still sees a lot of her old school friend, Joan Venne Youngerman, who now lives in Pennside, on the other side of Reading. When they get together and talk about John Updike, they keep leaping into each other's pauses.

Zug: Johnny took me to the junior prom, and we had a lot of movie dates. I can still see him leapfrogging over the parking meters in Reading as we walked to the movies.

Venne: Because of our last names, I always sat behind him or near him in school, and I used to copy from his paper. He always had the right answers.

Zug: He used to take a bunch of kids out in his father's car at lunch time, and he'd play chicken. He'd take his hands off the steering wheel and see who would be the first person to grab the wheel.

Venne: He used to smoke Kools because no one would bum them from him. I can still see him at Stephen's Luncheonette waiting for his father, hunched over the pinball machine with a cigarette dangling from his lips. He was the original flower child. His hair was always uncombed, his shirts always unbuttoned, and his fly always unzipped.

Zug: We all recognize ourselves in his writing. There's a scene in one of the Rabbit books where two neighbors are feuding. There's a narrow patch of grass between their houses, and each of them mows half of it. That was my parents' house, and it really happened. **Their neighbor house on the other side, across two cement sidewalks with a strip of grass between them, where lived the old Methodist. Mom used to fight about who would mow the grass strip** (*RAB*, 98).

Venne: We think his Rabbit character is a composite of several people. I always thought he looked like a rabbit, and once he came to a Halloween party dressed like a rabbit.

Zug: John and I used to say that everyone in our crowd reminded us of some kind of animal, and one time I told him that he reminded me of a rabbit. He agreed, and after that for a long time he went around making his nose and ears wiggle.

UPDIKE SLOWS ALMOST TO A STOP, then turns into a narrow dirt road. "This used to be a place where kids came to neck. . . . I suppose they still could." He sees the side of the road littered with beer cans. "I guess they still do. Who says time consumes all? That's very cheery."

"I'm not sure how I arrived at my Rabbit. Someone reminded me not too long ago that there was someone we went to high school with who was nicknamed Rabbit, and that may have been in my subconscious." Several scholars have concluded that Rabbit is rooted in the story of Peter Rabbit, and Rabbit Angstrom is hiding in the city of Brewer (Reading), which Updike several times describes as being the color of flowerpots. "That's an interesting theory," Updike says, peering left and right at a four-way stop sign. "I always liked the story of Peter Rabbit hiding under the farmer's flowerpot. I suppose I did it. Guilty as charged. There's one more Rabbit book to be written, but it won't come until the end of the decade, and I'll have to wait and see what happens in the '80s. I assume it will rather heavily involve Rabbit's granddaughter, who was born at the end of *Rabbit Is Rich*."

Updike parks near the Shillington Lutheran Church. **Of my family, only my father attended church regularly, returning every Sunday with the *Sunday Reading Eagle* and the complaint that the minister had prayed too long** (DG, 181). "I promised my mother I'd pick up some soap and bread at the old Variety Store" **where we bought punch-out licorice belts and tablets with Edward G. Robinson and Hedy Lamarr smiling on the cover** (DG, 170). "I won't be long."

He returns minutes later and points across the street. "That's where I went to elementary school." Though the building is now called Mifflin Plaza, the words "Shillington School" are chipped in the stone near the roof. **The elementary school was a big brick cube set in a square of black surfacing and painted with the diagrams and runes of children's games** (DG, 166). "And down there is the old movie house. You can still see the marquee." **It was two blocks from my home; I began to go alone at the age of six. My** mother, so strict about my kissing girls, was strangely indulgent about this (DG, 173).

Updike, originally reluctant to do the tour, has now been seduced by nostalgia and becomes apologetic because it is taking longer than he anticipated, yet he makes no attempt to truncate it. He turns right near the house on Philadelphia Avenue and directs the Rabbit up a steep hill. "This is Second Street. For some reason a lot of good-looking girls lived up here, and I used to walk to and from school with them." **As you walk beside them after school, they tighten their arms about their books and bend their heads forward to give a more flattering attention to your words** (IFS, 122). At the top of the hill is Fourth Street. "This is all new to me. I don't think it existed when I was a boy," Updike says, braking to a halt between two brick-and-aluminum ranch houses. There's a large open space between the two houses that offers a vista view of the city of Reading. **Chimneys like peony shoots thrust through the budding treetops. . . . Reading . . . who had ever heard of it? Yet to me Reading is the master of cities, the one at the center that all others echo** (PF, 160).

The Reading of John Updike's youth and adolescence was a symbiosis of idealism and corruption. It had a Socialist municipal government throughout much of the period, but the Ku Klux Klan and the Nazi party also were formidable presences. Reading also was known for pretzels and prostitutes, and an informal survey as late as 1966 found that more people recognized the name of the city's leading madam (Dutch Mary) than the name of the local district attorney. One of the nation's largest bootlegging operations had its stills hooked into the city water system. **Among cities Alton had a bad reputation; its graft and gambling and easy juries and bawdy houses were notorious throughout the Middle Atlantic States. But to me it always presented an innocent face; row after row of houses built of a local dusty-red brick the shade of flowerpots, each house fortified with a tiny, intimate, balustraded porch,** and nothing but the wealth of movie houses and beer signs along its main street to suggest that its citizens loved pleasure more than the run of mankind (FFP, 75).

Today along Penn Street, the city's commercial aorta, many of the stores have been torn down and replaced by parking lots to accommodate shoppers who seldom come in sufficient numbers. John Kissinger is a Reading native who works in a downtown bookstore and is an Updike aficionado.

"There's a funny attitude toward Updike in this area," he says. "You've got the whole local-boy-makes-good syndrome, and there is considerable demand for his books in the store. But people around here want him to do nothing but Olinger stories. They want him to keep feeding their nostalgia. Many local people were turned off by the sexual realism of *Couples*. And when the African novel, *The Coup*, came out, we had people coming in and asking for 'The Coop.'"

Kissinger has found that while Updike's early novels and stories generally offer precise geographical descriptions, the three Rabbit novels are more difficult. "The sequences of travel in the Rabbit books are all jumbled. I've tried to follow Rabbit in my car, but Updike has moved whole sections of the city to other places. It's a lot harder to pin down the places than it is in his earlier writing."

Updike is now more than an hour late, and he is pressing to get back to the farmhouse. Leaving Route 724 and beginning the long climb up Route 10, he says, "This is Eberly Hill, where my father and I got stuck in *The Centaur*." **The rear tires never cease slithering. The slits of vision in their windshield go furry and close; the heavenly bin from which the snow has been sifted now bursts its sides. Three times the Buick sloughs forward up the shallow slant only to have its motion smothered. The third time Caldwell grinds his foot into the accelerator and the crying tires swing the rear of the car into the untouched snow at the side of the road** (CEN, 263).

Like an admonishing finger, the steeple of the Robeson Lutheran Church appears on the left, and beside the church is a tiny

cemetery that is the final resting place of Updike's father, his grandparents, his great-grandparents, and his great-great-grandparents.
There's a stone with his mother's name on it. Only the final year
has been left blank. Linda Updike recently purchased another plot
at the cemetery. For her son:

> *I did resent my mother's heavy gift,*
> *her plot to bring me home, but slowly I*
> *have come to think, Why not? Where else? I will*
> *have been away for fifty years, perhaps,*
> *but have forever to make my absence up.*
> *My life in time will seal shut like a star.*
>
> (PL, 176)

Updike turns into the lane that leads to the farmhouse where his
mother is waiting. He answers the question before it is asked.
"Actually, I've come to think the idea is kind of nice. I came from
this soil, and I might as well go back to it." He says good-bye at
the car and walks toward the house balancing the brown bag of
soap and bread in his right palm. At the doorway he swivels and
shouts, "Thanks for letting me drive the Rabbit. It's a marvelous
machine."

Key to Sources

CEN: *The Centaur* (novel), New York: Albert A. Knopf, 1963.
DG: "The Dogwood Tree" (essay). *Assorted Prose.* New York: Albert A.
    Knopf, 1963.
FFP: "Friends from Philadelphia" (short story). *The Early Stories, 1953–
    1975.* New York: Random House, 2007.
HIP: "Harv Is Plowing Now" (short story). *The Music School.* New York:
    Albert A. Knopf, 1966.
IFS: "In Football Season" (short story). *The Early Stories, 1953–1975.* New
    York: Random House, 2007.
MID: "Midpoint" (poem). *Collected Poems.* New York: Albert A. Knopf,
    1993.

OTF: *Of the Farm* (novel). New York: Albert A. Knopf, 1965.

PER: "The Persistence of Desire" (short story). *Pigeon Feathers and Other Stories*. New York: Albert A. Knopf, 1962.

PF: "Pigeon Feathers" (short story). *Pigeon Feathers and Other Stories*. New York: Albert A. Knopf, 1962.

PL: "Plow Cemetery" (poem). *Collected Poems*. New York: Albert A. Knopf, 1993.

RAB: *Rabbit Redux* (novel). New York: Albert A. Knopf, 1971.

SH: "Shillington" (poem). *Collected Poems*. New York: Albert A. Knopf, 1993.

SN: "A Sense of Shelter" (short story). *Pigeon Feathers and Other Stories*. New York: Albert A. Knopf, 1962.

TA: "The Afterlife" (short story). *The Early Stories, 1953–1975*. New York: Random House, 2007.

TBM: "The Blessed Man of Boston" (short story). *The Early Stories, 1953–1975*. New York: Random House, 2007.

THIB: "The Happiest I've Been" (short story). *The Early Stories, 1953–1975*. New York: Random House, 2007.

Acknowledgments

MY DEBTS are substantial.

I joined the *Philadelphia Inquirer* in 1970 as its Harrisburg bureau chief. Ten years later, I was ready for a change. Among the most gratifying work I had done while covering state government was writing occasional articles for the *Inquirer*'s Sunday magazine, which was then named *Today.*

I went to Gene Roberts, the executive editor, and told him I wanted a change. I asked about becoming a staff writer for the magazine, which had just been renamed the *Philadelphia Inquirer Magazine* under a new editor, David Boldt, whom I had worked with and whom I admired. Roberts said there were no staff openings (it was a coveted post), but he asked, "Would you be willing to do it as a freelancer?" This was risky. Was I willing to give up a salary, benefits, and job security? But without hesitation, I answered, "Sure." It was one of the best decisions of my life.

Between 1980 and 1995, I wrote more than 100 articles for the magazine. It was a great spot on a great newspaper. I worked under three brilliant editors: the late David Boldt, Fred Mann, and Avery Rome. During those years, I teamed up directly with two superb deputy editors—Art Carey and Sue Weston—whose wise counsel shines through each of these articles. My deep gratitude goes to all five.

On behalf of this compendium, 100 or more people contributed their time and their sagacity. I want to single out one of them: the late Linda Hoyer Updike, who intervened and arranged for me to interview her famous son, whom she called "Chonny."

I also thank Aaron Javsicas, editor-in-chief at Temple University Press, for his immediate and enthusiastic support of this project, and Ken McClure, my brother-in-law, who several years ago suggested and then urged that I take on this project.

And finally, I express my gratitude and love to my wife, Susan, my first reader and unerring critic, for enduring life with a writer for more than a quarter century.

WILLIAM ECENBARGER, a freelance writer, is the author of *Walkin' the Line: A Journey from Past to Present along the Mason-Dixon* and *Kids for Cash: Two Judges, Thousands of Children, and a $2.8 Million Kickback Scheme* and the co-author of *Glory by the Wayside: The Old Churches of Hawaii* (with Susan Ecenbarger); *Catching Lightning in a Bottle: How Merrill Lynch Revolutionized the Financial World* (with Winthrop H. Smith Jr.); and *Making Ideas Matter: My Life as a Policy Entrepreneur* (with Dwight Evans).